EN ATTENDANT GODOT

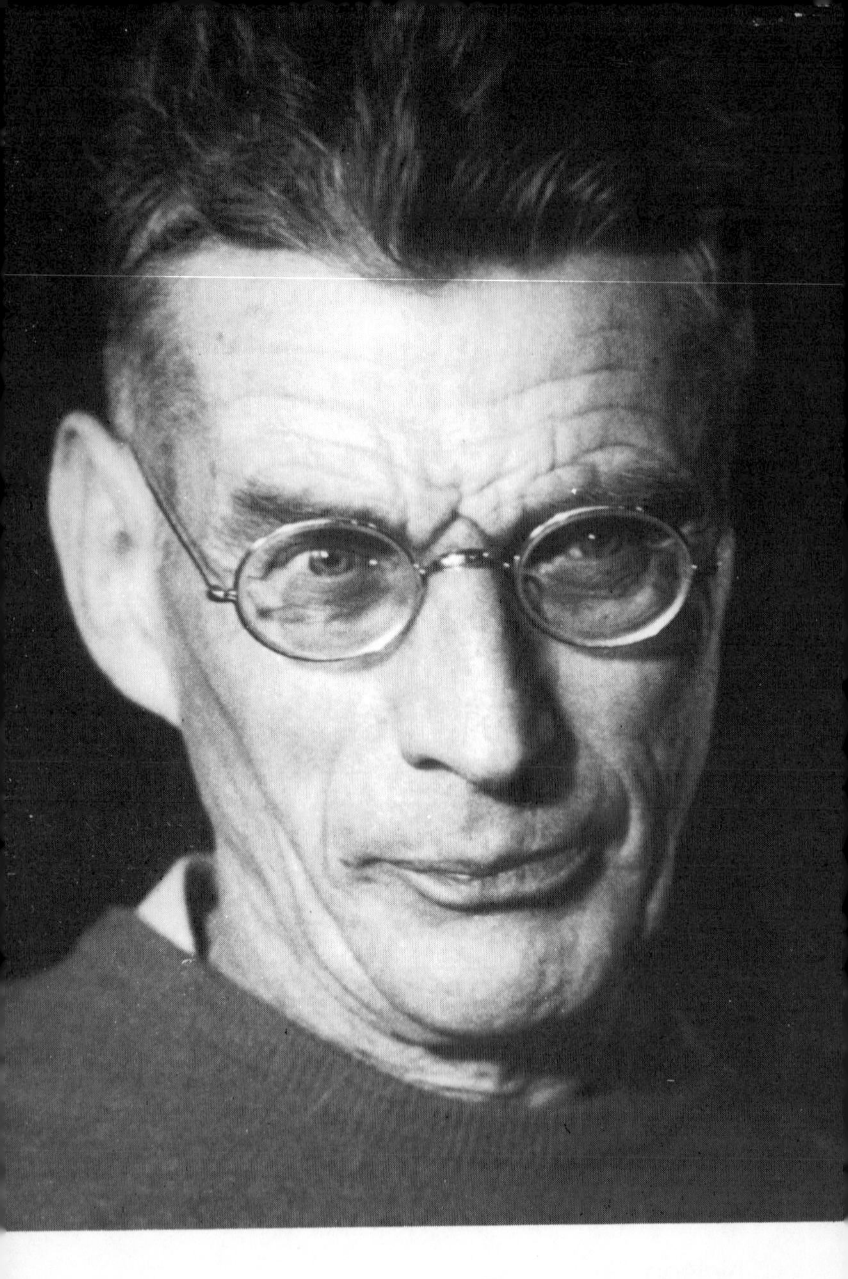

SAMUEL BECKETT

En attendant Godot

Pièce en deux actes

Edited by
COLIN DUCKWORTH, M.A., Ph.D.
Department of French, Bedford College
University of London

With a Foreword by
HAROLD HOBSON, M.A.

MODERN WORLD LITERATURE SERIES

Nelson

Thomas Nelson and Sons Ltd
Nelson House Mayfield Road
Walton-on-Thames Surrey
KT12 5PL UK

51 York Place
Edinburgh
EH1 3JD UK

Thomas Nelson (Hong Kong) Ltd
Toppan Building 10/F
22A Westlands Road
Quarry Bay Hong Kong

Distributed in Australia by

Thomas Nelson Australia
480 La Trobe Street
Melbourne Victoria 3000
and in Sydney, Brisbane, Adelaide and Perth

First published in the French language
by Les Editions de Minuit 1952

First published in Great Britain by George G. Harrap and Co. Ltd 1966
(under ISBN 0-245-52221-2)

Reprinted ten times
Twelfth impression published by Thomas Nelson and Sons Ltd 1985
Reprinted 1986, 1987

ISBN 0-17-444383-8

Print No. 04

Printed in Hong Kong

ACKNOWLEDGMENTS

I am glad to record my gratitude to the following:

Mr Samuel Beckett, for answering questions both in person and by correspondence, for allowing me to see and quote from the manuscript of *En attendant Godot*, and for permitting me to quote from his unpublished novel *Mercier et Camier*.

Mr Harold Hobson, for his foreword.

Dr John Fletcher, for lending me (with Mr Beckett's permission) a typescript copy of *Mercier et Camier*, and for some useful suggestions.

M. Jérôme Lindon, for sending me information about translations of *En attendant Godot*.

M. Jean-Louis Barrault, for revising the script of a radio interview and allowing me to quote from it.

The library staff of the British Drama League.

My wife, for her habitual help and encouragement.

LONDON, 1966. C.R.D.

FOREWORD TO

"WAITING FOR GODOT"

by Harold Hobson

Four times whilst I have been a professional drama critic I have found myself on the road to Damascus; four times I have been struck down and changed by the miraculous voice. No other love scene, not even that in *Romeo and Juliet*, no other soaring lyrical song has ever seemed quite the same to me since I heard the incomparable Edwige Feuillère in the great canticle in Paul Claudel's *Partage de midi* at the St James's Theatre in 1951. In 1958, at the Lyric Theatre, Hammersmith, at its first production in London (with a very fine performance by John Slater as Goldberg), Harold Pinter's *The Birthday Party* opened up to me a new world of unnamed and unidentifiable terrors, none the less frightening because they could not be isolated and analysed. In 1962, reading the brief text of Marguerite Duras's *The Square*, I experienced the feeling that never before anywhere, in literature or the theatre, had I known the fact of happiness to be so memorably realized, or its unrecognized fleetingness so poignantly seized.

The fourth occasion in the theatre that has marked me was the first night in 1955 at the Arts Theatre Club of Samuel Beckett's *Waiting for Godot*. It was the most unforgettable and important of all. I had not at that time seen *En attendant Godot* in Paris, and did not do so until a year later, so that it is Peter Hall's English production of the play that remains in my memory as the definitive interpretation. Whenever I think of Estragon and Vladimir I think of them as tramps in broken bowler hats and torn trousers and ragged boots, though it was not as tramps that Mr Beckett conceived them. In Paris they approximated more closely to circus clowns, which was what Mr Beckett wished. That today everyone in Britain who knows the play, and many thousands of people who do not, think of them as tramps is a curious tribute to the power of Mr Hall's creative imagination. If you ask Mr Hall why he thought of them as tramps, when there is nothing in the text of the play to suggest this, he says, "I don't know. I just saw them that way." I do not suppose that Shakespeare could explain *Hamlet*, either.

There is a famous story of how Mr Hall set about the production of *Waiting for Godot*. "I haven't the faintest idea what this play means", he said to his company. "Let's begin to rehearse it." In general it might be said that the critics who saw its first performance had also no idea what it meant. They were not haunted by Mr Beckett's preoccupation with the strangely different fates of the two thieves who were crucified, one of them damned, the other supping with Christ in Paradise. They were insensitive to the antiphonal rhythm, the solemnity of cry and response, in the exchanges between Vladimir and Estragon. They were, amazingly, unmoved by the appearances of the boy at the end of each act, appearances that have such exquisite echoes and are enveloped in so profound a mystery. They did not perceive the variations which the second act works subtly on the first, making the play a marvel of construction.

I cannot help feeling that if they had been able to read Dr Colin Duckworth's edition of the play, and his masterly introduction to it, they would have rendered a better account of themselves. For even critics, astounding as the statement may seem, are capable of learning.

The assumption that most people appeared to make when the play was first seen in England in 1955 was that its author was a dehumanized factory of poisoned misanthropy. Dr Duckworth very truly shows that few misapprehensions about a great writer could be more ludicrously unjust than this. No eminent man of our day is gentler or kinder than Mr Beckett, nor more solicitous of the welfare and happiness of others. Far from being cut off from all ordinary interests, Mr Beckett is the only dramatist ever known who has played first-class cricket. Terence Rattigan and Noël Coward are members of M.C.C., but I believe that their cricket is chiefly a matter of watching from the pavilion. But Mr Beckett has done battle on the field itself. Whilst he was an undergraduate at Trinity College, Dublin, he came with an Irish touring team to England, and played against all the first-class counties. My impression is that he used to bowl googlies, but of that I am not sure.

Dr Duckworth makes clear the enormous learning that lies behind Beckett's work. He shows the influence on it of Descartes and of French rationalism, and how the civilization of centuries has been summed up and assessed in one man. He stresses Beckett's preoccupation with the big, perennial philosophical problems, and with the existence or non-existence of God, and its influence on our lives. He traces the development of Beckett's thought and art through the early comic novels to the more difficult productions of later years. (It was *Murphy* that won Beckett the admiration before the war of Denis Healey, one of Harold Wilson's ministers, who used to recite long speeches from it to entranced circles of Oxford friends, including the young Iris Murdoch.) He even shows the curious, perhaps unconscious, influence of Paris street names. He reveals the humour, the style, the shape, purity, and musicality of Beckett's prose, and the importance of the strophe and anti-strophe; and he rightly condemns the folly of trying to force on to the anguish, grotesqueness and beauty of this great play the straitjacket of an exclusive meaning too narrow and literal. With his own learning and sensibility he enables us to enter into its riches.

March 1966 H.H.

CONTENTS

ILLUSTRATIONS

The photographs are reproduced by kind permission of the copyright holders: the frontispiece and plates 6, 7, and 8—Dominic; plates 1 and 2—Studio Lipnitzki; plates 3, 4, and 5—Houston-Rogers.

INTRODUCTION

CHAPTER 1

Samuel Beckett: A Man and his Mind

A completely bilingual writer who achieves world-wide renown as one of the most significant contributors to two cultures is a rarity. The critics and literary historians of France and of English-speaking countries share Samuel Beckett without quarrelling over him: he has translated (occasionally in collaboration) all his French works into English and his English ones into French with such complete command of style that only a bibliographical list will reveal the secret of which language any particular work was conceived in. What could be more Irish-sounding than *Malone Dies*? What more French-sounding than *Oh les Beaux Jours*? Yet the first was created in French, the second in English. One may not agree with Melvin Friedman's assessment of Beckett as "an amalgam of Joyce and Proust",[1] but it aptly illustrates the point that it is impossible to regard a certain proportion of Beckett's work as belonging to French literature, and the rest to English literature. His early works have an unmistakably Irish flavour (especially *Murphy* (1938), probably one of the great comic novels in the English tongue), but Beckett's preoccupations are so universal that he transcends all cultural limits. He has no time for what he contemptuously referred to in his great essay on Proust in 1931 as "the grotesque fallacy of a realistic art—'the miserable statement of line and surface', and the penny-a-line vulgarity of a literature of notations".[2] It is usually the 'naturalistic' elements of a literary work that tie it to its period and country of origin; these elements have gradually disappeared in his works since *Murphy*.

[1] In *Comparative Literature*, Winter, 1960, pp. 47–58.
[2] *Proust*, Calder (London), 1965, p. 76.

There are, however, reasons for considering Beckett as a French writer, despite the fact that he has never renounced his Irish nationality. The first is that he has adopted France as his spiritual home for the last thirty years. Secondly, he was almost ignored by public and critics alike until in 1948 he wrote a play in French, after writing in English for the previous twenty years. Thirdly, the works which seem, at the moment, to be his most profoundly original achievements, have all been written in French; namely, *Molloy* (1951), *Malone meurt* (1951), *En attendant Godot* (1952), *L'Innommable* (1953), *Fin de Partie* (1957), and *Comment c'est* (1961).

Samuel Beckett's life is almost totally irrelevant to an understanding and appreciation of his works. However, the man exists, and a brief account of the background to his literary career may not be entirely useless to those who are, for the first time, about to enter into the austere mysteries of the universe as seen by "perhaps the most difficult writer of his generation".[1]

Beckett will enter his sixty-first year of earthly existence at about the time this edition is published, so far as one can foresee. Almost exactly half his life has been spent in France; for, after two years of Parisian life, afforded by the coveted position of *lecteur d'anglais* at the École Normale Supérieure between 1928 and 1930, he found it impossible to settle again in Dublin, near to which city he had been born (in 1906) into a middle-class Irish family belonging to the Protestant faith.

His studies had been highly successful at Trinity College, Dublin, where he read French and Italian, gaining an outstanding First Class degree and a large gold medal in 1927. Although Dublin's atmosphere of theocracy and censorship was distasteful to him, he dutifully returned there to become the first Assistant to Professor Rudmose-Brown in 1930. But he could not settle down to the work, and so he resigned after

[1] Martin Esslin, 'Samuel Beckett', in *The Novelist as Philosopher*, ed. Cruickshank, 1962, p. 145.

four terms because—as he has said with the modest candour which is characteristic of those whose talents are beyond dispute—"he could not bear the absurdity of teaching to others what he did not know himself".[1] He took this decision despite the award of an M.A. degree in 1931 for a dissertation on Descartes, and despite the excellent study of Proust which he had just published. He went to live in London, in France, and in Germany; wrote a novel which is still unpublished, *Dream of Fair to Middling Women*; and finally settled in Paris in 1937, resolved to make his life there.

When he had first gone to Paris he had entered the *entourage* of James Joyce, who greatly appreciated—but probably failed to understand—Beckett's first published novel, *Murphy*, conceived during his stay in England between 1933 and 1935. The influence of Joyce on Beckett has been a source of controversy among critics and, as we shall see, an attempt has been made to show that their relationship is the key to the understanding of *En attendant Godot* and *Fin de Partie*. Beckett had in his own nature, however, qualities similar to those of the Master: irreverence for the established order, breadth and depth of learning, and mastery in the handling of words.

Between 1937 and the outbreak of war in 1939, Beckett continued to live in Paris on a small annuity, writing poetry, stories, articles, and reviews, mainly in English but sometimes in French. When the war started, Beckett was visiting his mother in Ireland. He went back to Paris where, as a citizen of Eire, he could have gone on living unmolested during the German occupation. But he put his contempt for Nazism into practice, and became involved in Resistance activities, until he was forced by the danger of imminent arrest to go into hiding in the Rhône valley. There, working on a farm in the Vaucluse—a part of France with which Vladimir and Estragon are acquainted—he wrote his third novel, *Watt*, setting it in the Ireland of his young days to try and get away from the horrors

---

[1] Quoted by Richard Coe, *Samuel Beckett*, Writers and Critics Series, Oliver and Boyd, 1964, p. 12.

of war and occupation. This was the last novel (to date) written in English, and was published (in a limited edition only) in 1953, when later works had made him better known.

After a short visit to Ireland in 1944 when France had been liberated, Beckett returned to Paris and began to write in earnest in the language of his country of adoption—a logical change, the need for which can be discerned from the gallicisms in *Watt*. Beckett has, on various occasions, given half-serious answers to the question of why he changed to French. To Israel Shenker he said that writing in French was a different and more exciting experience than writing in English.[1] Niklaus Gessner received the reply, "Parce qu'en français c'est plus facile d'écrire sans style"[2]—an ambiguous statement which could simply mean that by adopting French he was escaping from his own previous style and starting afresh. It was not merely a question of changing to another tongue; it involved a change of tone and outlook, and an urgent desire to treat new and deeper themes—themes of which *En attendant Godot* is the first dramatic expression: the identity of Self, reality, the dualism of mind and body, death, and eternity.

Whereas Beckett had, up to 1945, belonged clearly to the literary tradition of Swift, Sterne, and Joyce, his best post-war works reveal the sombre anguish that we associate with Dostoievsky, Kafka, Céline, and the existentialist writers and philosophers. The two influences which seem to remain undiminished—because they have now become totally assimilated into Beckett's own world-view—are Cartesian dualism and Dante; and the Swiftian bitterness and disgust at physical life still forces its way through the French style.

In 1945 Beckett made a false start with his first French novel (which he does not wish to publish), *Mercier et Camier*; of this more will be said, as it foreshadows *En attendant Godot* in many respects. Then between 1946 and 1950 there came a veritable creative explosion which produced, notably, the vast trilogy

---

[1] 'Moody Man of Letters', *New York Times*, 6 May 1956.
[2] *Die Unzulänglichkeit der Sprache*, Zürich, p. 32n.

Molloy, *Malone meurt* and *L'Innommable*, and *En attendant Godot*. With these works Beckett established himself as one of the most original and—within a short time—influential writers in the French language. For the next six years, Beckett's creative ability dried up completely, despite the worldwide success and renown brought by *Godot*. He described the situation in 1956, in words whose anguish can be judged only when one understands the nature of his fear of being reduced to silence, forced to abandon his desperate search for the identity of the Self. In 1956 Beckett stated:

> Since then (1950) I haven't written anything. Or at least nothing that has seemed to me valid. The French work brought me to the point where I felt I was saying the same thing over and over again. For some authors writing gets easier the more they write. For me it gets more and more difficult. For me the area of possibilities gets smaller and smaller. . . . At the end of my work there's nothing but dust. . . . In the last book, *L'Innommable*, there's complete disintegration. No "I", no "have", no "being". No nominative, no accusative, no verb. There's no way to go on.[1]

He tried several ways to get out of the attitude of disintegration, despite his conviction that he had come to the end of things to write about. First, by turning to the medium of radio, with its 'smaller area of possibilities' (smaller compared with visual theatre and extended narrative works). *All that Fall*, a one-act play for eleven characters, was broadcast on the Third Programme in January 1957. It is a violent protest against the monstrosity of God who condemns his creature, man, to suffering and death. The Irish setting is of only superficial realism. This venture into the realm of disembodied voices was highly successful; it suited admirably Beckett's desire to view human existence simply in terms of words, the externalization of thought. His second radio play, *Embers* (1959), has the same quality of compulsive talking, to keep out the silence;

[1] Quoted by J. Fletcher, *The Novels of Samuel Beckett*, Chatto and Windus, 1964, p. 194.

"You should do something about your talking, it's worse", the narrator is told by the ghost (or memory) of his wife. As Beckett said to Niklaus Gessner, "Words, that's all we have." Then in April 1957 Beckett's second long stage play, *Fin de Partie*, received its *première* (in French) at the Royal Court Theatre, London, together with the first of two mime plays, *Acte sans Paroles*. When Beckett's English translation, *Endgame*, was produced in October 1958, it was coupled with a short play originally written in English, *Krapp's Last Tape*, which, like *Embers*, is the musing of an old man. Here Beckett poses very movingly one of the fundamental preoccupations of all his writings, the meaning of Self, by means of juxtaposing a man, Krapp, and the tape-recorded manifestations of his past.

The year 1961 saw the appearance of a play first written and performed in English, *Happy Days*, but which has since received its most consummately beautiful realization in Madeleine Renaud's performances of Beckett's French version, directed by Roger Blin at the Théâtre de France. In that year also, 1961, appeared Beckett's most recent novel in French, *Comment c'est*, a long, unpunctuated, incoherent, but poetic narrative of great power, which took Beckett a year and a half to wrest from the silence. To say that this is the story of Bom's search for Pim, crawling through an endless mire, is merely to scratch the surface of the author's meaning, but will suffice for the moment in these brief biographical preliminaries.

The theme of questing, of searching for some ill-defined but all-important person or thing, which is a recurrent one in Beckett's works (it only momentarily ceases when the emphasis changes to waiting in *Godot*) is seen again in *Cascando*, another play for radio written in French (1963). The play is, as Beckett explained it briefly to me, "about the character called Woburn who never appears". The precise nature of Woburn is as mysterious as that of Godot, or Mr Knott (the mysterious master in *Watt*), or the object of the aimless searchings of the two old men in *Mercier et Camier*.

Beckett's most recent works are extremely brief: *Va et vient*, a 'dramaticule' for three women, lasting about five minutes; a short prose piece of about a thousand words, *Imagination Morte Imaginez*, appearing in Maurice Nadeau's *Lettres Nouvelles*; and a piece for television, *Eh, Joe* (*Dis Joe*), written for Jack MacGowran, lasting about twenty minutes.

The fate of Winnie (the heroine of *Happy Days*, who is seen uncomplainingly buried first to the waist, later to her neck), of Nagg and Nell (the father and mother in *Fin de Partie*, who live in dustbins), and (to go back to the prototype) of the legless, armless *je* of *L'Innommable*, "piqué, à la manière d'une gerbe, dans une jarre profonde, dont les bords m'arrivent jusqu'à la bouche" (p. 81), is extended in *Play* (1964) to the speakers—one can hardly call them characters—whose existence is restricted not only spatially and physically (they are also in jars and betray no visual or vocal expression), but temporally as well: they exist only when the spotlight is turned on them. The irony of the title is rather more obvious in the French: *Comédie*.

There is no doubt that Beckett is a man who suffers perpetually; not a self-pitying suffering, or physical suffering, but suffering caused by his unending consciousness of the suffering imposed on man by virtue of his existence. He lives in a state of existential anguish, and yet in person he gives every appearance of serenity and calm resolution. He now has the air of a man who knows what his purpose is, and how he has to fulfil it. Contrary to the legend that has been created (by such appellations as "moody man of letters") of aloofness and unapproachability, he is a man untouched by the success of the past fourteen years, modest and generous. His ability to inspire those who know him well—especially actors with whom he has worked on productions of his plays—with respect and affection is more significant than the antipathy he provokes in sensationalist journalists (he has been known to pose as his own brother when they have ferreted him out in his country retreat outside Paris, and then send them off on a wild-goose chase through the countryside). Beckett is "a truly compassionate man"[1]; but this did not prevent his speaking to me in harsh terms about "that dreadful man X, who asked me if I'd had an unhappy childhood, and was so disappointed when I told him, No, I'd been very happy and was fond of my parents".

He is notorious, of course, for his refusal to comment on the possible meanings of his works, and this uncommunicativeness —which is such a strong contrast to the self-explanation we have come to expect from, say, Ionesco or Montherlant—has resulted in some doubt as to his really having anything to say at all. Are we not being taken in? Is Beckett not laughing at the antics of commentators, editors, critics, and thesis-writers, who try to interpret his ambiguities as best they can? One cannot deny the possibility of this. It could, after all, be true of Dante, Cervantes, Kafka, Mallarmé, Proust, the writers of the Book of Revelation, and the author of any other text whose meaning is not elementary, simple, and immediately comprehensible in its totality to the average sixth-former. There is, however, an added safeguard in the case of Beckett for those who are afraid of being duped: Beckett wrote for twenty years without any expectation of having a public of more than a few hundred. His preoccupations as a writer were the same then as they have been since the 'break-through' of *Godot* in 1952. He has always written in response to the kind of irrepressible urge that pushes on every true writer. He has not developed a special kind of mystifying style or subject-matter just in order to set critics at loggerheads. But surely, one may ask, he himself must have the key to the meaning, which he mischievously declines to reveal? As I understand it from my conversations with him, his works should be treated almost as though they were not by a living author: "I produce an object. What people make of it is not my concern." Does he, in fact, understand the full

---

[1] Mr Paul Curran, in a letter giving me details of his interpretation of Pozzo in the Royal Court production of *Godot* in 1964–5.

implications of what he writes? "I'd be quite incapable of writing a critical introduction to my own works", he said. Everything that he does understand about the works is in them already. To the question, "Who or what is Godot?" he once replied: "If I knew, I would have said so in the play."[1]

It has been said that Beckett "produces his variations by ringing the changes on the same fundamental images . . . [his] skill in doing this is astonishing".[2] It is quite true that Beckett always seems to be digging in the same hole—an activity made respectable by Proust—but this is not necessarily limiting when the hole is the universe. As N. F. Simpson has shown in a masterly little play, *The Hole*, the visionary will find all he needs at the bottom of a hole. Mary McCarthy aptly pointed out, *à propos* of John Osborne, that "an author who is reluctant to repeat himself is in danger of repeating others".[3] Beckett has found his own voice with the certainty that customarily comes with experience and growing confidence, and we can hardly complain if this expatriate Irishman has developed a strongly idiosyncratic style in order to narrate his experiences of living with his mind in its quest for its own meaning.[4]

---

1 Alan Schneider, 'Waiting for Godot', *Chelsea Review*, New York, Autumn, 1958.

2 John Weightman, 'Talking Heads', *The Observer*, 3 May 1964.

3 'Verdict on Osborne', *The Observer*, 4 July 1965.

4 Beckett's attitude towards the indolence of a public unwilling to make any effort to understand what is not easily comprehensible is outspokenly stated in an essay written in 1929, 'Dante . . . Bruno. Vico . . . Joyce': "Here is direct expression —pages and pages of it. And if you don't understand it, Ladies and Gentlemen, it is because you are too decadent to receive it. You are not satisfied unless form is so strictly divorced from content that you can comprehend the one almost without bothering to read the other. This rapid skimming and absorption of the scant cream of sense is made possible by what I may call a continuous process of copious intellectual salivation."

CHAPTER 2

What are Beckett's Works 'about'?

"Prends un type par exemple qui n'a rien, ni au corps ni à l'autre truc. Comment va-t-il s'en sortir? C'est simple. En pensant au néant."
—*Mercier et Camier*

It is impossible to summarize Beckett's novels and plays without divesting them of almost all significance. If one does glimpse very occasionally (and more and more rarely) something like a sequence of events, this is quite unimportant. For this reason, the terms *anti-roman*, *anti-théâtre*, and *alittérature* have been applied to them, denoting a rejection of aesthetic conventions and commonly accepted literary preoccupations. Beckett distrusts 'literature' and the 'literary game'. He has said, "My little exploration is that whole zone of being that has always been set aside by artists as something unusable—as something by definition incompatible with art."[1]

Everything that is said about Beckett's works (other than *Godot*) in this essay is intended to prepare the reader for a fuller—*full* would be asking too much of the present writer—understanding of *Godot*. The various works will be mentioned *passim*, therefore, where reference to them would seem to illuminate some aspect of *Godot*. However, in the interests of initial orientation in the Beckettian wasteland, an attempt will first be made to suggest what his works are 'about' (I use the word more in the sense of 'approximation' than of 'subject'), on the most superficial level possible.

---

[1] Quoted by J. Fletcher, *op. cit.*, p. 232.

More Pricks than Kicks (1934), a collection of ten short stories, is 'about' the seedy Dublin adventures of Belacqua (the late-repentant, procrastinating Florentine mentioned by Dante in the fourth canto of the *Purgatorio*), whom Beckett makes into an eccentric *alter ego* full of pity for "all the living [who] dare . . . continue full of misery".

Murphy (1938) is 'about' the next incarnation of Beckett's *moi*, disguised as another Dubliner, Murphy. He leads a precarious life in London, and has two major occupations: trying to escape the attentions of a host of colourful characters—Neary, Wylie, Cooper, and the passionate Miss Counihan; and trying to stay out of work in the face of the subversive entreaties of the green-eyed, yellow-haired Celia.

Watt (written *c.* 1943, published 1953) is 'about' Murphy's reincarnation, Watt, who is much less of a distinct 'character' in the conventional sense than Murphy. Alienated from society, he goes to work as the servant of Mr Knott, an enigmatic, 'ineffable' master who is never more than glimpsed from a distance by his successive servants.

Molloy (1951), the first novel of the French trilogy, is in two parts. The first is 'about' a lame tramp, Molloy, who is wandering about on a bicycle searching for his mother and his home, and ends his journey in a ditch. In the second part, a sort of private investigator, Moran, receives orders (through a messenger, Gaber) to find Molloy. He fails, but returns strangely transformed: Molloy has become part of him.

Malone meurt (1951) is 'about' a reincarnation of Molloy, bed-ridden and completely solitary. His mind flits from one thing to another; he creates a character, Macmann, so as to slip into him. The novel ends with Malone's last breath.

The last volume of the trilogy, *L'Innommable* (1953), is told by an unnamed narrator who 'lives' in a world of half-light. He relates the story of one Mahood, who tried to reach the round-house in which his family lived; but as he had only one leg, his spiral progress was so slow that all his family died before he got there. The Unnamable narrator then conjures up Worm, 'a shapeless heap', 'a tiny blur', and is thus enabled to go on:

> ... il faut continuer, je ne peux pas continuer, il faut continuer, je vais donc continuer, il faut dire des mots, tant qu'il y en a... dans le silence on ne sait pas, il faut continuer, je vais continuer. (p. 261)

En attendant Godot (1952) is 'about' two destitute old men hopefully awaiting the promised arrival of a third, and not daring to move in case they miss him.

Fin de Partie (1957) is 'about' a family. The aged parents, Nagg and Nell, are legless and live in dustbins, one on each side of the stage. Now and then they lift their lids to ask for food or to interrupt briefly the dialogue between the son, Hamm, a blind old man who circles round the skull-like room in a wheelchair, and Clov, his rebellious servant, on whom Hamm is completely dependent. Outside the room, everything is dead, destroyed, 'corpsed', *mortibus*, even the sun is *néant*. Supplies are running out. Clov announces that a small boy is approaching, and finally puts on his hat and coat to fulfil his threat of leaving Hamm. As the play ends he is standing by the pantry door, still about to leave . . .

Acte sans paroles I (1957) consists of precise miming instructions for one man alone, who is pushed violently on to the stage which represents a desert with one palm-tree. Strange whistles come from all sides, but as soon as he goes off to investigate, he is projected on to the stage again. A carafe of water descends. However he tries to reach it—even with the aid of large cubes which are lowered to help him—it is always just too high. Eventually he sits motionless. The carafe is dangled right in front of his nose, the tree which has been protecting him with its shadow is hoisted aloft; he still sits without moving, looking at his hands.

"Progressivement, l'œuvre s'épuise; elle va vers une pointe." To P.-L. Mignon, writing this in 1964,[1] this point seemed to

---

[1] *L'Avant-Scène*, juin 1964.

be *Happy Days*, one of his most bleak and ferocious plays. The point has been even further reduced since then, but *Happy Days* serves as a good starting-point for a consideration of the kind of reactions Beckett's works inspire in readers and spectators, as it possesses to a remarkable degree two qualities which, although apparently contradictory, coexist in their most perfect equilibrium in *Godot*: utter despair, and the power to exhilarate:

> *Scene as before.*
> WINNIE *embedded up to neck, hat on head, eyes closed. Her head, which she can no longer turn, nor bow, nor raise, faces front motionless throughout act. Movements of eyes as indicated. Bag and parasol as before. Revolver conspicuous to her right on mound. Long pause.*
> *Bell rings loudly. She opens eyes at once. Bell stops. She gazes front. Long pause.*
> WINNIE: Hail, holy light.

This contrast between intolerable situation and unsinkable buoyancy runs right through Beckett's work. His comic insight prevents his ever becoming drab. The view that "from the beginning, his vision of the world has been that of a mild torture-chamber for incurables"[1] is one that has been unfortunately reinforced by BBC transmissions of selections of his works. These have been misleading, as they have given the general public no indication of Beckett's great comic qualities, or of the exhilaration his work can inspire by the juxtaposition of joy and despair. Jean-Louis Barrault has written with great perception about this play, *Oh les Beaux Jours*. In it, he says, we are at the end of life, at the end of everything. There are only a few seconds left, and only one couple:

> Et pourtant cette femme qui est là, est gaie et reconnaissante. Elle remercie. Elle comprend tout. Sa nature est obstinément braquée vers l'optimisme... C'est en côtoyant d'aussi près le

[1] John Weightman, *art. cit.*

néant et le désespoir que Beckett réussit cette espèce d'hymne à la vie, à l'amour, à la joie, à la reconnaissance, à la grâce. Peut-on dire grâce mystique?[1] //

The last two words of this eulogy go too far, perhaps, in the other direction. There is no evidence in anything Beckett has written or said to support the idea that the concept of divine grace enters into his world-view, but it is very important to remember that a highly literary actor of the calibre and sensitivity of M. Barrault is able to see this quality in Beckett's work. Less extreme is the equally sensitive appreciation of Martin Esslin:

//Beckett can give deep insights into human nature and the situation of man in the Universe, but above all he can make us see the world with serenity and a calm cheerfulness. . . . The idea that Beckett is a uniformly depressing writer is a misconception. . . /In Beckett's plays we are so harshly confronted with the mortality, evanescence, and ineffectuality of man that we look at our small daily predicaments with contempt and cheerfulness. . . .[2]

In all the characters, or figures, or *alter egos* who appear in Beckett's works, there is an irrepressible determination to remain human, to retain their dignity, irrespective of the degradation they undergo. Winnie, in *Happy Days*, with only her head radiantly visible above the ground, is able to say, in an epitome of courage on the brink of being sucked into the void: "Ah earth, you old extinguisher!" It is not the endless mire of *Comment c'est* that should strike one, but the dogged refusal of the creature crawling through it, to give up his search for a meaning in his existence, even though he knows this to be useless. Perhaps the secret of appreciating *Comment c'est* is to be found in a story by Kafka called *A Country Doctor*. The doctor is called in to treat a hideous wound in a boy's side. He can do nothing but comfort the boy with the words, "Es ist

[1] *L'Avant-Scène*, juin 1964.

[2] *Plays and Players*, November 1962.

wirklich so": '*That's how it is*'. All we can do is to face up to the hopelessness of the situation.

A highly literary and despairing, but nevertheless vigorously obscene gesture in the direction of Death is a common feature of Beckett's novels and plays. The tone is set already in *Murphy*, whose hero leaves instructions in his will for his ashes to be placed in a paper bag and

> brought to the Abbey Theatre, Lr. Abbey Street, Dublin, and [put] without pause into what the great Lord Chesterfield calls the necessary house, where their happiest hours have been spent . . . and I desire that the chain be pulled upon them, if possible during the performance of a piece, the whole to be executed without ceremony or show of grief.

In *Fin de Partie*, as in *Happy Days*, we are presented with the left-overs from some tragic, universal catastrophe, to which the play is a kind of epilogue, like a turntable still revolving after the motor has been switched off. The problem of existence, central to Beckett's work, is glimpsed in Hamm's anguished question, "Clov!... On n'est pas en train de... de... signifier quelque chose?" Clov's reply has the irreverent and ironic edge with which Beckett always cuts his writing off before it becomes pretentious or portentous: "Signifier? Nous, signifier! (*Rire bref.*) Ah elle est bonne!" (p. 49).

Writing of the Aldwych production of *Endgame*, J. W. Lambert struck a note of true feeling for the artistic and human qualities of this play when he emphasized

> Beckett's marvellous verbal mosaic . . . cadences which, shot through with rueful comedy, sing an unforgettable threnody for the human condition.[1]

One cannot stress too much, even at an early stage of this brief survey of the major characteristics of Beckett's works, the legitimacy of an exhilarated response to what J. L. Styan has called his "grim-gay nihilism".[2] Audiences at the recent production of *Godot* (at the Royal Court Theatre) found this

[1] *Sunday Times*, 12 July 1964.
[2] *The Dark Comedy*, p. 132.

the only possible response. Jack MacGowran, probably the definitive Lucky of our generation, has written of Beckett in terms which open up the important question of Beckett's style:

> He's opened a door and now there's no limit to how far he can go with his style. People get bored, depressed, and Beckett is bound to have his effect when he deals with these things on the stage. He is uplifting, exhilarating in the theatre. For an actor, to explore his compassion and his lyricism is very satisfying.[1]

Compassion[2] and lyricism. Even though the style of Beckett's novels is very different from that of the plays—his adaptation to the needs of the stage was as remarkable as that of Giraudoux—these qualities are constant. There is a purity, a density in Beckett's language when written for the spoken voice that has not escaped the ear of Jean-Louis Barrault who, in the course of a radio interview, was led to make a striking comparison[3]:

> Je vais peut-être vous étonner, sans le vouloir, mais l'auteur moderne qui me rappelle le plus Racine, cet auteur moderne que l'Angleterre et la France se partagent, est Samuel Beckett... Il y a dans Beckett ce souci de pureté, de simplicité, de musicalité et de sélection qui correspondent exactement au même souci, chez Racine. En examinant attentivement une œuvre comme *Oh les Beaux Jours* de Samuel Beckett on y découvre le premier germe du verbe de l'humanité. On y découvre une mosaïque harmonieuse, un

---

[1] 'Why Actors are Fascinated by Beckett's Theatre', *The Times*, 27 January 1965.

[2] Cf. Robert Shaw, *London Magazine*, 1960, p. 35: "Compassion's the thing. That's why I think I like *Waiting for Godot* more than anything I've seen since the war. I don't know why so many people call it a depressing play. Beckett writes about suffering in a way that makes me feel exhilarated—that I must get up and go out and do what I can."

[3] I am very grateful to M. Barrault and to Mr Carl Wildman of the BBC for permission to quote at length from this unpublished interview, broadcast in the Third Programme on 1 May 1965.

contrôle, un choix, un scrupule qui sont dignes de Racine. Citons dans *Oh les Beaux Jours*:

> "Fut-il un temps, Willy, où je pouvais séduire?
> Fut-il jamais un temps où je pouvais séduire?"

Eh bien, ce pourrait être deux alexandrins de Racine. Ces deux phrases sont aussi pures, aussi simples, aussi scrupuleusement choisies que deux vers de Racine. Elles sont aussi dépouillées de tout artifice inutile, de toute scorie... En France, Beckett a été pour les Lettres un phénomène très curieux. Il connaît le français mieux que moi.

The true subject-object of Beckett's writing is his Self—which is not the same as *himself*. He is engaged in a perpetual search for the nature of his personal identity. It is not Romantic introspection, vanity, egocentricity or narcissism that prompt this exploration, but a ruthless desire to expose the bottommost layer of being in the full knowledge—or belief—that there may in fact be *nothing* there. Novels and plays, for Beckett, have absolutely nothing to do with communicating information about 'living' characters in whom readers can 'believe'. They are imaginative speculations round the question, 'What do I mean when I say "I"?' As this question involves the most abstruse metaphysical, epistemological, and psychological problems man has ever perplexed himself with, it is understandable that the exploration could, given an indefatigable writer, continue almost indefinitely. Some of these problems are central to the meaning of *Godot*, and will be discussed at length in due course. For the moment, let us content ourselves with a simple statement of some of Beckett's basic preoccupations and beliefs:

—one cannot know what one means when one refers to 'I';
—definition of Self depends on memory, and this is imprecise;
—the writer (Beckett himself) *is* what he writes (cf. the existentialist 'je suis mes actes'). The words he writes *are* his constant search for his identity, for the meaning of his Self;
—our everyday existence is of doubtful reality;
—words give thoughts their existence, and are therefore the

only defence against being plunged into Nothingness (*le néant*), the Void (*le vide*) of silence and timelessness;
—earthly life is a punishment for an unknown crime, perhaps for the crime of being born;
—if a god exists, it is a malevolent entity, demanding and capricious;
—the body and everything else of a physical nature is worthy only of contempt and disgust, since it is something foisted on the Self as part of the punishment;
—the body and the mind are only tenuously connected;
—all Being is a unity; physical death is a trivial matter, as the Self continues eternally until the end of Time;
—the dividing-line between physical life and death is so vague that we might be existing now in limbo, waiting for eternity (timelessness);
—earthly existence is a state of exile from true reality whose essence is infinity;
—concern with earthly reality binds one to the finite. Conversely, being bound to terrestrial (linear) time enslaves one to materiality;
—there are only two possible states of Being: finite (in Time) and infinite (in silent Timelessness). Both are intolerable, but there is no third state to escape to;
—as the end of Time approaches, Time gradually decelerates, thus making successive events apparently occur more quickly. Thus, to the Self which is approaching the state of Timelessness, a recent event in linear Time seems like ancient history;
—the Self is a Void, like the centre of a circle. It awaits reunification with Nothingness, but this can only take place in a timeless (therefore changeless) state of motionless *waiting*.

These preoccupations enter into all of Beckett's writing, including *Godot*, with varying degrees of emphasis. They will be recognized, of course, as constituting also the major preoccupations of existentialist writers, but I have avoided using existentialist terminology so as not to prejudge the issue of whether Beckett is an existentialist writer. The problems of the absurdity (meaninglessness) of existence, the search for significance, authenticity, anguish, freedom, exile and separation, in-itself, for-itself, condemnation to existence beyond essence, and so on, which form the field of enquiry of phenomenological writers and philosophers,[1] are more technical and precise statements of the very same problems that torment Beckett. He has always refused allegiance to any religious creed or philosophical system. He regards any philosophical explanation of his works as unnecessary; as far as he is concerned they are self-explanatory.[2] He does not write with the intention of creating or expounding any metaphysical theory, unlike Sartre. A strictly philosophical approach to his works would, then, be irrelevant. It would, in any case, have to take in more than existentialism, for the influence on Beckett of dualistic philosophers (Descartes and Geulincx) is, as we shall see, better established than existentialist influence.

As an eclectic, widely-read, cultured intellectual, Beckett has manured and cultivated his garden with many philosophical droppings; therefore it is natural that the blossom (cankered though some consider it to be) should contain the essence of the compost that has fed it. The philosophical approach, however interesting for those trained in philosophy, tends to seek to prove the validity of the theories involved, and is of little use if it results in making the literary text more inaccessible. This has frequently happened in the field of Beckettian studies. Literature must be assessed in literary terms; if philosophical terms help to elucidate humanity,

---

[1] For an eminently readable comparison of different approaches to these problems, see Colin Smith, *Contemporary French Philosophy: A Study in Norms and Values*, Methuen, 1964.

[2] "If the subject of my novels could be expressed in philosophical terms, there would have been no reason for my writing them", he said, on being asked if they had existentialist foundations. (G. d'Aubarède: interview with Samuel Beckett, *Nouvelles Littéraires*, Paris, 16 février 1961.)

meaning, beauty, and originality when dealing with the texts, we should avail ourselves of them with gratitude. There is a rich allusiveness in his work which often needs to be pointed, and there is some deliberate (or inescapable) incoherence which—although it would be folly to reduce it to mere coherence since it expresses a universe without a system—needs to be partially unravelled in order to distinguish the golden thread of meaningfulness.

Beckett's work is, then, 'Self-centred'—which is very different from being 'self-centred'. We have seen that as Beckett's individual 'heroes', 'vice-existers', or 'other selves', progress, or are reincarnated—Belacqua, Murphy, Watt, Molloy, Moran, Malone, Mahood, Worm, Winnie[1]—they are deprived of all appendages—limbs and organs—not absolutely essential to stay alive. In this way Beckett makes these creatures less distinguishable as individuals, thus enhancing their ability to represent and express our common human condition. "What Moran calls 'that most fruitful of dispositions, horror of the body and its functions' pervades and informs Beckett's work from this book [*Molloy*] onwards."[2] In the two major plays, *Godot* and *Fin de Partie*, the physical side of life is also reduced to its barest essentials. There is a striking difference between the novels and the major plays, however; it is that the Self becomes split in two, forming what Beckett has called a *pseudocouple*: Vladimir and Estragon; Hamm and Clov. This dual nature had its roots in *Murphy*, was first explored in a novel still unpublished, *Mercier et Camier* (written *c.* 1945), and blossomed forth in *En attendant Godot*.

The relationship of the body with the mind, and the interaction of the two, is in our days primarily a psycho-physiological problem. But from the days of Ancient Greek philosophy, through Cartesian metaphysics, until the advent of

---

1 The M and the W beginning these names are inverted forms of Sigma—Σ—presumably S for Samuel.

2 J. Fletcher, *op. cit.*, p. 142.

empirical psychology, this problem came solely within the purview of metaphysics.

Rather more than by Descartes, Beckett was affected by the reasoning of the second-generation Cartesian, Arnold Geulincx (1624–69) who, with his 'beautiful Belgo-Latin', is mentioned in *Murphy* and in *La Fin* (in the *Nouvelles et Textes pour rien*). He maintained that the mental and physical modes are completely distinct, the only interaction between them being miraculously occasioned by the intervention of God who, however, has control only over the body: the mind is free. The man of good sense, realizing that he has power only over his mental processes, gives up all hope of governing any aspect or parts of the world outside his own mind, thus developing a total lack of involvement in any material or emotional stimuli and withdrawing to the inner recesses of the mind which alone is autonomous—but only over itself.[1] The body and the mind, according to Geulincx, interact by the action of God upon the body. The fact that a decision to perform a certain act can be followed immediately and spontaneously by the performance of the act is explained by Geulincx by the analogy of two clocks which keep perfect time quite independently of each other. Beckett does not accept the hypothesis of an intervening God. Hence the lack of co-ordination that frequently characterizes his heroes. Their bodies do not seem to 'belong' to them, and the will dictates movement in vain. The resultant inaction and lethargy are features common to Murphy, Watt, Molloy, and all four characters in *Godot* at various times.[2]

---

[1] In *Godot*, the two tramps' withdrawal from society into a limbo where physical preoccupations are of the most elementary kind and their possessions almost nil can be seen as an example of this dualist retreat from physical contingencies.

[2] *E.g.*, Vladimir and Estragon cannot leave when they express their wish to do so. In Act 2 their will to help the fallen Pozzo is followed by very delayed action. When they fall themselves, they cannot will their bodies to stand up again; they have to wait until the physical 'clock', which has apparently got out of

Again it should be stressed that Beckett is not concerned with illustrating the 'truth' of Geulincx's theories. He is not interested in contributing to the metaphysical debate that has gone on between Cartesians, interactionists, epiphenomenalists, behaviourists, and parallelists, all attempting to explain the mysteries of body-mind dualism. The Belgian, Geulincx, seems to have appealed to Beckett more than Plato, Aristotle, Descartes, Malebranche, Spinoza, Leibnitz, or other philosophers speculating about this problem, probably because Geulincxian *askésis* (ascetic withdrawal from society) accords with his personal proclivity to introspection.

Apart from Geulincx there is one other profoundly influential writer who must be mentioned in general terms before we turn our attention specifically to *En attendant Godot*. This is Dante. The link between the Belgian and the Italian is—if one needs to find a link—dualism, which in Dante takes the form of the 'cleft consciousness' that is a commonplace in Christian thinking. Beckett studied Dante at university (he reads Italian fluently), and introduced the indolent, phlegmatic character of Belacqua Shuah, the guitar-maker of Florence, for the first time into a prose text, *Sedendo et Quiescendo* (1932), and made him the hero of the ten short stories that constitute *More Pricks than Kicks* (1934). "Dante . . . comes back into his own again in the works Beckett wrote in French after 1945 . . . not only did he not forget the *Divine Comedy*, he even steeped himself more deeply in its atmosphere, and the Inferno especially became one of his most habitual points of reference."[1] Dr Fletcher's main concern, it is true, is with the novels, but the remark is important for *Godot* which was also written during this period of renewed interest in Dante. It is not merely particular points of simi-

---

phase, catches up with the mental one that is vainly dictating action to the body. The possibility that Vladimir and Estragon represent body and mind respectively will be discussed later.

1 John Fletcher, 'Beckett's Debt to Dante', *Nottingham French Studies*, vol. IV, no. 1, May 1965, pp. 41–52.

larity that are involved,[1] but rather the fascination, for Beckett, of the vivid representation Dante gives of the everlasting monotony, the eternal unchanging sameness, which make the limbo of Purgatory so completely different from Paradise, with its eternal progress and ascent from one state of knowledge and blessedness to another.

The experience upon which Dante had to build was scarcely different from that of Beckett, in that it was bounded by the miseries of earthly existence; but the visionary intuition of Beckett leads him to extend the lines of his meditation through limbo to eternal Nothingness. There is no sublime state, no *Paradiso*; on the other hand, there are none of the violent tortures of the *Inferno*. Although the creatures struggling through the mire in *Comment c'est* are made to suffer abominably, Beckett's works are "... incantations that the mind transmits from limbo, for Beckett's *Inferno* is rather an eternal and solitary state of suspension than a Dantesque torture-chamber ..."[2] This limbo resembles the state of *l'homme absurde* in Camus' *Mythe de Sisyphe*, in which the same act has to be repeated indefinitely. As the hero says in a short story Beckett wrote in 1945 (*Le Calmant*), "tout est dit, tout sera à recommencer".

Molloy fears that God does not exist; or that even if he does it does not really matter since in any case he probably 'will not come'. Life is reduced to an alternation of going on and waiting. Beckett presents humanity as aimlessly questing or endlessly waiting—but having the courage to continue living even though it is far from being sure what (or whom) it is searching or waiting for, and far from being convinced that there is anything, anyway. In *Mercier et Camier*, Watt says during his brief appearance at the end, "Moi aussi, j'ai cherché, tout

[1] *E.g.*, the late repentance of Belacqua *and* of the tramps in Godot: reason enough to put them all in Antepurgatory to await idly their summons to Purgatory. Murphy, too, imagines himself to be in Antepurgatory, dreaming away until the time comes for "the toil up the hill to Paradise".

[2] John Fletcher, *The Novels of Samuel Beckett*, p. 108.

seul, seulement moi je croyais savoir quoi. Vous vous rendez compte... incroyable mais vrai." The journey theme recurs in Beckett's novels, beginning in a recognizable geographical *milieu* with Belacqua's meanderings in Dublin, and Murphy's in London. In *Watt* the landscape is more immaterial and unreal, but not entirely so. Nevertheless, the journey in this novel is partly that of Watt's

dim mind wayfaring
through barren lands
of a flame with dark winds
hedged about
going out
gone out . . .

The element of myth becomes very much stronger in *Molloy*, where the theme of one man's search for another, leading to physical disintegration and mental isolation, is grossly underestimated if taken at its face value. The journey Moran undertakes is ordered by a tyrannical master whose name, Youdi, can be associated (through Yahudi) with Yahweh, Jehovah. These journeys are notable for their lack of success: Watt does not discover anything about the mysterious Mr Knott, Moran fails to find Molloy, Mercier and Camier forget what they set out to search for (if they ever knew).

The usual result of constant frustration and failure in the face of a task is apathetic indifference. Beckett illustrates this clearly in *Acte sans Paroles I*. If constant searching proves fruitless, the temptation to sit and wait for the object of the search to turn up is very strong. *L'Innommable* and *Godot*, written at about the same time, have in common an absence of those distractions which, in our socially-orientated existence, shield us from the basic problem of waiting for eternity. In these works, as in *Oh les Beaux Jours* and *Fin de Partie*, there is no escaping the unrelenting presence of the problem which underlies them all, irrespective of the different artistic terms Beckett uses to express them; that problem is, *when will the end come?* Viewed on this level, these works are allegories or, more precisely, symbolic representations of our mortal condition.

Although we may find it difficult to associate ourselves with the destitutes and abandoned remnants of humanity who haunt Beckett's works, we may begin to do so with something of a shock (intended) when we realize that they are not alone in their tragi-comic occupation of aimless searching and fruitless waiting. We are in it, too, but we can have the fact brought home to us only by a form of literature which reduces social, political, civic, and ideological elements to zero. Beckett presents us with a definition of man in terms of solitude and exile, as Camus does in *La Peste*. But whereas Camus places his exiles *en situation*, in a precise social setting, and presents them with social duties and dilemmas, Beckett's more visionary eye is focused on man divested of his social functions and set outside any historical context—in the context of eternity. This archetypal, mythical literature is the antithesis of a literature which —like that of Balzac or Zola or modern Marxist writers—seeks representation and explanation of human problems in terms of social causality, physical determinism, or the class struggle. "Beckett is more of a seer than a moralist. He views the human predicament; he does not prescribe for its alteration."[1] The visionary, apocalyptic quality of Beckett's writing is at its most striking in *Fin de Partie* which, whilst developing the master-slave relationship of Pozzo and Lucky as seen in *Godot*, seems to herald the very end of existence.

The explorations Beckett undertakes into the depths of Time and Being, and the horror he experiences at the faint glimmer of timeless eternity he has witnessed, are of the same order as the experience Victor Hugo records in *La Pente de la Rêverie*. The poet-seer's vision momentarily transcends the illusion of everyday reality and glimpses the reality of the great illusion:

> Oh! cette double mer du temps et de l'espace
> Où le navire humain toujours passe et repasse,

---

1 Jerome Ashmore, 'Philosophical Aspects of *Godot*', *Symposium*, vol. XVI, no. 4. Winter 1962, pp. 296–306.

> Je voulus la sonder, je voulus en toucher
> Le sable, y regarder, y fouiller, y chercher...
> Et dire si son lit est de roche ou de fange.
> Mon esprit plongea donc sous ce flot inconnu;
> Au profond de l'abîme il nagea seul et nu,
> Toujours de l'ineffable allant à l'invisible...
> Soudain il s'en revint avec un cri terrible,
> Ébloui, haletant, stupide, épouvanté,
> Car il avait au fond trouvé l'éternité.
>
> (*Feuilles d'Automne*, XXIX)

Beckett echoes this in *Molloy*: "le fond c'est mon habitat, oh pas le fin fond, quelque part entre l'écume et la fange" (p. 19). We are in the same realm of experience in Baudelaire's *Le Voyage*:

> Plonger au fond du gouffre, Enfer ou Ciel, qu'importe,
> Au fond de l'Inconnu pour trouver du nouveau!

But it is above all in Pascal that one finds the most simple and the most majestic visionary expression of infinity:

> Nous avons beau enfler nos conceptions au delà des espaces imaginables, nous n'enfantons que des atomes au prix de la réalité des choses... Qu'est-ce qu'un homme dans l'infini?... entre ces deux abîmes de l'infini et du néant, il tremblera dans la vue de ces merveilles... Toutes choses sont sorties du néant et portées jusqu'à l'infini.
>
> (*Pensées*, éd. Brunschvicg, II, p. 72)

Pascal's awe quickly turns to admiration, however; the Author of these wonders understands them—we do not need to. Hugo concludes that the reason why "le sentiment de l'infini plane sur le monde moderne" is because "pour nous, tout est Dieu". This solace, which is evidence of *mauvaise foi* for the Sartrian existentialist, is denied to Beckett, who has said: "I'm not interested in any system. I can't see any trace of any system anywhere."[1]

---

[1] I. Shenker, 'Moody Man of Letters', *New York Times*, 6 May 1956.

The lines from *Watt* quoted above ("the dim mind way-faring") epitomize the anguish caused by confrontation with man's situation in the universe, "un néant à l'égard de l'infini", as Pascal said. Beckett is far from being the only writer to have felt this anguish, of course. It has been a common experience since 1930, and especially since 1945. This is hardly surprising; as the Jungian analyst Dr Eva Metman has pointed out, the type of drama with which we are concerned here "has its roots in the general cultural situation and in the increasingly unbearable contrast between conscious aims and unconscious needs".[1] For example, consciously we respond to the constant encouragement we are given to improve our social and material conditions, but unconsciously we fear that the ultimate absurdity of it all may not be just the fantasy of a few too intellectual Weary Willies.

One may wonder at the comparison suggested above between the majestic evocation of infinity attempted by Pascal, and the diminutive, whining, grinding *homunculi* of Beckett. Jean Anouilh had the insight to see the connexion straight away after the first production of *Godot*, when he likened it to "a music-hall sketch of Pascal's *Pensées* performed by the Fratellini clowns".[2] For Pascal, however, the *néant* of man is balanced by the *toute-puissance* of God. One side of the equation has disappeared for Beckett. All that is left is Nothing—and, to quote Beckett's favourite saying from Democritos the Abderite: "Nothing is more real than nothing." Beckett has therefore had to tackle the problem of rendering by very different means the nothingness of man seen *sub specie æternitatis*, in relation to infinity. He cannot even evoke the nobility of the existentialist hero who accepts *le néant* and the anguish of utter freedom. The artistic procedure he has adopted may seem to be lacking in spectacular grandeur and in ima-

---

1 'Reflections on Samuel Beckett's Plays', *Journal of Analytical Psychology*, January 1960.

2 *Arts*, 27 January 1953. Quoted by Edith Kern, 'Drama stripped for Inaction', *Yale French Studies*, no. 14, p. 41.

ginative *élan*, but another comparison may help one to evaluate its effect in a way that comparisons with Pascal, Hugo, Baudelaire, or Rimbaud cannot. The Swiss sculptor Giacometti impresses the same spare, dwindling, disintegrating qualities on the clay and bronze as Beckett does on his invisible creations; but it is a remark made by Jean Genet about one of Giacometti's drawings which seems more strikingly analogous. It showed "a minute figure placed right at the bottom of an enormous white expanse", and the effect was to "bring out such a vast white surface by means of such a tiny figure".[1] Similarly, the very destitution and insignificance of Beckett's characters, diminished in a world which becomes more restricted in each successive work, suggests more forcibly than the grandest of Hugo's visions the limitless engulfing Void.

There are, certainly, moments when Beckett evocatively suggests the absurd, useless immensity in which man is held prisoner with not only no means of escape but nowhere to escape *to*:

> Énorme prison, comme cent mille cathédrales, plus jamais autre chose, dorénavant, et là-dedans, quelque part, peut-être, rivé, infime, le détenu, comment le trouver, que cet espace est faux, quelle fausseté aussitôt, vouloir y nouer des rapports, vouloir y mettre un être, une cellule suffirait... il n'y a qu'ici, il n'y a pas deux endroits, il n'y a pas deux prisons, c'est mon parloir, c'est un parloir, je n'y attends rien, je ne sais pas où c'est, je ne sais pas comment c'est, je n'ai pas à m'en occuper, je ne sais pas s'il est grand, ou s'il est petit, ou s'il est fermé, ou s'il est ouvert, c'est ça, réitère, ça fait continuer, ouvert à quoi, il n'y a que lui, ouvert au vide, ouvert au rien, je veux bien, ce sont des mots, ouvert au silence...[2]

---

1 'Giacometti's Studio', *The Observer*, 11 July 1965.

2 *L'Innommable*, pp. 250–253.

CHAPTER 3

GODOT: Genesis and Composition

"Je n'attends rien..."
"On attend Godot."

These two statements together, the first from *L'Innommable*, imply many of the major problems of interpretation we are likely to encounter in dealing with *En attendant Godot*, this amalgam of simplicity and complexity which suddenly brought Beckett into the forefront of contemporary theatre after twenty years of semi-obscurity as a novelist. How did it come to be written? How was it created? Does the genesis of *Godot* throw any light on its possible meanings?

The first page of the manuscript of *En attendant Godot* bears the date '9 October 1948'; the last '29 January 1949'. Between these dates Beckett put aside *Malone meurt* and wrote the play which was due to cause as much controversy among scholars and critics as Goethe's *Faust* and Kafka's *Castle*. "I began to write *Godot*", Mr Beckett told me, "as a relaxation, to get away from the awful prose I was writing at that time." Although *Godot* was in many ways—structurally, stylistically, thematically—a new development in Beckett's writing, it expressed his basic concerns as faithfully and sincerely as his novels.

In *L'Avant-Scène* of June 1964, P.-L. Mignon wrote: "Pour Samuel Beckett chaque travail nouveau procède du précédent, chaque travail secrète le suivant." It was with this in mind that I asked Beckett if he would throw any light on the way *Godot* might have grown out of his previous works which might illuminate the study of the genesis of the play. In the first place, he confirmed that, as Mignon records, the source of the dialogue between the boy and Vladimir is to be found in the unpublished play *Eleutheria*. He then added: "If you want to find the origins of *En attendant Godot*, look at *Murphy*." The most significant connexion between the two works—but far from being the only one—can be discerned in the description of Murphy as "split in two, a body and a mind. They had intercourse, apparently, otherwise he could not have known that they had anything in common. But he felt his mind to be bodytight and did not understand through what channel the intercourse was effected nor how the two experiences came to overlap. He was satisfied that neither followed from the other." The description continues with a detail which one cannot help associating with the unfortunate Estragon crippled by Lucky: "He neither thought a kick because he felt one, nor felt a kick because he thought one."

Murphy, then, feels his body and mind to be divided into separate entities. This idea has its roots in a very respectable philosophical tradition, as we have seen. Beckett has readily acknowledged the profound effect upon him of the occasionalist Arnold Geulincx. In *Godot* Beckett consummates the division, thus making the monologue of the novels—the exploration of the depths of one central solipsistic character—into dialogue. It is too simple to call one of the two tramps 'the Mind' and the other 'the Body', as Ruby Cohn does ('mental versus physical man').[1] They are nevertheless a *pseudocouple*. It is not without significance that Beckett applies this term, in *L'Innommable*, to the protagonists of the unpublished novel *Mercier et Camier*—the only one of Beckett's French novels not to be written from the point of view of 'I'.

A careful reading of the typescript of *Mercier et Camier*[2] discloses many clues to the 'making' of *En attendant Godot*, but

---

[1] *Samuel Beckett: The Comic Gamut*, Rutgers, 1962, p. 213.

[2] I am very grateful to Dr John Fletcher, author of an excellent study of Beckett's novels, for placing at my disposal in a spirit of great scholarly generosity a typescript copy of *Mercier et Camier*. Mr Beckett had told me he no longer possessed *any*

it should be stressed at the outset that to compare them is not to infer that the play is in any way a deliberate transposition or adaptation of the novel. Such a conclusion would misconstrue the purpose of the comparison, which is twofold: to show the uses to which elements common to both works were put; and to throw light on the artistic superiority of *Godot* by showing what it grew out of and what it might have been but for the magical transformation wrought by a true artist.

Beckett knew instinctively that *Mercier et Camier* was but an experimental approximation to what he was trying to achieve. Hence his refusal to publish it and his complete lack of interest in it. His refusal must be respected, of course, and I reproduce here—with his kind permission—no more than is necessary for the genetic study of *Godot*.

When I told Mr Beckett that I was struck by the similarities between the two works and that, to put it crudely, they seemed to have come out of the same stable, his only comment was to the effect that he could remember nothing about *Mercier et Camier* ("a dreadful book"), and had cast it completely out of his mind. Seeing that it was written in 1945, four years before *Godot* (with *Molloy*, *Eleutheria*, and *Malone meurt* in between), it is quite credible that a writer with a headful of dying worlds crying out to be drawn into existence should drive an unwanted embryo from his conscious mind. But any work of art, once it has been created, never leaves its author intact, whatever he might think of it. As Dr Fletcher points out, for example, Part II of *Molloy* derives from *Mercier et Camier* and in places follows it quite closely.[1] The resemblances

---

copy of the work, and that Dr Fletcher might be able to lend me his. Dr Fletcher has recently completed a study of the novel *per se*; my present study and his article ('Sur un roman inédit de Samuel Beckett', *Annales* (Toulouse), t. 1, fasc. 3, novembre 1965, pp. 139–154) have quite different aims and have been done independently.

1 *The Novels of Samuel Beckett*, Chatto and Windus, 1964, p. 129.

between *Mercier et Camier* and *Godot* are of quite a different order, however. That they are unconscious similarities one need have no doubt, but they are none the less highly informative and, together with the manuscript of *En attendant Godot*, throw some new light upon the question of the making of *Godot*.[1]

There are many coincidences of style and theme in *Mercier et Camier* and *Godot*. Particular attention will be paid to the most interesting points illuminated by the unpublished documents—namely, the setting of the play; the origins and meaning of the tree; Godot; the rendezvous and the theme of waiting; the creation of the characters and the relationships between them; the perfection of the dialogue and the suppression of certain precise details to be found in the manuscript.

The essential difference between *Mercier et Camier* and *Godot* is that the two old men in the novel are completely *disponibles*, able to wander aimlessly on their vague quest, whereas the two tramps in the play are tied to one spot. This results in radical dissimilarities in structure. Mercier and Camier dissipate their energies in the search for divers objects—their bag, their umbrella, their bicycle—as well as for the ultimate unspecified thing or person motivating their wanderings. In *Godot* all this is streamlined, as all the hopes of Vladimir and Estragon are concentrated upon one objective: the meeting with Godot, with whom a rendezvous has been

---

[1] The manuscript of *En attendant Godot*, which Mr Beckett kindly allowed me to read, thus making this study possible, consists of an exercise book measuring 8½ in. × 7 in. Beckett wrote on each right-hand page to the end of the book, then continued on each left-hand page beginning at the beginning of the book again. He told me that there were several typescript versions between the manuscript and the first edition. The 2nd edition (also 1952) contains minor textual changes, and constitutes the definitive edition upon which the present text is based.

arranged. Vladimir and Estragon do, in fact, go away from the meeting place at night, and they lose sight of each other during the action of the play, greeting each other like long-lost friends a few moments later. Similarly the journey of Mercier and Camier is punctuated by regular returns *chez* Hélène (a singularly accommodating acquaintance). The centre of interest in the novel is in the time spent away from 'base'; in the play, the centre is in the returning and the waiting. The importance of waiting and meeting is a notable feature of the novel too, together with the questing theme which Beckett took up again in *Molloy*.

Mercier and Camier arrange to meet at a place called le Square Saint-Ruth. "C'est ce qui les amena sans doute à s'y donner rendez-vous. Certaines choses, nous ne les saurons jamais avec certitude." In *Godot*, Vladimir retorts to Estragon's insinuation that they have come to the wrong place, "Pour jeter le doute, à toi le pompon" (p. 9). Mercier and Camier miss each other several times at the rendezvous, but eventually both arrive at the spot at the same moment:

> Leur joie fut donc pendant un instant extrême, celle de Mercier et celle de Camier, lorsqu'après cinq et dix minutes respectivement d'inquiète musardise, débouchant simultanément sur la place, ils se trouvèrent face à face, pour la première fois depuis la veille au soir.

The similarity of situation and emotion with that of the beginning of Act 2 of *Godot* is striking:

> Ils se regardent longuement, en reculant, avançant, et penchant la tête comme devant un objet d'art, tremblant de plus en plus l'un vers l'autre, puis soudain s'étreignent, en se tapant sur le dos. (p. 50)

So strong is the theme of joyful reunion that Beckett returns to it very much later in *Mercier et Camier*:

> Ta main, dit Camier, tes deux mains.
> Pour quoi faire? dit Mercier.

Pour les serrer dans les miennes, dit Camier.

Les mains se cherchèrent sous la table, parmi les jambes, se trouvèrent, se serrèrent, une petite entre deux grandes, une grande entre deux petites.

Je nous aurais bien proposé de nous embrasser, dit Mercier, il y a si longtemps que nous ne nous sommes pas embrassés, mais j'ai peur des représailles.

In Act 2 of *Godot*, Vladimir and Estragon make up after quarrelling:

— Ta main!
— La voilà!
— Viens dans mes bras!
— Tes bras?
— (*ouvrant les bras*) Là-dedans!
— Allons-y. (*Ils s'embrassent.*) (p. 67)

Mercier and Camier wait in a public shelter for the rain to stop. Their conversation has the same qualities as that of their two counterparts in *Godot*; it is that of two people forced into passive waiting by something beyond their control. The "agent complaisant de la malignité universelle" which forces them to wait is in this case nothing more mysterious than the rain; the strong term applied to it might seem more appropriate to Godot.

Mercier and his companion argue about who kept whom waiting. Camier replies, "On n'attend ni ne fait attendre qu'à partir d'un moment convenu d'avance."

This statement is the very core of *Godot*. The very fact that Vladimir and Estragon are waiting presupposes that a time was fixed. In the manuscript of the play this arrangement is not just verbal, as in the published text (p. 9), but *written down by Godot himself*:

— Tu es sûr que c'était ce soir?
— Quoi?
— Notre rendez-vous.
— Diable! (*Il cherche dans ses poches.*) Il l'a écrit.

[*He pulls out a number of pieces of paper and hands one over.*] Qu'est-ce que tu lis?

— "Samedi soir et suivants." Quelle façon de s'exprimer!
— Tu vois!
— (*rendant le papier*). Mais sommes-nous samedi?

For Godot to have written the words himself, he must have a physical reality; this obvious consequence led to the omission of the piece of paper. But we see from this first version something not entirely without significance, that Beckett originally envisaged the two characters to be waiting for a real person.

We see in *Mercier et Camier* the seeds of doubt about the precise nature of the arrangement to meet. Camier concludes, "Nous ne saurons jamais à quelle heure nous nous sommes donné rendez-vous, aujourd'hui. Ne cherchons donc plus." The importance which Mercier and Camier attach to this matter is curious, since in their case it is in fact a very trivial point. Only when it was later transferred to the cosmic situation of Vladimir and Estragon did it assume its full latent significance.

A clearer pre-echo of the waiting for Godot makes itself heard half-way through *Mercier et Camier*. A mountaineer called M. Conaire—whose idiosyncrasies give him a likeness to both Pozzo and Vladimir—tells the barman, "(Camier) m'a donné rendez-vous, ici même, pour le début de l'après-midi". But Camier and his friend are upstairs in a drunken stupor, so they miss M. Conaire. The following day, however, Camier accidentally meets M. Conaire, and explains that he, Camier, is no longer interested in him: "C'est que j'avais compris, ou plutôt décidé, que mon travail était fini... et que j'avais eu tort en pensant que vous pourriez vous joindre à nous..." The nature of the work and the reason why M. Conaire was to join them are never precisely revealed. Here, it is Camier—whose *projet* the journey is—who plays a kind of Godotesque rôle. Because he is drunk upstairs he fails to turn up at the rendezvous with M. Conaire, who expects Camier to find him some sort of business partnership with them. In the first act of *Godot* the expectations of the two tramps are expressed in similar terms: Godot would have to consult his friends, his registers, his bank account, before deciding. The manuscript does not mention "ses agents, ses correspondants"—these are included in the final text to stress further the idea of a business relationship.

The setting of *Godot* seems at first sight so simple and stark as to make any research into its origins unnecessary: a country road with one tree. But one gradually builds up enough of a picture of the locality to make one want to know where the tramps are—because the nature of the place may have some connexion with the identity of the person for whom they are waiting, and with the reasons why they are waiting. Where? For whom? And why? Much has been written on these three basic questions posed by *Godot*. The evidence of the unpublished material will certainly not provide any definite answers, but it may help us to pick our way among the many possible interpretations by revealing something of the author's intentions during the process of gestation and creation.

The deserted plateau on which Vladimir and Estragon spend their days was in process of creation in *Mercier et Camier*. Let us first consider the setting of a story told, in the course of the novel, by a barman, M. Gast, "tout en choisissant avec soin ses termes et en calculant ses effets", in the manner of Pozzo.

> ... un paysage plat, net et vide. C'est une lande, et un chemin étroit, sans bordure ni ombre, y déroule à perte de vue ses douces courbes alternantes. L'air gris pâle est sans un souffle. On voit au loin, entre terre et ciel, une sorte de commissure qui laisse passer par endroits comme le trop-plein d'un monde ensoleillé.

A little later, Mercier and Camier find themselves out in the wilds: "Le champ s'étendait devant eux. Rien n'y poussait, rien d'utile aux hommes."

Le Square Saint-Ruth, where Mercier and Camier meet at the beginning of their journey, has a tree—"un hêtre pourpre immense et luisant"—planted more or less in the centre "par un maréchal de France de nom Saint-Ruth". The square owes its name and what little charm it still has to the tree, which is nearing its term and will wither away, "jusqu'au jour où l'on l'enlèverait, par morcellement". Then everyone will breathe better, for a little while.

The tree was planted by a soldier; it has charm, but it will be better for everybody when it is removed. Now let us move on to the striking and vivid scene near the end of the novel (Chapter 10), in which we observe the two exhausted old men wandering about in the pitch blackness of night over a plateau:

> Un chemin carrossable traverse la haute lande... Il coupe à travers de vastes tourbières, à cinq cents mètres d'altitude, mille si vous aimez mieux... Tout semble plat, ou en pentes douces, et cependant on passe tout près de hautes falaises... La ville non plus n'est pas loin...

There are no trees; only a cross over the grave of a soldier, "une croix fort simple".

In *Godot*, Vladimir draws attention to "cet arbre... cette tourbière" (p. 9). Many ingenious arguments have been elaborated to try and identify the tree in *Godot* with the Cross or with the mythical trees of life.[1] Professor McCoy's argument, in the article just quoted, rests very cogently upon the foliation of the tree in Act 2. The English and French versions have an interesting variant here: the French tree is "couvert de feuilles" (the manuscript already has this), but the English one "has four or five leaves". Mr Beckett has given me the following reason for the difference: quite simply, he and Roger Blin realized, when the first production was staged (after the

[1] *E.g.*, "They miss the appointment [with Godot]. The tree, the Cross, becomes a tree of life. But those who wait in self-satisfied blindness remain dead." C. McCoy, '*Waiting for Godot:* A Biblical Appraisal', *Religion in Life*, Fall, 1959. L. C. Pronko says the tree recalls a gallows, a cross (both instruments of torture and religious symbols), and the various trees of mythical literature—the sacred Bo-tree, or Yggdrasil's ash, the 'world-tree'. (*Avant-Garde: the Experimental Theatre in France*, pp. 26–27.)

first edition of the French text had gone to press) that it was more effective to have a few sparse leaves. However, this does not explain why the post-production editions and reprints of the French text (all dated 1952) still read "couvert de feuilles". The sparse foliage is certainly more in the Beckettian style (a *satirical* comment upon the passage in Proverbs 13, xii: "Hope deferred maketh the heart sick . . .". Vladimir's memory gives up at this point of the quotation in the English text of *Godot*—the reference is missing altogether from the French text. It continues thus: ". . . but when the desire cometh, it is a tree of life"; some tree of life, one might retort!). It is, after all, the sparse foliage that appears in the final version of the play (i.e., in the Grove Press (1954) and Faber (1956) editions).

Let us return for a moment to the tree in le Square Saint-Ruth, to which Beckett gives a good deal of attention. It was planted by a soldier whose name is commemorated by a plaque on the tree. The solitary cross on the plateau also commemorates a soldier. Is it too fanciful to see some connexion between the tree and the cross (no doubt unconscious, but that hardly matters in these post-Freudian days)? One can interpret the statement that it will be better for everybody when the tree withers either by identifying it with Yggdrasil's tree (ash, not beech, it is true)—in which case the implication is that humanity will benefit from the death of that divine power which (supposedly) shelters and protects it. This would coincide with Beckett's familiar views on the desirability of total extinction, life being the horrible thing it is.[1] Or the interpretation might read, through the association of tree and cross, that the world will be better off without a suffocating Christianity. The two possibilities are not, of course, mutually exclusive.

We have, then, a tree and a cross occupying positions of

---

[1] *E.g.* 'Il faut manger, dit Mercier.
Je n'en vois pas l'utilité, dit Camier. Plus vite on crèvera, mieux ça vaudra.
Cela est vrai, dit Mercier.'

importance in the two most crucial scenes in *Mercier et Camier*: the first meeting-place from which they set off on their quest, and the night on the plateau. At the forking of the ways, as they leave the plateau, there stands "un arbre géant, fouillis de branches noires". The tree (of life?) being now dead, the two old men separate and 'un-know' each other, only to be brought together again later by Watt, that great seeker of truths about the unseen master who has negation in the very heart of his name: Knott. As the three of them, Mercier, Camier, and Watt, walk along, "ils sentent la décomposition".

The tree which provides the focal point of the setting of *Godot* can therefore be considered as 'growing' out of an unconscious amalgamation of these two crucial scenes. Any misplaced hopes that might have been (and have been) pinned by commentators on the healthy foliation of that tree[1] are undermined by the pathetically comic four or five leaves.

The plateau on which Vladimir and Estragon wait has confines which are explored by Estragon during his panic-stricken sorties just before the arrival of Pozzo and Lucky in Act 2 (pp. 65–66). He is absent for only a moment, and yet Vladimir welcomes him back like a long-lost friend. How long was that apparently momentary separation? Estragon gasps: "Je suis maudit", and says he has been "Jusqu'au bord de la pente." Vladimir is sure Godot is coming: "Nous sommes sauvés!" Estragon dashes off the other side. Vladimir again acts as though they have not seen each other for a long time. "Je suis damné!" shouts Estragon—in the English text he says more tellingly, "I'm in hell!" He has been "jusqu'au bord de la pente" on that side too. Vladimir concludes, "nous sommes servis sur un plateau".

---

1 *E.g.*, J. R. Moore, 'A Farewell to Something', *Tulane Drama Review*, 1960, p. 58: "The tree, that ever-present reminder of the Cross, stands for the resurrection (as the leaves show) that comes from sacrificial death."

Immediately after this Vladimir nearly pushes Estragon off their 'plateau' into the audience to enable him to escape: "Là il n'y a personne. Sauve-toi par là" ("There! Not a soul in sight!"). Estragon "recule épouvanté". "Tu ne veux pas?" asks Vladimir; he contemplates the auditorium. "Ma foi, ça se comprend."

Before trying to make sense of these rather mystifying and fearful reactions to whatever lies beyond their plateau, let us refer again to *Mercier et Camier* and to the manuscript of *En attendant Godot*. First, Camier encourages Mercier as they continue their aimless journey: "Courage, dit Camier, c'est bientôt la station des damnés. Je vois le clocher." And later on, the two meet again after a short separation:

> Qu'est-ce qui t'est arrivé? dit Camier.
> Voilà le dialogue qui reprend...
> Quelle tête tu fais, dit Camier. On dirait que tu sors des enfers...
> Je n'en connais qu'un, dit Mercier.
> On ne t'a pas battu? dit Camier.

Vladimir similarly asks Estragon if he has been beaten during the night, and he replies that ten men did so (only four in the manuscript). This merely underlines how close the situation of the two couples of old men is, thus allowing us to treat them as parallel with textual justification. Thus, the answer to the question, 'Where did Estragon get beaten up?' is to be found, by implication, in *Mercier et Camier*: in the nearby town. For the lights of the town are to be seen from one spot on Mercier and Camier's plateau. When they leave it, "c'est bien entendu vers la ville qu'ils vont, comme à chaque fois qu'ils la quittent..." What town is this? This question needs to be looked into, because it is related to the problem of the tramps' very existence.

In the novel, Camier asks, "La petite voix implorante qui nous parle parfois de vies antérieures, tu la connais?" Mercier replies, "Je la confonds de plus en plus avec celle qui veut me faire croire que je ne suis pas encore mort." Vladimir and

Estragon speak of "Toutes les voix mortes... Elles parlent de leur vie... Il ne leur suffit pas d'être mortes" (pp. 54–55). A little later Estragon asks hopefully, "On trouve toujours quelque chose, hein, Didi, pour nous donner l'impression d'exister?" (p. 61). Vladimir, thinking over the day's events, muses, "dans tout cela qu'y aura-t-il de vrai?" (p. 84). He asks the boy to tell Godot that he has been a witness to their existence (p. 86). Mercier similarly remarks, "Je crois que nous avons eu des témoins, depuis ce matin." Vladimir concludes with a statement which is not in the manuscript: "Seul l'arbre vit". Only the tree is alive. We are not.

"Insecurity of identity is only one aspect of doubt about the whole of reality", remarks John Fletcher (*op. cit.*, p. 217). In the passages quoted above, however, there are indications that the heroes of *Mercier et Camier* and *Godot* are not simply non-existent; they exist—in limbo; in a limbo of eternally repetitious monotony which owes much of its conception to Dante's *Purgatorio*. Beckett's intimate knowledge of, and debt to, Dante is well established, as is the obvious fact that Beckett's writing is full of ambiguous Christian allusions. He remarked to me, "Christianity is a mythology with which I am perfectly familiar, so I naturally use it." With this in mind, we should look again, with particular attention, at *la pente* from which Estragon returns, panic-stricken.

In the manuscript, the passage reads:

— J'ai été jusqu'au haut de la côte.
— Ils étaient loin?
— Oui.
— Avec ça la visibilité est mauvaise.
— Oui.
— C'est Godot! (cf. p. 65)

This, the only mention of poor visibility, occurs only in the manuscript. *All* mention of *la pente* is omitted from the English text. Certain 'clues', then, have been progressively suppressed—clues which the reader of Dante will follow without hesitation (hence, no doubt, their suppression).

Dante tells us that over the Marsh of Styx which surrounds the *city of Dis* hangs *a fog* exhaled from the mire (*tourbière*).

> Vero à che 'n su la proda mi trovai
> della valle d'abisso dolorosa
> che truono accoglie d'infiniti guai.
> Oscura e profonda era e nebulosa...
> "Or discendiam quagiù nel cieco mondo..."
> (*Canto IV*)

This is translated by Dorothy L. Sayers thus:

> I stood on the steep brink whereunder
> Runs down the dolorous chasm of the Pit,
> Ringing with infinite groans . . .
> "Down must we go, to that dark world and blind . . .[1]

One can now begin to see something other than pure poetry or mere mystification in the extraordinary reference to "Toutes les voix mortes" and "tous ces cadavres" which draw their gaze (pp. 54–56). It is true that 'la pente' is less steep than 'la proda', but it approximates to it more closely than 'la côte' of the manuscript. The reason for Estragon's horrified retreat from 'the brink' of the 'pit' is understandable.

Crawling about in the Marsh of Styx (by the side of which Dante and Virgil wait for the heavenly messenger to come) are hosts of lost souls—clearly the *point de départ* for *Comment c'est*, in which two old men, Bom and his creature Pim, crawl along in an eternal muddy limbo. Bom and Pim are not the only couple there; Bem and Pem are mentioned, and it is implied that innumerable others also unite and separate. It is in accordance with Beckett's habitual practice of referring obliquely in one work to names which occur in others, that the clowns Bim (or Pim) and Bom are to be found in *Godot*—in the manuscript and in the first edition. But they are cast into oblivion in later editions. The manuscript reads:

— Charmante soirée.
— Inoubliable.

---

[1] Penguin Classics, no. 6, p. 91.

— Et ce n'est pas fini.
— On dirait que non.
— On se croirait au spectacle.
— Au music-hall.
— Avec Bim et Bom.
— Les comiques russes.[1]
— Mais... (*etc.*) (cf. p. 28)

It would be pointless to maintain that Beckett places his characters in Dante's Purgatory. When I mentioned the possibility to Mr Beckett, his comment was characteristic: "Quite alien to me, but you're welcome." However, given his close acquaintance with Dante, and his view that all existence is a pointless, aimless, tortured, monotonous experience under the aegis of a universal malignant force, it is reasonable to expect oblique references to well-known landmarks and features of the Dantesque landscape. In the light of this purgatorial-limbo hypothesis, the no doubt misplaced interest shown by Vladimir in repentance, being saved, and *le Sauveur* is understandable. The manuscript varies slightly when the Saviour is referred to (cf. p. 7):

— Engueulé qui?
— Mais Jésus, nom de Dieu!

Changing this to 'Le Sauveur' obviously stresses salvation as the precise function of Jesus which interests Vladimir. It gives more sense to Estragon's standing with his arms out (like a tree/Cross) and asking for God's pity (p. 68), as well as to the request they think they made to Godot for "une sorte de prière".

The manuscript contains a few lines about the probable direction from which Godot will come (cf. pp. 7–8):

—Endroit délicieux. (*Il se retourne, avance jusqu'à la rampe, regarde vers le public.*) Aspects riants.

---

[1] In the first edition this was given a political overtone ("Les comiques staliniens") which, being quite misplaced, was rightly deleted. On the recurrence of these clowns in Beckett's work,

The other tramp, "*le rejoignant*", goes on:

> — J'ai dans l'idée qu'il arrivera par là.
> — Tout est possible. (*Ils retournent au milieu de la scène.*) Tu es sûr que c'est ici?

If Godot were to come from the direction indicated, from over the *tourbière*, the marsh, he could come from only one place in the Dantesque landscape, and that is the City of Dis. And the lord of Dis is Satan. An ironic possibility which would accord well with Beckett's idea of *la malignité universelle.*

The malignant character of Godot is implied in several ways: he is indifferent to the tramps' anxiousness to meet him, and keeps breaking his promise, even though—as the boy says—he has nothing to do (p. 85); he dispenses or withholds punishment for no clear reason (p. 45); the two tramps are afraid of being punished by him if they leave (p. 87); he does not give the boy enough to eat (p. 46). It is true that the boy says Godot is nice to him, but his subsequent replies make this sound more like charity or fear than truth. On the whole, Godot seems to have very few redeeming qualities likely to inspire confidence in his beneficence.

One of the many equal possibilities with regard to the identity of Godot is that he is Pozzo. The unpublished evidence I have to offer on this fundamental point is fortunately contradictory (it would be an impoverishment of the text if one were able to give a definite answer to this). To my verbal question, "Is Pozzo Godot?" Mr Beckett replied, "No. It is implied in the text, but it's not true." However, when I visited him in Paris several months later, he opened the manuscript of *Godot* and said, "It's a long time since I looked at this." He glanced at the page where it had fallen open in his hands. "This, for example," he went on, "I'd completely forgotten about it: 'Suggérer que Pozzo est peut-être Godot après tout, venu au

---

see Ruby Cohn, *Samuel Beckett: The Comic Gamut*, pp. 203–204.

rendez-vous, et qu'il ne sait pas que Vladimir et Estragon sont Vladimir et Estragon. Mais le messager?' "

From this note we can deduce, first, that Beckett's mind was not made up on the matter even when he had written much of Act 1 (the reference to the characters by name proves this was not a *preliminary* note—see later remarks on naming). Secondly, we can deduce that he was aware of the complication introduced by having the message brought—reputedly—by the boy. Thirdly, the note suggests that if the message brought by the boy could be reconciled with the identification of Pozzo with Godot, such an interpretation would not greatly distort Beckett's original intentions. It is possible to reconcile the two things: if the two tramps are mistaken about Godot's name ("—Il s'appelle Godot?—Je crois", p. 15) Pozzo would not recognize them because they tell him they are waiting for another man called Godot. He would therefore return to his castle[1] and give the boy orders to look for Monsieur Albert and say he will not be coming—with reason, especially after going blind. If he really is blind.

What the tramps expect of Godot—which is extremely vague—and what he may in fact be capable of, could be very different indeed. We should not, therefore, be surprised if he is a personification of evil, disintegrating at an even faster rate than the tramps themselves. It will be remembered that when Bom eventually finds Pim, in *Comment c'est*, he discovers that the Absent One's state is no improvement on his own. Judging by this, the tramps would seem doomed to disappointment

---

[1] In the *Textes pour rien*, published in 1955, the question is asked: "Pozzo pourquoi est-il parti de chez lui, il avait un château et des serviteurs?" We know he left in order to sell Lucky. He would need a replacement, and he might well be going to consider M. Albert for the job. Hence his repeated question, "Ce nom ne vous dit rien?" (p. 17), and his intuition that the tramps' immediate future depends on "ce... Godet... Godot... Godin..." (Vladimir cannot understand how Pozzo knows this.)

with respect to their hopes of Godot's powers to give meaning to their existence.

Another note in the manuscript gives a precise indication of Pozzo's slyness: "Après départ deuxième acte de Pozzo et Lucky suggérer que celui-là fait seulement semblant d'être aveugle." Such a pretence deals a severe blow to interpretations which have been built up on the assumption that Pozzo's blindness is real.[1]

In *Mercier et Camier* there is a link between *êtres malfaisants* (to whom Pozzo is undoubtedly related) and the kind of physical attacks to which Estragon is subjected, during the night by the ten men, and on stage by Lucky: "Alors jaillit le premier d'une longue série d'êtres malfaisants." He is a pompous *gardien* who questions the two old men aggressively. "Serait-ce le coup de fouet dont nous avions besoin, pour nous mettre en route? dit Mercier." He threatens them. "Je crois qu'il va nous attaquer, dit Camier. —A toi les couilles, comme d'habitude, dit Mercier."

As well as resembling the whip-carrying Pozzo, the *gardien* (who in fact carries a walking-stick, not a whip at all) has certain of the less endearing qualities of Vladimir: "L'envie d'uriner quasi incessante", "haleine fétide"—thus adding strength to the possibility that Vladimir and Pozzo are doubles (the same applies to Estragon and Lucky, since they are poet/thinker and suffer more acutely—see p. xcix).

The manuscript reveals that none of the characters are individualized to the extent of having names when they first appear on the written page—proof enough that it is the original draft. The opening stage direction reads, "Un vieillard assis"... "Entre un deuxième vieillard, *ressemblant au premier*" (my

[1] *E.g.*, J. R. Moore, *art. cit.*, p. 58: ". . . Lucky and Pozzo . . . subsist on 'blind' instinct and thought now reduced to silence . . . the hell of the truly damned represented by Pozzo and Lucky." Jacques Guicharnaud maintains—very cogently, if Pozzo is really blind—that Pozzo's definition of life is drawn from his blindness (*Modern French Theater*, Yale University Press, 1961, p. 207). See p. ciii.

italics). Differentiation between them only gradually crystallizes. Vladimir is the first to receive his name. The other *vieillard* is called "Lévy" right up to the end of Act 1. The word "Estragon" is written on the back of the last page of Act 1, and he becomes Estragon from that point on.

The first entrance of Pozzo and Lucky reads thus in the manuscript: "Entrent deux messieurs, un très grand et un petit." They are then referred to as "le grand" and "le petit". Pozzo is not given a name until he introduces himself (p. 16)—which he does in the manuscript with the words "Je m'appelle Pozzo." Of particular interest is the fact that the reason why Lucky is so named is clarified by the context in which he first receives his name. Pozzo is explaining the protocol with regard to the bones (p. 21): "Mais en principe les os reviennent au porteur"—the manuscript reads "...à Lucky"; that is to say, he is lucky *because he gets the bones*. Just to keep the spirit of contradiction alive, however, it must be stressed that this is not the only 'official' explanation. Mr Beckett's verbal reply to my question, "Is Lucky so named because he has found his Godot?" was: "I suppose he is Lucky to have no more expectations."

With regard to the names the two tramps give themselves, the manuscript has Estragon replying thus to Pozzo's "Comment vous appelez-vous?": "—(*du tic au tac*) Magrégor, André." He is, then, one of the great family of Beckett's *M*s, at the beginning of his existence. He calls himself "Catulle" in the published French version, "Catullus" in the Faber English edition—no doubt in sarcastic reference to his status as an impoverished poet. In the Grove Press edition, however, he replies "Adam" instead of "Catullus". This has led B. F. Dukore to maintain that the name appropriately recalls the expulsion from the Garden of Eden.[1] Why did Beckett make Estragon reply "Adam" instead of "Catullus" in the American edition? His explanation to me was this: "We got fed up with

---

1 'Gogo, Didi, and the Absent Godot', *Drama Survey*, Winter, 1962, pp. 301–307.

Catullus." If this were the only reason, one could justifiably take the author of *Godot* to task for indulging in deliberate mystification. Why not choose a name like 'Bill' or 'Jones' which would conform more with Beckett's avowed principle of "no symbols where none intended"?

When the boy enters and asks for "Monsieur Albert", the manuscript reveals some hesitation from the other tramp—he does not appear to be acquainted with the name:

GARÇON. Monsieur Albert?
LÉVY. Qui? (*Silence*.)
GARÇON. Monsieur Albert.
VLADIMIR. C'est moi. (cf. p. 43)

The similarity between Lucky and the beast of burden is fairly obvious, but the development of this character can be traced back to two scenes in *Mercier et Camier*, neither of which has any significance or relevance in itself with respect to the quest of Mercier and Camier. The first occurs in M. Gast's story, part of which has already been quoted above. It continues:

> La petite masse sombre qui approche si lentement, on finit quand même par savoir ce que c'est. C'est une voiture bâchée tirée par un cheval noir. Il la tire avec aisance et comme en flânant. Le conducteur marche devant, en balançant son fouet. Il porte un manteau ample, lourd et clair, qui lui tombe jusqu'aux pieds.

But this driver is young, happy, and singing. In the second passage the relationship between driver and animal is equally good; they are in complete harmony. Mercier has gone off alone:

> Mais son chemin ne tarda pas à croiser celui d'un vieillard hirsute, plus hirsute que lui, et déguenillé, qui marchait à côté d'un âne. L'âne, qui n'avait pas de bride... portait deux paniers, dont l'un était plein de coquillages, et *l'autre de sable*. [My italics.]

It is Vladimir who thinks he hears Godot shouting in the

distance. "Et pourquoi crierait-il?" asks Estragon. "Après son cheval" is the answer. The horse turns out to be Lucky. The analogy with the horse is strengthened by Pozzo's shouting "Woooa!", '*comme à un cheval*'. The exclamation is not in the manuscript; Beckett stressed the equine analogy at a later stage in composition. Both master and slave/beast have degenerated by the time they appear in *Godot*, as has the relationship between them, despite the more noble natural status of Lucky compared with his animal prototypes in *Mercier et Camier*.

The origins of Pozzo can be seen in M. Madden, with whom Mercier and Camier share a train compartment for a short while. He directs an interminable monologue at the two old men: "Je survivais en parlant," he says, with a truly Beckett-ian fear of silence, "tous les jours un peu plus, tous les jours un peu mieux." He wears gaiters, a yellow bowler hat, and a knee-length frock-coat.[1] As they leave him on the platform, he cries, "Adieu, adieu! Ils m'aimaient toujours, ils m'ai-maient —." His despondency is that of Pozzo (cf. p. 27): "Mercier le vit, indifférent aux gens qui affluaient vers la sortie, poser sa tête sur ses mains qui, elles, s'appuyaient sur la pomme du bâton." Another character, M. Conaire, resembles Pozzo when he asks Mercier, Camier, and the barman to guess his age, removing his hat and taking up "une pose avantageuse".

> Allez-y, dit-il, ne me ménagez pas.
> Monsieur Gast nomma un chiffre...
> C'est la calvitie qui trompe, dit Monsieur Gast.

The 'routine' in which Estragon tries to ask Pozzo a question

---

[1] Cf. also the description of Watt's dress in *Mercier et Camier*: "Il portait, malgré la chaleur, un immense chapeau melon enfoncé jusqu'aux oreilles et un lourd manteau boutonné de tous ses nombreux boutons et dont les pans balayaient le sol." The three great Pozzos to date—Roger Blin, Peter Bull, and Paul Curran, have all assumed a very close resemblance to these characters who appear in *Mercier et Camier*—but the latter are manifestly of the same family as many other bowler-hatted men in Beckett.

(pp. 23–24) may be developed from a simple and amusing attempt at interrogation in *Mercier et Camier*:

> Je voudrais te poser quelques simples questions, dit Camier.
> Simples questions? dit Mercier. Tu m'étonnes, Camier... Je ne connais pas de réponses... J'en ai connu dans le temps, et des meilleures. C'était ma seule compagnie. J'inventais même des phrases à l'interrogatif pour aller avec...

The manuscript reveals very little hesitation over Pozzo's precise and lengthy orders to Lucky (pp. 18–19), involving stage directions as detailed as the *Actes sans Paroles*. There are, however, enough changes (with original words all scored out) to show that this is a working draft.

There is considerable—one might almost say, anguished—hesitation starting with Pozzo's words, "Voilà qu'il m'adresse la parole" (p. 23), as far as Vladimir's hopeful "Je crois qu'il t'écoute"; this is revealed not in the writing but in the 'doodles' with which Beckett has adorned the *verso* of the manuscript pages: monstrous, tortuous, distorted, convoluted, very complex shapes, vaguely human but using rather some part of the human body as a *point de départ*; finely penned, and reminiscent of Max Ernst's illustrations of Lautréamont. They occur yet again, in this scene, at p. 28 ("il m'assassine"), p. 29 ("*Vladimir s'arrête...*"), p. 30 ("Rasseyez-vous, Monsieur, je vous en prie", which is followed immediately by "Insistez un peu", the mock coyness being *corsé* at a later stage in composition), p. 31 ("Catulle", or rather "Magrégor, André"—one would have expected hesitation here, and it is interesting to have it confirmed), p. 36 ("enchaînez"—there are eighteen exchanges here which do not appear in the published text). With the exception of one enormous monster opposite the very last page of Act 1, revealing the prolonged hesitation necessitated by the ever difficult process of rounding off an act, the biggest concentration of hesitation-doodles occurs in this scene with Pozzo in Act 1. Lucky's speech, however (pp. 37–39), shows no such evidence of irresolution. The manuscript contains the directions regarding the other characters' reactions almost without intercalation or correction, but among the few changes and hesitations one sees the names of 'Steinweg et Petermann' noted on the back of the page previous to that containing the sentence, "...des expériences en cours de ? et ?" (cf. p. 38).

The manuscript has Lucky beginning his monologue with "*débit précipité*" (instead of "*monotone*"); "quaqua" is an undisguised "quoique"; "sa divine apathie sa divine athambie sa divine aphasie nous aime" originally appears as "apathie pour ne pas dire athambie nous aime". The reference (p. 37) to "la divine Miranda" is more direct: "à la façon de la Miranda du divin Shakespeare"; the repetition of "feux" is absent—"tourment dans les flammes, pour peu..."; "n'en est pas moins le bienvenu" reads "moins d'un secours indéniable"; the vague obscenity of "l'Acacacacadémie d'Anthropopopométrie" is not in the manuscript, in fact the spelling of these words is normal throughout. "Berne en Bresse" is not mentioned, and the repetitions following the second "il est établi" are more coherent: "...il est établi, établi, établi ce qui suit, à savoir, à savoir, à savoir...". Lines 10–12 of p. 38 are more recognizably allusive than the final "l'homme en Bresse de Testu et Conard", as the manuscript reads "l'homme en Europe tout au moins malgré les progrès..."; "on ne sait pas pourquoi" does not appear so frequently (e.g., "parallèlement en même temps en dépit de l'essor de la culture physique"; and for "des sports tels tels tels le tennis" the manuscript sports only one "tels".[1]

We can see, therefore, that part of the process of mystification through the disintegration of language originates from post-manuscript stages in composition. Repeated, deformed, and nonsensical words replace some earlier coherent expressions. But the overall impression is one of sureness of touch—this is hardly surprising since Beckett had had a fair amount of practice at this style of writing in *Watt* between 1942 and 1944. Watt develops the same formless, incoherent speech

[1] A commentary on Lucky's speech will be found on pp. cvii–cx.

with "cracks" in it which he is "too tired to repair"; and the echo of that endless, circular, resumptive speech is heard again, of course, in *L'Innommable*. Vladimir's round-song at the beginning of Act 2, which so perfectly epitomizes the circularity of the whole structure of *Godot*, is seen, in the manuscript, actually being worked out on the page from its English original; "dans l'office", for example, was at first "dans la cuisine".

It is now common knowledge that the origin of the scenes between Vladimir and the boy is in *Eleutheria*; but do we not also glimpse the boy *and* his brother in *Mercier et Camier*? Monsieur Madden, the old man in the train, treats the two travellers to his life story:

> Mes parents... étaient sévères avec moi, mais justes. Au moindre écart de conduite mon père me battait... Même comme berger, comme vacher et comme chévrier, j'avais beau m'évertuer, je n'arrivai pas à donner satisfaction. (cf. *Godot*, p. 45)

The boy's brother (in *Godot*) who keeps the sheep, does not give satisfaction either, since he gets beaten by the white-bearded father-figure, Godot.

The most human quality of the two tramps is the ambivalence of their feelings for each other. They want to be independent but dread being parted. They pretend to get on famously alone, but know they are destined to remain together. These contradictory emotions govern the relationships between Mercier and Camier also: for example, Camier offers to go off and buy Mercier a cream cake:

> Attends-moi là.
>
> Non non, cria Mercier, ne me quitte pas, ne nous quittons pas.

Camier returns with a rum-baba, with which Mercier finds fault:

> Je m'en vais, dit Camier.
>
> Tu m'abandonnes, dit Mercier. Je le savais.
>
> Tu connais mon caractère, dit Camier.
>
> Je ne connais rien de ton caractère, dit Mercier, mais je comptais sur ton affection pour m'aider à purger ma peine.

> Je peux t'aider, je ne peux pas te ressusciter, dit Camier.
> Prends-moi par la main, dit Mercier, et emmène-moi loin d'ici. Je trottinerai bien sagement à tes côtés, comme un petit chien, ou un enfant en bas âge.

Dependence has a slight edge over independence for the two characters in the novel:

> Certes il fallait de la force pour rester avec Camier, comme il en fallait pour rester avec Mercier, mais moins qu'il n'en fallait pour la bataille du soliloque.

And yet for Camier, the possibility of separation is always there, sometimes as a threat to the slightly less self-reliant Mercier:

> ... je me demande souvent, assez souvent, si nous ne ferions pas mieux de nous quitter sans plus tarder.
> Tu ne m'auras pas par les sentiments, dit Mercier.

This is clearly echoed in *Godot* (p. 54), when Estragon suggests, "On ferait mieux de se séparer."

The fatality of Mercier and Camier's 'togetherness' is epitomized in words which are more applicable to Vladimir and Estragon, since Mercier and Camier do, in fact, part and cease to know each other (or pretend to):

> Les voilà donc sur la route, sensiblement rafraîchis quand même, et chacun sait l'autre proche, le sent, le croit, le craint, l'espère, le nie et n'y peut rien.

Estragon's crowning, pathetic appeal for confirmation of their ability to get on together ("On ne se débrouille pas trop mal, hein, Didi, tous les deux ensemble?"—p. 61) has its counterpart when Camier remarks:

> Il y a des fois où c'est un véritable plaisir de causer avec toi.
> Je ne suis pas méchant, au fond, dit Mercier.

The fraternity of the two couples, so mysteriously destroyed at the end of the novel (whereas it just as mysteriously avoids destruction at the end of both acts of the play, thus becoming one of its major themes) is a very important element of their common origin; Vladimir looks after Estragon, feeds him, protects him, and Camier plays the same rôle. He makes Mercier eat—much against his will, since he has sunk into a state of nauseated depression during Camier's absence:

> Je me demandais si tu allais revenir...
> Mercier réfléchit un instant. Il faut être Camier pour ne pas abandonner Mercier, dit-il.

Camier does not simply become Vladimir, however. He is the more sceptical of the two, and this equates him more with Estragon. The manuscript of *Godot* is more self-consistent than the final text in regard to Vladimir's intelligence; when Vladimir and Estragon contemplate hanging themselves from the tree (p. 11), Estragon has to explain why they cannot both do it. The manuscript reads:

> VLADIMIR. Je ne comprends pas.
> LÉVY. Mais... voyons. Ça marcherait avec moi. Ça pourrait très bien ne pas marcher avec toi.
> VLADIMIR. Je n'avais pas pensé à ça.
> LÉVY. Qui peut le plus peut le moins.
> VLADIMIR. Attendons voir ce qu'il va nous dire.

There is no condescending pigeon-English, and the oblique reference to the thieves on the Cross ("Il y a une chance sur deux") is thus shown to be an afterthought. However, the point is that there is a slight discrepancy in the final text, since it is Vladimir who seizes Pozzo's meaning first (p. 32) when he asks how his little speech went ("Bon? Moyen?", etc.). The manuscript reads differently:

> LÉVY (*comprenant*). Oh très bien, tout à fait bien.
> VLADIMIR. Oh très très bien, très très très bien.

There is no comic *accent anglais*.

The manuscript makes Estragon (Lévy) alone guess the name of Lucky's dance. He suggests simply "La mort du canard"—all the obscene and symbolic overtones of the final version are later elaborations.

Vladimir's horror of hearing about dreams, however, is inherited from Camier, who reminds Mercier, "Tu n'ignores pas cependant ce que nous avons arrêté à ce sujet: pas de récits de rêve, sous aucun prétexte." Another of Vladimir's little idiosyncrasies is to be found in M. Conaire: 'Peu et souvent' is his motto. He goes off. " 'Dans le cour, vous dites?' 'Au fond et à gauche,' dit Monsieur Gast" (cf. *Godot*, p. 28).[1] The same two characters have something else in common: "Monsieur Conaire enleva sa casquette et la secoua avec violence dans tous les sens. Puis il la remit..."

If the general 'philosophy of life' of Mercier and Camier is more bitter than that of the heroes of *Godot*, this is due to the softening effect of Vladimir's more affectionate character, and his determination to go on hoping. The lack of sympathy he and Estragon show for the blind and fallen Pozzo (pp. 69–72) is somehow out of character, and savours of the lack of warmth underlying the couple in the novel. There is, for example, a not dissimilar scene where a fat old woman is knocked down by a car. She lies there, "s'agitant faiblement par terre":

> Ah, dit Mercier, voilà ce dont j'avais besoin. Je me sens tout ragaillardi. Il avait en effet l'air transformé.
> Que cela nous serve de leçon, dit Camier.
> C'est-à-dire? dit Mercier.
> Qu'il ne faut jamais désespérer, dit Camier. Faisons confiance à la vie.[2]

And so they go on panglossizing, just as Vladimir and Estragon do over the helpless Pozzo, as if the need to be of assistance were an abstraction.

---

[1] In the manuscript, the reference to Vladimir's incontinence is rather more delicate (cf. p. 51):

VLADIMIR. Je ne me suis pas levé de la nuit, *ce qui ne m'est pas arrivé depuis des années.*

ESTRAGON (*tristement*). Tu vois, tu *vas* mieux quand je ne suis pas là." [My italics]

[2] Cf. Pozzo's affirmation to the crippled Estragon, that "the tears of the world are a constant quantity" (less strikingly phrased in the French text, p. 26 ('*immuables*'). Pozzo's unsympathetic response to Estragon's bleeding leg (*ibid.*) is that of Camier:

Je suis un peu souffrant, dit Hélène.
C'est d'un bon augure, dit Camier.

Estragon's need for food, satisfied minimally by the raw vegetables offered by Vladimir, has its counterpart in Mercier, who is dissatisfied when Camier returns with the wrong kind of cake. The gradual deterioration in food is common to play and novel ("Hier des gâteaux, aujourd'hui des sandwichs, demain du pain sec et jeudi des pierres" is the way the situation is summed up in the novel); this reminds us that in *Godot* Beckett has taken the men to the absolute extreme of destitution. They begin and end just this side of the stones.

There are a number of similar exchanges in the novel and the play which it would be tedious to quote in full. The 'after you—no, after you' routine (p. 67), the frequent references to the thief who was saved (a recurrent theme throughout Beckett's works), the compulsive talking to fill the void (p. 54), the self-awareness and self-depreciation (*passim*). The comedy extracted from the subject of suicide is subtly caught in the novel too:

> Où allons-nous de ce pas mal assuré? dit Camier.
> Nous nous dirigeons je crois vers le canal, dit Mercier.
> Déjà? dit Camier.

Pozzo's disquisition on the horrors of night (p. 31) is foreshadowed in three quite separate parts of the novel, and yet there is no repetition of words; this is an important point in comparing the two works as a whole, for while much of the dialogue in *Mercier et Camier* consists of short, sharp, pithy exchanges in a style strongly resembling that of *Godot*, and while there is the same need to make conversation out of nothing—for example, on the subject of whether to open an umbrella when it is pouring with rain or wait until the sun is hot and then use it as a sunshade—very little of the actual dialogue of the novel is repeated in the play.[1]

---

[1] Had Beckett intended to re-use the material, he would hardly have been able to resist including the 'Hugolian' reference to the Relief of Ladysmith in 1900: Camier reminisces, and says, "Le siècle avait deux mois", to which Mercier rejoins, "Regardez-le maintenant."

The dialogue of *Godot* is a great improvement on that of *Mercier et Camier*. The manuscript of *Godot* shows that Beckett has an infallible ear for what to cut. In Act 2, for example, there were originally about ten additional pages of dialogue inserted between p. 66 and p. 68 of the final text. They contain an argument (of which the 'Oh pardon' routine is the essence) elaborately built round the question 'Est-ce que c'est la peine?' This question takes them ten pages to formulate, just as it takes them many pages to ask Pozzo why Lucky does not put down his bags. Beckett rightly saw the danger of tedium and repeated effect here—although it would have stood in a novel, as it is a true *tour de force*.

Another example occurs on p. 36 of the final text of *Godot*. Between the juxtaposed words "Enchaînez" and "Assez" the following originally appeared:

> POZZO. Ou bien il ne fait rien.
> LÉVY. Le salaud.
> VLADIMIR. Et quand vous ne lui demandez rien?
> POZZO. Ça ne change rien.
> LÉVY. Il sait ce qu'il veut.
> VLADIMIR. Quand il veut.
> LÉVY. Comme il veut.
> VLADIMIR. Que vous lui demandiez ou non.
> POZZO. Plus ou moins.
> LÉVY. Et quand vous lui demandez de s'arrêter?
> POZZO. Ça ne change rien.
> LÉVY. Il ne s'arrête pas.
> POZZO. Quelquefois.
> VLADIMIR. Mais pas toujours.
> POZZO. Non.
> LÉVY. Et il a toujours été comme ça?
> POZZO. Non.
> VLADIMIR. Depuis quand?
> POZZO. Je ne sais pas.
> LÉVY. Assez.

This long quotation is given because it is instructive. It shows how miraculously the final text of *Godot* manages to avoid the tedium of this suppressed page even though the intellectual substance of much of the play is no greater than this. The danger of taking the quality of the dialogue for granted, of failing to appreciate the manipulation of language and the flow of words, is diminished by the realization that a lesser writer would have finished with a book full of passages like the suppressed one quoted, no doubt congratulating himself on creating the Theatre of Inaction in a massive prefatory note.

It is for similar reasons that Beckett has declined to publish *Mercier et Camier*, with its frequently cyclic, hair-splitting dialogue tediously dependent upon forgetfulness of what has just been said or decided. These features are to be found in *Godot* as well, but used with great discretion, with an eye and an ear for the shape of sentence, exchange, scene, act, and total structure.

Mercier et Camier illuminates the situation of the characters in *Godot* by showing that Beckett does not push them to the extreme suffering of self-aware solitude. Those who think *Godot* depressingly morbid, exploiting *ad nauseam* the basic misery of a godless universe, would realize on reading the novel that the hours or days of anguish on the *haute lande*, when the narrative becomes turgid and incoherent, mark the mysterious transformation of the *pseudocouple* Mercier/Camier into the *pseudocouple* Vladimir/Estragon. They become imbued with a totally different quality. Whereas Mercier and Camier rarely rise above the level of two rather dirty old men, Didi and Gogo positively *glow* by comparison; their condition is so infused with timeless, tragic quality that it acquires a density and depth quite lacking in the novel.

We see, from *Mercier et Camier* and *Godot*, that it is the reliance upon each other in waiting which keeps the couple together. The relationship between Mercier and Camier begins to disintegrate as soon as they leave the *haute lande* to go their separate ways. Had they stayed there, they would have continued to face 'things' together; but the rain is endless (at least Vladimir and Estragon do not have to put up with this outpouring from "la malignité universelle"). The rain drives them on, and they cannot face the constant wandering for ever. Vladimir and Estragon, on the other hand, cannot resist the attraction of the spot to which they return as surely and (we suppose) as regularly as the moon shoots up into the sky the moment the boy leaves. Even though they separate at night, they have a point to return to, a base: the tree on the plateau outside the city.

The change from wandering to waiting was no doubt dictated by the exigences of the kind of austere dramatic unity Beckett wanted to achieve, as an antidote to the exaggeratedly discursive style of the novel then being written. The classical concentration upon one place and short duration rectify the major weaknesses of *Mercier et Camier*: loose construction, aimlessness, repetition of effects already used in earlier novels, for example. Had *Godot* been conceived as a novel—recording the characters' movements beyond the existential limits set by the stage—it would no doubt have been a greatly improved form of *Mercier et Camier*; but as the scope for dialogue would have been circumscribed by the need for narrative, description, and the other elements of fictional writing, the result could only have been diffusion and dispersal of interest.

We have seen that the problem of the genesis of *En attendant Godot* is closely linked with the thorny problems of interpretation which, during the past twelve years, have inspired as wide a diversity of views as, for example, the *Divine Comedy*. However, genetic study and reference to statements of intention by the author himself cannot produce definitive solutions, even if these were considered desirable. To curtail speculative exegesis would result in impoverishment, but if unpublished material and the author's own comments help to rectify the wilder flights of fancy, no harm has been done.

The problems of interpretation and meaning-potential of *Godot* which have been introduced in the course of this chapter will be examined in greater depth and detail in the remaining pages of this study of the play.

CHAPTER 4

Approaches to GODOT

The interpreter of Beckett's work is faced with the same problems as face interpreters of two other writers whose preoccupations frequently resemble those of Beckett: Dante and Kafka. Dr Karl Witte's essay on 'The Art of Misunderstanding Dante'[1] will one day have its counterpart in Beckett studies; a similar exercise in comparative criticism has also been performed (on a more modest scale than that of Dr Witte) in the study of Kafka's *Castle* by Ronald Gray.[2] In this he draws attention to the many conflicting interpretations of *The Castle*, each claiming to reveal its true meaning, but succeeding only in making the reader conclude that Kafka cannot really be worthy of attention since his writing is so unclear, vague and ambiguous. "Any further attempt at interpretation can only add to the numbers on one side or the other", he concludes.

The situation is very similar in regard to *Godot*, and rather ironically, Mr. Gray has helped to make it so by his own Christian interpretation of *Godot*![3] The dangers of adding just one more interpretation to those already available (they range from the fanciful to the flat-footed) are such that it is tempting simply to give a *recensement* of views and leave the reader to take his choice. After all, ". . . in many instances, to interpret is to transform", as Professor Gombrich has pointed out.[4]

Mallarmé wrote in his *Enquête sur l'Évolution littéraire*,

---

1 In *Essays on Dante*, London, 1898.
2 *Kafka's Castle*, C.U.P., 1956.
3 *The Listener*, 24 January 1957.
4 *Art and Illusion*, Pantheon Books, New York, 1960.

"Nommer un objet, c'est supprimer trois quarts de la jouissance du poème qui est faite du bonheur de deviner peu à peu; le suggérer, voilà le rêve." It is our intention not to deprive anyone of this happiness, but to increase it by opening up the reader's awareness of the text's potential meanings. Beckett has, of course, *nommé* the object: 'Godot'. But it is a word still —*still*—undefined, still infinite in its potential attachments to persons, beliefs, ideals, or objects.

"What we are all arguing about in London is the meaning of *Waiting for Godot*", said Harold Hobson; to which Beckett quickly responded, "I take no sides about that."[1] His refusal to narrow down the field makes it more difficult for the interpreter to reproduce the author's own intentions. In terms of *what* exactly should one write about *Godot*? If one is dealing with a play by Sartre, Camus, or Genet, the writers' verbal intention is fairly clear on account of their interviews, journals, prefaces, and theoretical works. With Ionesco the problem is more complex, as even the recognizable social setting he gives his plays may be misleading. In the case of Beckett, no firm pathological, poetic, dramatic or philosophical basis presents itself as the obviously *correct* one. Hence the danger of going to extremes—either restricting oneself to one pet exclusive theory of meaning, or giving up in despair, with the hopeful excuse that it is not worth the trouble. *Godot* does seem to be a rather trivial affair until one begins to look at it on Beckett's own level of intended meaning, so far as this can be deduced from his other—more explicit—works. Then the problems it raises can be seen to be the same forbidding, enigmatic epistemological ones as those from which the novels grew.

The reader—or spectator—of *Godot* should feel flattered that a large degree of active participation in the creative act of giving meaning to the text is expected of him. But this should not allow the floodgate of subjectivism to be flung open: it is not true that any interpretation is as good as any other. Even

---

1 'Samuel Beckett, Dramatist of the Year', *International Theatre Annual*, no. 1, 1956, pp. 153–155.

if one admits that the question 'What does *Godot* mean to me?' is as legitimate as 'What does *Godot* mean to Beckett?' or simply 'What does *Godot* mean?', it remains true that each interpretation will be generally valid to vastly differing extents. When fourteen hundred convicts in San Quentin penitentiary saw *Godot* in 1957, they knew what it meant—to them. The prison newspaper reviewed it thus:

> It was an expression, symbolic in order to avoid all personal error, by an author who expected each member of his audience to draw his own conclusions, make his own errors. . . . We're still waiting for Godot, and shall continue to wait. When the scenery gets too drab and the action too slow, we'll call each other names and swear to part forever—but then, there's no place to go.[1]

We may retort that the play's associations in the minds of long-term convicts have no relevance to us. But those men had first-hand knowledge of exile, solitude, and degradation within the walls of the prison, and this brought them nearer to understanding and sympathizing with the very same feelings Beckett has within the boundless walls of the universe: there is no escape, "no place to go". Their reaction, albeit a personal and unsophisticated one, was *relevant* to Beckett's own preoccupations, therefore it had validity. To the convict with a sentence of many years, existence becomes absurd, and Beckett's total intention in *Godot* has been described as "the artistic portrayal of man's absurd existence as it appears to Beckett".[2]

The failure of many cultivated and sophisticated critics and audiences to appreciate *Godot* at first was partly caused by its lack of conventional ingredients (plot, action, 'message', etc.); but more important was the lack of *rapport* between the audiences and what was being enacted. For centuries the public has liked to see itself on the stage, even if its ideals and pre-

---

[1] Quoted by Martin Esslin, *The Theatre of the Absurd*, p. 14.

[2] J. Rechstein, 'Time and Eternity meet in the Present', *Texas Studies in Literature and Language*, vol. VI, no. 1, Spring 1964, pp. 5–21.

judices are being ridiculed. But the situation of the two tramps in *Godot* was, to the average citizen free to go about his fairly lucrative daily business, an *alien* one. A clue to this incomprehension (which was particularly strong, and even violent, in the more prosperous cities of the United States) is given by Dr Metman (*art. cit.*) in her Jungian analysis, which deserves to be quoted *in extenso*:

> In contemporary drama . . . man is shown not in a world into which the divine or demoniac powers are projected but alone with them [whereas] in times of religious containment [dramatic art] has shown man as protected, guided and sometimes punished by . . . the great archetypal powers.
>
> This new form of drama . . . creates a vacuum between the play and the audience . . . By far the most profound and daring writer associated with this new development in drama is Samuel Beckett . . . he strips his figures so thoroughly of all those qualities in which the audience might recognize itself that, to start with, an *alienation effect* is created that leaves the audience mystified.

In thirteen years the bemused bewilderment of those early audiences has changed to enthusiastic appraisal—sometimes for the wrong reasons, one suspects. Public taste has undeniably changed as more people have become attuned to more and more *avant-garde* plays both in Paris and in London. There is, however, little room for complacency or self-congratulation. As Edward Albee has written:

> The basic crisis the theatre's in now is that the audience primarily wants a reaffirmation of its values, wants to see the *status quo*, wants to be entertained rather than disturbed, wants to be comforted and really doesn't want any kind of adventure in the theatre, at least from living playwrights—they'll take it from dead ones because that's part of the lit-cult.[1]

---

1 'The Stage Today', *The Observer*, 18 April 1965. [Reprinted from the *Atlantic Monthly*: extracts from a conversation between Sir John Gielgud and Edward Albee, recorded by R. S. Stewart.]

The first performance of *Godot* in Paris in January 1953, at the little Théâtre Babylone (now defunct) was reminiscent of *la bataille d'Hernani* in 1830. The audience was quite unprepared for the impact of its originality. After the first act, many left—some engaging the *godotistes* in fisticuffs on the way out. At the end, the enthusiastic applause was just about equalled by the bewildered silence. Beckett had not expected *Godot* to have any success at all, but through the good offices of a few enlightened critics, it stayed alive long enough to become established. It had more than four hundred performances in Paris, and has since been performed in the United Kingdom, U.S.A., Scandinavia, Finland, Spain, Portugal, Italy, Germany, Holland, Turkey, Greece, Indonesia, Japan, Mexico, Israel, Brazil and other Latin-American countries, Poland, Hungary, Jugoslavia, and Rumania.[1] It has been translated into English, German, Italian, Spanish, Catalan, Japanese, Serbo-Croat, Danish, Norwegian, Swedish, Dutch, Portuguese, and Finnish.[2]

The first American production, in Miami, in January 1956, was received even more antipathetically than the first Paris production. In New York clever advertising for '70,000 Playgoing Intellectuals' had the right snob appeal. As for the London production at the Arts Theatre Club in August 1955, it was so successful that it moved to the Criterion Theatre (suitably emasculated, of course, by the Lord Chamberlain). Kenneth Tynan wrote that the play's enemies were vexed because "it was not pretentious enough to enable them to deride it", and continued: "It forced me to re-examine the rules which have hitherto governed the drama; and having done so, to pronounce them not elastic enough".[3] Beckett

---

[1] I am grateful for the assistance of the Société des Auteurs et Compositeurs dramatiques in obtaining information about performances, which is true up to June 1965.

[2] Fuller details of translations, given to me by Les Éditions de Minuit, will be found at the end of this Introduction.

[3] Reproduced in *Tynan on Theatre*, Pelican Books, 1964, p. 53.

did not like this production by Peter Hall, feeling that too much stress was laid on the farce and not enough on the tragic quality. These two qualities were balanced with exquisite perfection in the 1964–5 production by Anthony Page at the Royal Court Theatre, London. Although this was, of course, a production of Beckett's own English text of the play, the fact that the author supervised the production himself makes it something of a definitive production. It is to be noted, for example, that although it was found very amusing, the farcical element was kept to a minimum. The laughter in no way destroyed the sheer anguish and pathos of the last few minutes of each act. The play's triumph could be measured by Bernard Levin's admission in the *Daily Mail* (31 December 1964) that nine years previously Harold Hobson, "who waged war single-handed on behalf of Mr Beckett", had been right: "*Godot* is a great play". The reviewer in *The Times* (31 December 1964) summed up the play's originality in these terms:

> When we first saw it in London, the play was obviously recognizable as a work of the highest originality and talent; nine years later, it stands revealed as the work that gave the theatre a new language and created a world of its own which has passed into folklore: these are the highest achievements within the range of literary composition, and they establish its greatness as a matter of more than personal opinion.

Philip Hope-Wallace had a strong personal opinion (*The Guardian*, 31 December 1964) that "*Godot* seemed to me last night not so much classical as already dated". Perhaps in another nine years he will be doing a Levin and admitting that Mr Hobson was right.

Today, *Godot* has become almost a myth. No lecture, book or conversation about modern theatre can go on for long without its being mentioned. "Today there is little point in defending Beckett's play. The play is 'important', it is new, it lives, it represents a true insight into a way of feeling typical of our times."[1] To a large extent the fascination of the play lies in its combination of sheer simplicity of form and complexity of metaphysical implication.

---

[1] J. Guicharnaud, *Modern French Theater*, Yale University Press, 1961, p. 193.

CHAPTER 5

GODOT: Structure and Style

"It is the shape that matters."
—*Samuel Beckett to Harold Hobson.*

With more wit than precision, Vivian Mercier described *Godot* as a play in which "nothing happens, twice". If one thinks of the two pairs of characters, or figures, in the play as a microcosm of humanity, then each minute action and occurrence takes on a heightened significance. What we should ask ourselves is not so much why something important does not happen, as how Beckett manages to hold our interest and prevent the play from falling apart, even though the action is circular and almost static. "While many dramas of intrigue in which a great deal happens leave us cold, this 'nothing happening' of *Godot* keeps us in suspense", comments the Spanish playwright Alfonso Sastre; "does this seem no small achievement to you?"[1]

Godot is a rejection of what Shaw nicknamed 'Sardoodlum', that is to say, the sentimental well-made play perfected by Scribe and Sardou in the nineteenth century, with its mingling of melodrama, farce, and social realism. *Godot* has no more plot than a quadrille or a quartette; but its structure is tight and economical—a fact overlooked by Hugh Hunt when he says:

> The approach made by Samuel Beckett in *Waiting for Godot* . . . symbolizes that chaotic state of existence by a corresponding anarchy in the construction of the play itself. Play archi-

---

[1] 'Siete notas sobre *Esperando a Godot*', *Primer Acto*, no. 1, April 1957.

> tecture as it was understood by the writer of the well-made play . . . has given place to a seemingly abstract void in which plot, or dramatic story-telling, is almost non-existent.[1]

This is true of many *avant-garde* plays, but not of the two most outstanding: Ionesco's *Rhinocéros* and *Godot*. Indeed, as Professor N. A. Scott has noted, "if its meaning is obscure or ambiguous, it has the kind of absolute clarity of form that is possessed by such modern masterpieces as Kafka's *Das Schloss* [*The Castle*] and Faulkner's *As I lay Dying*, Camus' *La Peste*, and William Golding's *Lord of the Flies*".[2]

It is not easy to differentiate between action and dialogue in *Godot*. Nevertheless, visual occurrences succeed one another with an underlying pattern of repetition:

	Act 1	*Act* 2	
p. 3.	E alone, struggling with boot.	V alone, looks at E's boots.	p. 49.
p. 3.	V enters.	E enters.	p. 50.
p. 3.	E beaten during the night.		p. 50.
p. 16.	P and L enter.		p. 68.
p. 42.	P and L leave.		p. 83.
p. 43.	Boy enters.		p. 85.
p. 46.	Boy leaves, night falls, moon rises.		p. 86.
p. 48.	"Allons-y." *Ils ne bougent pas.*		p. 88.

Within the symmetrical, circular structure of each act there are smaller circles, represented by
—Vladimir's repetitious pantomime, taking off his hat and knocking out an invisible foreign object[3];
—Estragon's repeated fussing with his boots;

---

[1] *The Live Theatre*, O.U.P., 1962, p. 155.
[2] *Samuel Beckett*, Bowes and Bowes, 1965, p. 83.
[3] Cf. Clov's *jeu de scène*, going up and down the ladder, in *Fin de Partie*; the academic committee in *Watt*; in *Acte sans Paroles I*, the futility of repeated attempts to reach the water-carafe. *Acte sans Paroles II* is a telescoped pantomime of our daily ritual of getting dressed and undressed.

—Lucky's recurrent acts of picking up and putting down the luggage;
—the hat-exchanging routine;
—Vladimir's endlessly repeatable round-song at the beginning of Act 2.

The most important of the circular eddies within the main stream is created by the repeated line "On attend Godot". This recurs, like the refrain of a ritual or of a ballade, three times in Act 1 and a dozen times in Act 2, thus indicating an increased impatience as time goes on, which has to be contained by more frequent self-reminders of the obligation to wait. The monotony becomes imperceptibly cumulative and more unbearable for the two tramps, miraculously not becoming so for the spectator. The fact that Act 2 is only a little more than three-quarters the length of Act 1 accounts partly for the avoidance of boredom, but interest is maintained in a number of other ways: by the creation of suspense; by the renewal of the dialogue through the asymmetrical introduction of new themes; by the constant oscillation between the metaphysical and the comic, the eternal and the *terre à terre* (or between "surface patterns and the universal themes of human existence"[1]); by the poetic action of images, the rhythm of words and silence; and by the gradual downward linear movement of the total structure towards disintegration.

Waiting is by its very nature suspended action. Everything that goes on in the play—talking, speechifying, play-acting (miming), arrivals and departures—is pseudo-action, substituting for genuine action which can take place only if

(a) Godot arrives *or*

(b) Vladimir and Estragon abandon their vigil in order to search elsewhere or to stop trying to communicate with Godot altogether.

As their lives are dominated by the suspense of wondering if

---

[1] Lawrence Harvey, 'Art and the Existential in *En attendant Godot*', *P.M.L.A.*, LXXV, March 1960, pp. 137–146.

and when Godot will come, this suspense is transmitted to us every time their conversation returns to the subject of Godot. However, Godot is not mentioned for the first five pages or so of Act 1; until then we have little idea of what the two men are doing in that deserted spot. The title gives a fairly obvious clue, of course, but we cannot be sure until we hear this exchange:

ESTRAGON. Allons-nous-en.
VLADIMIR. On ne peut pas.
ESTRAGON. Pourquoi?
VLADIMIR. On attend Godot. (p. 8)

Until this point in the dialogue the theme of waiting is dormant. What happens, then, during these first vital minutes in the play when, traditionally, the audience is presented with the exposition of the dramatic action? We are presented, in fact, with nothing less than a synthesis of most of the themes forming the total meaning of the play. As the lights go up, we see a leafless, lifeless tree, and a decrepit old man wrestling painfully with his boot. The underlying themes of suffering, and of life and death, are *suggested*—not stated—even before a word is spoken. The first exchange has a double level of meaning which takes us straight away from the immediate triviality of removing an old boot to the fundamental problem of whether there is anything man can do to improve his existence:

ESTRAGON. Rien à faire.
VLADIMIR. Je commence à le croire. J'ai longtemps résisté à cette pensée, en me disant, Vladimir, sois raisonnable, tu n'as pas encore tout essayé. Et je reprenais le combat.

The theme of physical deterioration (an inevitable part of man's lot on earth) is immediately suggested by Vladimir's condition (he walks "à petits pas raides, les jambes écartées", and the theme of man as the victim of unknown forces for reasons unknown appears when we hear that Estragon has been beaten up again (—"Toujours les mêmes?" — "Je ne sais pas.").

Also established within a few lines is the conflict between the need for friendship and the desire for independence, when Estragon rebuffs Vladimir's affectionate impulse, only to be reminded that but for his friend he would be "un petit tas d'ossements".

The first reference to suicide ("La main dans la main...") heralds the subsequent importance of this pseudo-solution to problems. The word 'éternité' (p. 4) is more than a cliché (the Grove Press edition has "a million years ago") and gives us the feeling that time is going to be an important dimension in this strange little corner of the universe. In the middle of comic exchanges about Estragon's boots and Vladimir's fly-buttons, Vladimir repeats *rêveusement* his friend's reproach, "tu attends toujours le dernier moment"—which suggests the important theme of the late-repentant—and makes a statement ("C'est long, mais ce sera bon") which is not only a comment on his physical condition, but also a meditation on their long purgatorial wait.

Vladimir's first important speech is another characteristic *double-entendre* ("Des fois... je me sens... épouvanté") in which the word *ça* ("ça vient quand même") is to be understood in terms of his urinary problems (he suffers from some kidney disease), *and* (not or) in terms of his intuition that they are nearing the last moment of time. This premonition is in some way connected with the irritation caused by his hat: the hat, as we shall see later, is indispensable to thought; as the symbolic organ of thought is becoming uncomfortable, it is an implicit sign that thought (and therefore existence—*cogito ergo sum*) will soon cease. When Vladimir removes his hat again almost immediately after this with the mystified comment, " Ça devient inquiétant", he launches immediately into the question of salvation and repentance, and despite minor deviations and irrelevances from Estragon, he manages to keep alive the theme of Hell, damnation, and the salvation of one of the thieves on the Cross, until Estragon kills the subject with his obscene oath, an expression of all the bitterness and resentment born of an eternity of unfulfilled hopes and disillusionment. They then come to the question of waiting for Godot, and we thus come to the end of the first phase, the initial enunciation of the important themes of the play.

If we now look at the beginning of Act 2, we see that the themes of affection and victimization alone fill the time until the first "On attend Godot" which, with its ensuing pause, marks the end of the first phase of the act.

Both acts continue with references to the tree, and to the capriciousness of memory. In Act 1 it is Estragon who remembers that they were by that tree the day before; in Act 2 it is Vladimir, and Estragon remembers nothing: a little diversity within the repeated pattern. The distance Estragon has moved along the road to despair can be judged by his reponses to Vladimir's questions about the place they are in:

VLADIMIR. L'endroit te semble familier?
ESTRAGON. Je ne dis pas ça. (*Act* 1)

ESTRAGON. Et tu dis que c'était hier, tout ça?
VLADIMIR: Mais oui, voyons.
ESTRAGON. Et à cet endroit?
VLADIMIR. Mais bien sûr! Tu ne reconnais pas?
ESTRAGON. Reconnais! Qu'est-ce qu'il y a à reconnaître? J'ai tiré ma roulure de vie au milieu des sables! Et tu veux que j'y voie des nuances! (*Regard circulaire.*) Regarde-moi cette saloperie! Je n'en ai jamais bougé!

(*Act* 2)

The structural balance of the two acts is subtly varied by the relation of each Pozzo-Lucky scene to the structure of each act. It is most simply described thus:

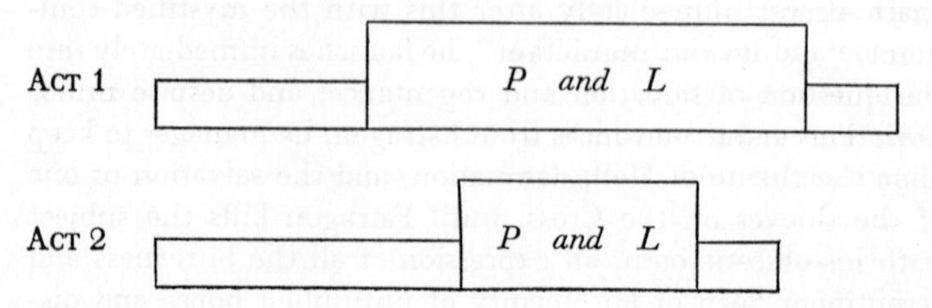

The overwhelmingly dominant factor in Act 1, as can now be easily observed, is the Pozzo-Lucky scene, whereas the first half of Act 2 is weighted by the dialogue between the tramps preceding the return of master and slave, which occurs exactly mid-way through the act. This structural balance is matched thematically, for the 'core' of Act 1 is the long monologue by Lucky, and the 'core' of Act 2 is divided between the impossibility of escape (either *via* 'la pente' or the pit into the audience) and Pozzo's impassioned disquisition on Time ("un jour nous sommes nés...", p. 83). Estragon's panic-stricken attempts to hide or escape in Act 2 cause a much stronger dramatic suspense than that caused by Vladimir's false alarm ("Écoute!") in Act 1. The excitement created by Estragon's fear offsets the difficulty encountered by the tramps throughout the first half of the second act to 'keep the ball rolling' ("Nous commencions à flancher. Voilà notre fin de soirée assurée", says Vladimir with relief when Pozzo's voice is heard).

The similarity of the end of each act stresses the circularity of the whole structure; the return to zero leaves us with an overall impression of the monotony and futility of the eternally repeated ritual enacted on that deserted road. The asymmetry, and the differences between the two acts—by which our interest has been kept alive—are quietly subordinated. Beckett thus solves the immense problem of how to create repetitious monotony without being repetitious and monotonous. It is, as Pronko remarks, "a precisely structured play". But it is not really true to say that "the categories of exposition, inciting moment, rising action, turning point, falling action, climax, and conclusion are not observed in any strict sense".[1] These categories do exist in each act—with the notable and inevitable exception of the inciting moment (i.e., incitement to action), for this is theatre of situation, of inaction. The order in which they appear is changed, however: exposition (of underlying themes)—rising action (in the sense

---

[1] L. C. Pronko, *Avant-Garde: The Experimental Theater in France*, University of California Press, 1962, p. 26.

of increased activity), especially in Act 2—climax (arrival of Pozzo and Lucky)—turning point (the boy's announcement that Godot is not coming)—falling action. It has been suggested that the placing of Lucky's great speech in Act 1 makes the structure defective, "for after it there is nothing to be said".[1] But even though this speech contains many of the fundamental themes of the play, it could hardly be called a coherent exposition of them! Even the intelligent spectator can make sense of it only when the gist has been clarified by subsequent references to the themes in the rest of the play.

As each act can be considered as more or less complete in itself, and the overall effect of the second is the same as the first, why are there two acts? Robert Poulet does not see why there are two acts rather than just one, or ten all the same.[2] Thomas Barbour thinks that Act 2 is essentially a repetition of Act 1, but less successful.[3] All of Beckett's other plays except *Happy Days* have only one act; as they were written after *Godot*, is this not evidence that Beckett realized the two-act structure was a mistake?[4]

In *Fin de Partie* and *Happy Days* the situation is different at the end from what it was at the start. For example, a boy has appeared outside, showing for the first time that there is life outside the room; Clov has revolted and is about to leave (although we are not certain that he will). In *Happy Days*, Winnie is buried only up to her waist at the beginning of Act 1, and up to her neck at the beginning of Act 2; by a logical completion of the series we can foresee that she will be totally engulfed at the beginning of a non-existent Act 3. But in order to start the series off, a second act is essential. Any two num-

---

[1] *The Times*, 31 December 1964.

[2] *La Lanterne Magique*, Debresse, 1958, p. 241.

[3] 'Beckett and Ionesco', *Hudson Review*, Summer 1958, pp. 271–277.

[4] *Molloy* (in which the 'mania for symmetry' is mentioned) is divided into two chapters, with parallels and cross-references, forming an elaborate pattern prefiguring that of *Godot* (see J. Fletcher, *Novels* . . . pp. 131–132).

bers may begin a series which can continue to infinity. Winnie will presumably go deeper and deeper into the ground, no doubt entering the muddy limbo of Pim and Bom (in *Comment c'est*). The situation in *Godot* is one of monotonous sameness, and Beckett had to suggest this perpetual recurrence in the most economical way possible. One act would have been too little, three too much. Two is the magic number denoting *continuous* repetition—not just a *single* repetition—in our everyday vocabulary (it went on and on, it grew smaller and smaller, it went round and round, they went down and down, for ever and ever . . .). Sartre suggests eternity in *Huis Clos* in a single act, but he does not suggest eternal repetition. The possibility of change or development in the situation of Garcin, Estelle and Inès is left open. Not so in *Godot*: in Act 1 it is hinted that exactly the same things happened *before* the beginning of the play; by the end of Act 2 we realize that the cyclic pattern will continue like an unbroken circle until the end of time.

Although the pattern is cyclic, there is an accompanying downward movement, a "linear downward line"[1] which is suggested in many ways: Lucky has degenerated, and does so further in Act 2; Pozzo loses his possessions one by one, his whip loses its crack, he goes blind and he cannot stand up in Act 2; Vladimir and Estragon have degenerated—they were once presentable enough to be admitted up the Eiffel Tower, Estragon was a poet, Vladimir resents Estragon's begging for bits of food and money off Pozzo; the chicken bones of Act 1 are called fish bones in Act 2—suggesting that there may have been another 'day', another visitation (between the two 'days' enacted on the stage), during which Estragon was reduced to begging fish bones from Pozzo; in Act 2 Pozzo has nothing to eat at all; the more Estragon eats of the carrot, the worse it gets; the carrot is followed by a turnip, then a black radish. The two tramps find it more difficult to converse in Act 2.

---

[1] L. Harvey, *art. cit.*, p. 141—an excellent analysis of the theme of degeneration in *Godot* to which I am indebted.

Estragon is more sulky and depressed, and Vladimir agrees at the end of the play to the idea of suicide.

The downward movement is quite clearly indicated and brought into relief in Act 2 by the striking image of the ephemeral nature of earthly life, in terms of the course of a day. "Elles accouchent à cheval sur une tombe, le jour brille un instant, puis c'est la nuit à nouveau" (p. 83). The combination of monotonous repetition within the circularity of the total structure, and the line of life leading sharply to the grave and beyond to eternity is one of great aesthetic simplicity and beauty, which can be seen immediately in geometrical form:

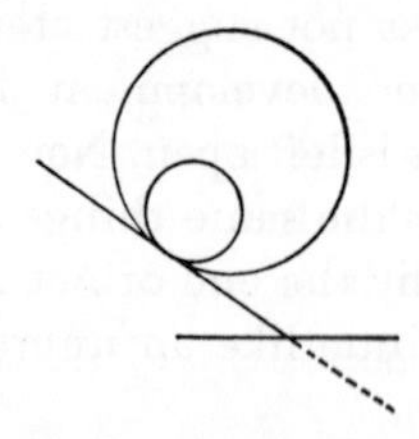

The structure of *Godot* thus achieves the rare quality of being both static and dynamic—a quality which is defined for us at the beginning of Act 2 with Vladimir's round-song.

The first exchange in the dialogue of the play is characteristic of the dual function given to many of the *répliques*. The effect of this has been well expressed by H. A. Smith: "Beckett has succeeded in *fusing* the ordinary and the poetic, and in establishing an ironical counterpoint between a surface triviality or banality and overtones which are infinitely varied in their power of suggestion and often vast to the point of [being] cosmic in their implication."[1] In Act 1 Vladimir and Estragon look at the tree:

ESTRAGON. Qu'est-ce que c'est?
VLADIMIR. On dirait un saule.
ESTRAGON. Où sont les feuilles?

[1] 'Dipsychus among the Shadows', in *Contemporary Theatre*, Stratford-upon-Avon Studies no. 4, Arnold, 1962, p. 157.

VLADIMIR. Il doit être mort.
ESTRAGON. Finis les pleurs. (p. 8)

This is about the most simple and magically concise throw-away line imaginable on the subject of this Vale of Tears, and death as release from it. There is a similarly ironical allusion to the Way of Righteousness shortly after:

VLADIMIR. Tu n'irais pas loin.
ESTRAGON. Ce serait là, en effet, un grave inconvénient... Étant donné la beauté du chemin. (*Un temps.*) Et la bonté des voyageurs. (p. 10)

The sudden transition from the transient to the transcendent, which we see in Pozzo's cliché-variant, "Un beau jour je me suis réveillé aveugle *comme le destin*", can be extremely moving and memorable. Estragon decides to leave his boots for someone with smaller feet and, passing on by way of ironic litotes, ends up with the Crucifixion:

VLADIMIR. Mais tu ne peux pas aller pieds nus.
ESTRAGON. Jésus l'a fait.
VLADIMIR. Jésus! Qu'est-ce que tu vas chercher là! Tu ne vas tout de même pas te comparer à lui!
ESTRAGON. Toute ma vie je me suis comparé à lui.
VLADIMIR. Mais là-bas il faisait chaud! Il faisait bon!
ESTRAGON. Oui. Et on crucifiait vite.
Silence. (p. 47)

At other times, the effect is comic rather than momentous, usually through *non sequiturs*, misunderstandings, talking at cross-purposes, and pratfalls. The intention is none the less serious, however, underneath the clowning:

VLADIMIR. Nous ne sommes pas en train. Faisons quand même quelques respirations.
ESTRAGON. Je ne veux plus respirer.[1] (p. 68)

When Lucky kicks Estragon, Vladimir complains angrily to Pozzo, "Il saigne!", to receive only a terse "C'est bon signe" in reply.

---

[1] The English text is frequently more amusing than the French, as here:—"What about a little deep breathing?"—"I'm tired

The short alternate lines of dialogue are sometimes on the level of music-hall patter, but still the cosmic undertone can be picked out.[1] Estragon inspects his half-eaten carrot:

ESTRAGON. C'est curieux, plus on va, moins c'est bon.
VLADIMIR. Pour moi c'est le contraire.
ESTRAGON. C'est-à-dire?
VLADIMIR. Je me fais au goût au fur et à mesure.
ESTRAGON (*ayant longuement réfléchi*). C'est ça, le contraire?
VLADIMIR. Question de tempérament.
ESTRAGON. De caractère.
VLADIMIR. On n'y peut rien.
ESTRAGON. On a beau se démener.
VLADIMIR. On reste ce qu'on est.
ESTRAGON. On a beau se tortiller.
VLADIMIR. Le fond ne change pas.
ESTRAGON. Rien à faire. (p. 15)

The deep vein of humour running through *Godot* is obvious to those who have seen a good production of it, but it may be missed on the printed page because of the difficulty of accepting the close juxtaposition of tragedy and comedy. On the stage these moments of comic release are realized by the actors' art of inflexion and timing. The attitude underlying this tragicomedy is that even though suffering is the hallmark of man's existence, it is not to be taken seriously as nobody sees it. When Estragon asks, in his ridiculous posture, wobbling on one foot, "Tu crois que Dieu me voit?", the implied answer is 'No'.

---

breathing." The same is true of the following, for example:
POZZO. Is it evening?
Silence. Vladimir and Estragon scrutinize the sunset.
ESTRAGON. It looks as if it was rising backwards.
VLADIMIR. Impossible.
(Cf. p. 78.)

[1] "In *Waiting for Godot* . . . the vaudeville techniques . . . simultaneously cloak and reveal the metaphysical farce of the human condition. Stale gags, shoes that pinch and stink, hats that shift from head to head—Beckett bends these worn-out techniques to his purpose." Ruby Cohn, *op. cit.*, p. 211. "Beckett is the first great academic clown since Sterne." Hugh Kenner, *Samuel Beckett*, Calder, 1962, p. 204.

Beckett makes quite frequent use of the device of stychomythy (dialogue in the form of strophe and antistrophe, with antithesis and rhetorical repetition or taking up of the other speaker's words), in conjunction with highly stylized language attaining a considerable poetic value through the rhythm of words and silence and the pervasive action of images. The most extended examples of this occur in Act 2 (p. 54 onward), where the dialogue attains the rare incantatory power of a broken, plaintive melody.

"In all the sentences that Beckett writes it is the shape that matters."[1] The "souci de pureté, de simplicité, de musicalité et de sélection" to which M. Barrault drew attention[2] are to be seen not only in the relationship of the words within the sentence, but just as clearly in the movement from sentence to sentence, and from silence to silence.

> VLADIMIR. Nous ne sommes plus seuls, à attendre la nuit, à attendre Godot, à attendre — à attendre. Toute la soirée nous avons lutté, livrés à nos propres moyens. Maintenant c'est fini. Nous sommes déjà demain.
> ESTRAGON. Mais ils sont seulement de passage.
> POZZO. A moi!
> VLADIMIR. Déjà le temps coule tout autrement. Le soleil se couchera, la lune se lèvera et nous partirons — d'ici. (p. 69)

No better example of Beckett's handling of contrast could be found than in Pozzo's *discours public* in Act 1, which is too long to be quoted (see pp. 30–31). We are given here a striking paraphrase of Beckett's world-view illustrating admirably the dramatist's ear for the inflexions and timing of the spoken voice, the sense of balance, the interplay of harmony and contrast, which match the qualities of the overall structure. *Godot* has the kind of beautiful inevitability of a flower or a butterfly's wing. It grows out of nothing, without any obvious plan, like a richly imaginative, symmetrical, poetic doodle with one large question-mark hidden in its convolutions.

---

[1] Harold Hobson, *International Theatre Annual*, 1956, p. 154.
[2] See p. xxxii.

CHAPTER 6

Symbolism and Characterization

"No symbols where none intended."—*Samuel Beckett.*

We are given the impression that the four characters in *Godot* are placed in a situation whose significance is beyond their understanding. They are not mere abstract figures, however, achieving meaningfulness only in terms of a carefully worked-out allegory. The 'meaning' of the play is inseparable from the 'meaning' of the characters. If the play is an allegory, they must be allegorical figures; if it is symbolic, they are symbols. If the play has no meaning beyond the literal, they are simply two seedy, prolix men down on their luck in a country where slavery is still legal. We must seek the most complete and satisfactory level of interpretation; that is, the one which is the least obscure.

A definition may be helpful at this point:

> An allegory is a paraphrase of a conscious content, whereas a symbol is the best possible expression for an unconscious content whose nature can only be guessed, because it is still unknown.[1]

Guicharnaud states that "*Godot* is totally symbolic without being traditionally allegorical", noting that allegory consists of "an analysis, an exteriorization, and a concrete representation of the elements of the analysis", and concluding that "this is surely not the case in *Godot*".[2]

---

[1] C. G. Jung, *The Archetypes and the Collective Unconsciousness*, Routledge and Kegan Paul, 1959, Part 1, p. 6.
[2] *Modern French Theatre*, p. 193.

No single scale of analogies can be applied to *Godot* in order to 'explain' it. As in Camus' *La Peste* no single level of meaning is sustained long enough for it to be understood as an allegory in the way Swift's *Tale of a Tub* or Bunyan's *Pilgrim's Progress* can be. It suggests a whole range of preoccupations. "The range of Beckett's devastating account of the human predicament includes the fields of politics, economics, theology, society, education, metaphysics, discourse, physical science, and history. . . . The work is a searching exposure of man's limitations."[1] The terms 'account' and 'exposure' adroitly avoid the pitfalls of the term 'symbol'. Some critics have been aware of the dangers of imposing a tidy allegorical pattern and of seeing "symbols where none intended". Jean Vannier, for instance, saw the play as being great enough when considered as "le déroulement de la parole... le lieu fascinant où se révélait la solitude du langage".[2] In 1956 Samuel Beckett remarked to Alec Reid that "the great success of *Waiting for Godot* had arisen from a misunderstanding: critics and public alike were busy interpreting in allegorical or symbolic terms a play which strove at all cost to avoid definition".[3]

Winnie, in *Oh les Beaux Jours*, issues a warning about the assignment of meaning: "'Ça signifie quoi?' dit-il. 'C'est censé signifier quoi?' Et patati... et patata... toutes les bêtises habituelles..."

Although the warning not to say *bêtises* should, of course, be heeded, we should not allow ourselves to be ridiculed into silence either because of the more grotesque interpretations that have been proffered, or because Mr Beckett tries to put us off. It is significant that although he replied to Peter Hall (who first produced the English version in London) that his interpretation would be as good as anyone else's, Beckett subsequently expressed disapproval of the play, thus implying that Mr Hall's interpretation was not as good as his own. Further-

---

[1] Jerome Ashmore, *art. cit.*, p. 296.

[2] *Théâtre populaire*, juillet 1957, no. 25, pp. 69–72.

[3] *Drama Survey*, Fall, 1962.

more, Beckett has since taken a very active part in productions of *Godot*--proof enough that he thinks interpretation does matter. What is not acceptable, and for good reason, is any attempt at exclusive definition, or reduction of total implication to a single idea.

According to various interpretations, the play has been seen as:

—a dramatic representation of the wretchedness of man without God;

—"a general expression of the futility of human existence when man pins his hope on a force outside of himself" (Dukore, *art. cit.*);

—"the artistic portrayal of man's absurd existence as it appears to Beckett" (Rechstein, *art. cit.*);

—"an existentialist play [arguing] against the assumption of an image that drains off the energy of stark human responsibility" (Hoffman, *op. cit.*, p. 150);

—a revelation of "man's anguish as he waits for the arrival of something that will give life meaning and bring an end to his suffering" (Pronko, *op. cit.*, p. 34);

—"a profoundly anti-Christian play" (C. Chadwick, "*Waiting for Godot:* A Logical Approach", *Symposium*, Winter, 1960);

—a Christian play (Ronald Gray, C. McCoy, Pronko);

—"a modern classic affirming man's dignity and ultimate salvation" (L. J. Marinello, *Drama Critique*, Spring, 1963);

—"a picture of unrelieved blackness" (G. E. Wellwarth, *Kansas City Review*, XXVIII, 1961);

—"a modern morality play on permanent Christian themes" (G. S. Fraser, *Times Literary Supplement*, 10 February 1956);

—"an atheist existentialist play" (*Times Literary Supplement*, 13 April 1956).

When one adds that Beckett has been described as a disciple of Sartre and of St Thomas Aquinas, and as a lapsed Catholic, one sees that the no-man's-land between wishful thinking and scholarship is almost without bounds—a view which is strengthened by interpretations which have equated Godot with de Gaulle; Pozzo with Capitalism and Lucky with

Labour; Pozzo with the U.S.S.R. and the enslaved Lucky with the East European satellite countries; the two tramps with Britain and France, waiting for Godot (the U.S.A.) to come to their aid. A detailed hypothesis has been built up 'proving' that Pozzo is James Joyce and Lucky Beckett himself.[1]

Ingenuity has been unbounded in the amusing exercise of ascribing meanings to the names of the characters. The very nicknames epitomize their dichotomy, maintains Ruby Cohn.[2] Gogo (< go—walk—feet) has stinking feet, and Didi (< *dire*) stinks from his mouth. B. F. Dukore constructs a wonderful psychological theory[3]: Didi reversed is Id-Id, and Gogo is formed from (e)go-(e)go. The Id is the primitive, instinctual part of the psyche, out of touch with the world; its relations to the body are dominated by the pleasure principle. The Ego, on the other hand, is that part of the psyche which is conscious and in closest touch with social reality. According to Freud, Mr Dukore goes on, the Ego is the principle that perceives reality; the Ego and the Id are inseparable and indivisible, some psychoanalysts maintain.

Now, the theory continues, Didi has a backward Id, and Gogo has an incomplete Ego (the E is missing). So Gogo is dominated by the Id (or pleasure principle), and Didi—having a backward Id—has an overdeveloped Ego (or rational principle). This, it is claimed, explains why Gogo and Didi must be together, and why Gogo cannot withstand the pressures of the external world with which Didi, having a strong Ego, can cope. Gogo, having an incomplete rational sense, has great difficulty in remembering and reasoning, whereas Didi, having a dominant Ego, meditates and reminds Gogo of the people they met the day before. Pozzo, according to Mr Dukore, is an extension of Gogo, and Lucky of Didi; their function is to show the personality traits of Gogo and Didi in a different relationship—that of master and slave instead of companions. In fact, Didi

1 Lionel Abel, *Metatheatre: A New View of Dramatic Form*. New York, 1963.

2 *Op. cit.*, p. 214.

3 *Drama Survey*, Winter, 1962.

and Gogo will become Lucky and Pozzo in time. The missing element of the psyche is the Superego, or the sense of Moral Standards. Didi and Gogo are without moral values, and instead of searching for a system of values within themselves, they wait for an outside force (God?) to supply them. But they will wait in vain. This, Mr Dukore concludes, is in line with Sartre's existentialist viewpoint.

The theory summarized above is an interesting and ingenious amalgam of existentialism and a form of dualism based on the similarities and differences that link the two couples. There is just enough similarity between Vladimir and Lucky, Estragon and Pozzo, for the contrasting natures of Vladimir and Estragon to be seen more clearly in Pozzo and Lucky. Mr Dukore's 'extension' theory ignores the fact, however, that it is the Gogo/Lucky couple who are the poet/thinker, and that when Didi assigns to himself the rôle of Lucky in the play-acting scene in Act 2, he is unable to perform. Furthermore, it is Didi who, Pozzo-like, shouts "porc!" at Gogo (p. 61). These examples indicate that the 'extensions' have crossed wires, along which this particular 'message' becomes rather garbled.[1]

The main disadvantage of Mr Dukore's theories is that they are not in terms of anything that remotely interests Samuel Beckett—and the author's intention cannot be entirely discounted. They do reveal, however, that the two characters, Vladimir and Estragon, are psychologically coherent, whereas Dr Eva Metman disputes their ability to exist as 'persons':

> Significantly, all Beckett's works are mainly monologues, or rather musings, of some solitary person, and from this we may take the hint that the various figures which he puts on the stage are not really persons but figures in the inner world.[2]

What, though, is meant by the phrase "not really persons"? Imaginary fictional characters are frequently emanations of their creator's own psyche, and this in no way detracts from

---

[1] Concerning the possibility that in some respects it is Didi and Pozzo who are doubles, see Ch. 3 above, p. lxii.

[2] *Art. cit.*, p. 44.

their *vraisemblance*. According to Guicharnaud (*op. cit.*, p. 197) they are much more coherent and individualized than Ionesco's 'characterless' characters. "Each has a coherent and original personality, a body, a past. Yet they are often treated anonymously." Edith Kern (*art. cit.*) says they are as anonymous as A and B in *Molloy*.

The anonymity of Vladimir and Estragon comes more from their lack of a background to which we can attach them firmly, than from vague delineation. It resembles the anonymity of stock characters in farce and *commedia dell'arte* with their conventional theatrical names, rather than the abstractions A and B referred to by Edith Kern. Estragon and Vladimir are not interchangeable; they are unforgettable, each in his own right. Clearly they are symbiotic—that is to say, they have a common life source. Each one makes up for the deficiencies of the other, and this can be understood in ordinary human terms without having recourse to psychoanalytical jargon that adds nothing to our appreciation of the play's artistry. All around us there are couples who are bound together by their individual strengths, weaknesses, and needs.

Vladimir is the more intelligent, sensitive, analytical, dignified, philosophical, altruistic, protective, cultured, active, articulate, buoyant, and strong-willed of the two. Estragon is the more spontaneous, animal, instinctual, sulky, childish, lethargic, egotistic, obstinate, forgetful, victimized, acutely anguished, dependent, bitter, and impatient. That is quite an array of well-defined characteristics for figures who are "not really persons"! What keeps these two together? The relationship between them resembles the idea of friendship which, according to Beckett, is to be found in Proust, who situates friendship "somewhere between fatigue and ennui" (*Proust*, p. 65). They are mutually dependent, and not only from the point of view of needing each other's company. Each needs the other in a far more urgent way: to give constant reassurance of his existence, his identity. "On trouve toujours quelque chose, hein, Didi, pour nous donner l'impression d'exister", says Estragon. "Mais oui, mais oui, on est des magiciens", retorts Vladimir in one of his rare moments of impatience (p. 61). In the absence of Godot, only the other partner can give life a meaning—a truly existentialist concern, this mutual dependence on others to give meaning to one's existence, in the absence of any external, independent witness. Vladimir and Estragon enable each other to avoid the torment of solitude, which can only be filled in with faulty memories of an old song, endlessly repeated. Like the vast majority of humans, they have no inner resources. Beckett deprives his heroes of all the aids to which we commonly resort to enable us to escape from the vacuum of inactivity and thus to make ourselves forget the dimension of time. They have great verbal talent, but because of their faulty memory they cannot narrate tales or even talk of books (Vladimir resorts to a story from the Bible, Estragon to a bawdy story). They have no knowledge of music, cannot sing songs or whistle symphonies. So they are forced to fall back on picking quarrels with each other over nothing, doing their exercises, thinking up little gags, play-acting—anything to ward off the surrounding silence to which all human voices must ultimately be reduced. This silence threatens to envelop the characters—Pozzo feels it too, and finds it difficult to drag himself away from the tramps' company although he pretends to be favouring them with his.

Vladimir and Estragon leave us with the impression of fortitude and humour and irrepressible mental activity, just as Winnie does in *Happy Days*. But to recognize this, one has to have the courage to accept the fact that here Beckett is setting before us, in this pathetic couple, the condition each one of us is placed in by virtue of being born. At birth we are forced to take part in a game we must lose. Whilst realizing fully and without self-deception (or *mauvaise foi*) the absurdity of the game, we must keep our dignity. Vladimir and Estragon perform no act of importance in itself: the implication is that nothing *is* important in itself. Even a call for help is met with inertia and acquisitiveness—as calls for help to the infirm and the hungry on a massive scale are ignored every day by all of us as we go on talking about trivialities.

If these two pathetic tramps succeed in involving us—not alienating us—to the extent of making us wonder how far we simply cover up our expectation of things to come by absorbing ourselves in activities which are fundamentally of the same order of meaninglessness or absurdity (the tennis, winter sports, swimming, golf, skating, cycling, etc., mentioned by Lucky in his synthesizing 'think'), then we may regard them as successful both as human characters and as symbolic figures.

Dismal though the existence of Vladimir and Estragon is, it is bearable by comparison with that of Pozzo and Lucky, which becomes increasingly unbearable and deteriorates apparently at an alarming rate. They have been described as "a terrifyingly ambiguous paradigm" presenting "quite a problem to the philosopher".[1] There is no doubt that by introducing this itinerant pair into the inert and stationary locus of the tramps, Beckett has taken every opportunity to provide a contrast which will bring out the fraternity of the tramps into stronger relief. Master and slave, tyrant and martyr, villain and victim, exploiter and exploited, dictator and subject; all are symbolized by this couple. But they are also made subtly relevant to the vigil of Vladimir and Estragon in various ambiguous ways. There is the similarity of names—Pozzo, Godot—which leads to a misunderstanding both comic and pathetic. In Act 1 they arrive, with one end of a rope round Lucky's neck and the other clutched in Pozzo's hand, immediately after Estragon has asked "si on est lié... à ton bonhomme"; in Act 2, no sooner has Vladimir said "il faut fermer les yeux" than they appear again, this time Pozzo being blind. What is behind these coincidences? Has Pozzo been eavesdropping, waiting for a good 'cue' for him to make his entrance into the company of the two trespassers? The coincidences have led one commentator to be very suspicious: "Vladimir's recommendation that [Estragon] should close his eyes inspires Pozzo with a fresh idea for a cruel practical joke . . . he is apparently blind, but there are in fact

---

[1] J. R. Moore, *art. cit.*, pp. 55 and 58.

clear indications that he is not blind at all."[1] Pozzo's inability to get up is, in the light of this, a "monstrous hoax". Lucky's dumbness is, equally, a trick, "manifestly a lie since Pozzo's complaint, a few lines before, about Lucky not answering when he called presupposes that Lucky is not really dumb" (*ibid.*).

The first point, about Pozzo's blindness, is a serious one. The latter is less so, since it is natural that if Lucky had only recently been struck dumb, Pozzo would not be accustomed to this, and would regard the affliction with suspicion himself. Pozzo's blindness has been discussed in Chapter 3 above, but here it is perhaps relevant to add the opinion of Mr Paul Curran, whose performance as Pozzo at the Royal Court Theatre in 1964/5 owed much of its authenticity to the close collaboration of Mr Beckett himself. Mr Curran wrote to me on this point as follows:

> Obviously we queried and debated many alternatives in *Godot*—but the truth of Pozzo's blindness was not one of them. There is no doubt in my mind that he is blind nor, I am sure, is there any doubt in Sam's mind. I remember he gave me a note in rehearsal once that I was looking too directly at Vladimir; I must look further "off" for if I didn't it gave him the impression that I could see Vladimir. Doesn't that seem to you conclusive?

It is certainly conclusive so far as Beckett's ideas *at that time* are concerned, but it is far from certain that his ideas do not evolve—as the question of identifying Pozzo with Godot will show.

When Pozzo and Lucky first appear, their afflictions are already foreseeable. Pozzo suffers from his heart; a stroke could bring on blindness. Lucky's incoherence in Act 1 merely degenerates from faulty communication to silence. Between them they share the afflictions of Watt, who is both dumb and blind when he leaves Mr Knott's house—because of his disappointment ("This body homeless . . . This emptied heart"). Apart from the simple cause of physical degeneration, what else

[1] C. Chadwick, *art. cit.*, p. 256. See also above, p. lxii.

could lie behind their decline? On the socio-political level, it is the sign of the degradation that must befall the master-slave relationship (Guicharnaud, *op. cit.*, p. 207). On the purgatorial level, they are having fresh punishment meted out to them, perhaps for the sin of pride (intellectual and social). In Dante, loss of voice is the punishment for suicide; it is the fate of Pier delle Vigne, once poet and orator. By committing suicide, a man

> casts himself back to the stage from which he started. In this low vegetative stage, all the customary avenues to the outside world are necessarily closed. The human body is a mysterious system of such avenues, eye, ear, touch, and so on; but the suicide flings the mysterious system away, and with it the power of communication. Dante indicates this by the difficulty of speech under which these vegetative souls labour.[1]

Were Beckett's debt to Dante in other contexts not already well established, it would hardly be worth while trying to find a literary antecedent for Lucky; but the influence being what it is, and Dante being such an integral part of Beckett's highly literary vision, the example of Pier delle Vigne deserves to be cited as a possible model.

As for the physical appearance of Lucky, we see it in a description of one of *l'Innommable*'s 'delegates':

> Ployé, il semble porter à bout de bras des objets pesants, je ne sais lesquels. Ce que je vois le mieux de lui, c'est son chapeau. Le sommet est tout usé, comme une vieille semelle, laissant passer quelques cheveux gris. Son regard, levé assez longuement vers moi, je le sens implorant, comme si je pouvais faire quelque chose pour lui. (pp. 22–23)

It is not possible to say whether this was written just before or just after *Godot*. To all intents and purposes, Lucky and 'the delegate' were conceived together.

Kafka writes in his *Diaries* that "Dumbness is one of the

---

[1] J. S. Carroll, *Exiles of Eternity: An Exposition of Dante's Inferno*, Hodder and Stoughton, 1903, p. 212.

attributes of perfection". Lucky has the qualities of a saint[1]—total submission to the Master, accepting humiliation without a murmur, bearing the burden uncomplainingly. The possibilities of Biblical irony are, therefore, considerable in his case. For example,

> Come to me, all those whose work is hard, whose load is heavy; and I will give you relief. Bend your necks to my yoke, for I am gentle and humble-hearted . . . (Matt. xi, 28, 29).

Again according to Matthew, Lucky is really lucky:

> You know that in the world, rulers lord it over their subjects, and their great men make them feel the weight of authority; but it shall not be so with you. Among you, whoever wants to be great must be your servant, and whoever would be first must be the willing slave of all . . . (Matt. xx, 25, 27)

This is not to claim that Beckett set out with the object of writing an ironical commentary on St Matthew's Gospel; but given his strict Protestant upbringing, his familiarity with the Bible, and his religious scepticism, the chances of subconscious covert allusion are great.

If one wants further proof of the validity of this approach to the underlying significance of Lucky as a symbolic figure, one has only to look at his long speech in Act 1, which is a "parody of the Christian liturgy which, for many people, has indeed become a mere ritual whose words are devoid of all meaning".[2]

Richard Coe begins his useful study of Beckett's works with a quotation from and comment on Lucky's 'think' because it is "an extraordinary *résumé*—in a form which is by no means as garbled as might at first appear—of the Beckettian uni-

---

[1] His ingratitude when he kicks Estragon would seem to contradict this, but one may appeal to L. Harvey's view that "he causes pain, for he is a teacher who reveals the hard facts of the human condition" (*art. cit.*, p. 146).

[2] C. Chadwick, *art. cit.*

verse". It constitutes the only utterance made by Lucky. Apart from this his only actions are to pick up, put down, do a pathetic little dance, weep, and kick Estragon. The incoherence of his speech is part of his own being, but it has a significance beyond that; it is a complex expansion of the nonsensical and incoherent answers Rabelais and Voltaire imagined being given to our questionings about the nature of the infinite and the Almighty. When Lucky begins his speech he assumes the rôle of man trying to apply his reason to the task of explaining the mysteries of the universe—and failing utterly, painfully, pitifully.

The existence and nature of God are Lucky's first concerns. Two phony-sounding and non-existent authorities, Poinçon [Grove and Faber editions[1]: 'Puncher'] and Wattman [= a tram-driver who cannot go off the rails laid down for him] have postulated the existence of a personal God with a white beard (the boy's description of Godot also conforms to this comforting picture-book image). But, paradoxically, God is "hors du temps de l'étendue" (*G*, *F:* "outside time without extension"] and suffers from apathia (insensibility to suffering), athambia (imperturbability) and aphasia (inability to understand or use speech—i.e., to hear prayers and supplications or to communicate with man). This venerable God, the two authorities have asserted, loves us dearly with a few mysterious exceptions, "on ne sait pourquoi" (a refrain stressing human ignorance)—"mais on a le temps" to find out why: "ça viendra", it will come to our knowledge. God suffers (despite his apathia) with those who are tormented in the fires of Hell and who "mettront le feu aux poutres" [*F*, *G:* "will fire the firmament"] and take Hell up to heaven.

Lucky quotes other authorities of equally suspicious authenticity, revelling in names concocted with Rabelaisian irreverence out of the private parts and the excretive functions. They have proved at the 'Academy of Anthropometry' (man-measurement) that in spite of progress made in the fields of

---

[1] Will be referred to as *G* and *F*.

nutrition, physical culture, hygiene, medicine, and communication—all the discoveries of which man is so proud—man is shrinking, "est en train de maigrir... de rapetisser... de rétrécir... depuis la mort de Voltaire..." [*F:* "Samuel Johnson"; *G:* "Bishop Berkeley"[1]] "...étant de l'ordre de deux doigts cent grammes par tête de pipe" [*F:* "to the tune of one inch four ounce per capita"]. Ever since the eighteenth century, then, the age of the so-called Enlightenment, when we began to take the idea of Progress and Science seriously, man has been dwindling, shrinking, wasting. There is nothing man can do about this universal running-down of things.

Furthermore, "ce qui est encore plus grave", Lucky has a prophetic intuition of some great catastrophe; "à la campagne, à la montagne et au bord de la mer... l'air et la terre par les grands froids, l'air et la terre faits pour les pierres" [*F, G:* "the abode of stones"] "au septième de leur ère" [*F, G:* "in the year of their Lord . . ."—not necessarily *our* Lord—". . . six hundred and something"]... "par les grands fonds" [*F, G:* "in the great deeps"] "...la tête" (the organ of thought, therefore of existence), "...la barbe" (of the personal God), "...les flammes" (of Hell), "...les pleurs" (of man), "...les pierres si bleues si calmes" (the earth, abode of stones, will all be blown to "les nues si bleues si calmes").

The end, laments Lucky, must be accompanied by disintegration into the calm azure of the sky. The rising tide of hopelessness and the increasing frenzy of his speech are too much for his three listeners, and they hurl themselves at him. Only when his 'thinking hat' is removed does he stop. He has become a mere piece of mechanism, switching himself on when ordered, and being put out of action by the removal of a part.

By reducing Lucky's 'think' to a semblance of coherence, one destroys the parodic effect, the pathos, the growing tension, and the brilliance of the speech which demands an equal

[1] The significance of the choice of Bishop Berkeley is discussed on p. cxvi.

brilliance in performance. After establishing in our minds the three key thoughts (God is cut off from us—human progress is an illusion—the universe is moving towards disintegration) we must return to the text and see how Beckett the *artist* has achieved his effects, which are far more important than the ideas, for which he would claim no originality. We have here an example of disintegration of speech, the rebellion of a former thinker (Pozzo tells us Lucky was this) against conventional, literary language. We find other examples in Beckett's writings. Watt's speech becomes formless and incoherent; it develops 'cracks' which he is too weary to mend. In *L'Innommable*, written at the same time as *Godot*, the style develops into a similar 'endless stream', and *Comment c'est* is completely devoid of all syntactical and typographical conventions (sentences or paragraphs). It is readable only by virtue of the division into 'blocks' varying from three to fifteen lines in length.

Lucky's speech has a form of punctuation—an unwritten pause before each "je reprends"—which is supplied by the actor. If this is borne in mind, together with repetition of leitmotifs ("quaqua" (*quoique*), "on ne sait pourquoi", "n'anticipons pas"), repetition of syllables, and slipping back to earlier themes in the 'argument', the reading of it becomes a simple matter (especially if it is done quickly so that the needle is forced over the cracks in the record).

Lucky is ordered to speak, against his will. This leads Mr Dukore to see his 'think' as "a dramatic demonstration of man's intellect used as a slave to man's physical activities" (*art. cit.*), whereas M. Guicharnaud regards it as "a farcical satire on the condition of professional intellectuals. Supported by a society for whom . . . they 'produce' thought . . . [they] exasperate their masters by their verbal delirium" (*op. cit.*, p. 209). The logic of this argument is not quite clear; intellectuals who are *supported* by society surely have to give what can be readily understood? In totalitarian states, where the intellectual is, like Lucky, *inescapably* dependent on Authority, he dare not exasperate, displease or mystify, under pain of being 'silenced'.

If one must look for a social significance in Lucky's performance, it would seem to have its strongest analogy here. Perhaps Pozzo, a Stalinesque character in his despotism, could once dictate Lucky's thought, but now he refuses to 'toe the party line'. In Act 2, he has been silenced, but Pozzo disclaims all knowledge of the cause. Fantastic? Perhaps. But we should remember that in the first edition of *Godot*, Pozzo and Lucky are referred to as "les comiques staliniens".

Mention should also be made of Lionel Abel's views on the question of the origins of Pozzo and Lucky.[1] "From *Endgame*", he writes, "I think I have learned that Pozzo is none other than Beckett's literary master and friend, James Joyce" (p. 135). Hamm (the father) is Joyce, Clov (the son) is Beckett. Pozzo and Lucky have the same rôles. "It is abundantly clear now", Mr Abel goes on, "why Lucky, in his monologue, parodied the Joycean manner." The truth of this is unlikely. Lucky's speech has none of Joyce's style. As Martin Esslin has said, "it is, if anything, a parody of philosophical jargon and scientific double-talk—the very opposite of what either Joyce or Beckett ever wanted to achieve in their writing".[2]

This autobiographical approach is based on a set of faulty analogies; the Joyce-Beckett relationship was very different from the Pozzo-Lucky one. Pozzo has no artistic talent—Joyce was extremely gifted; Lucky performs at Pozzo's bidding—Beckett never did this for Joyce. Mr Abel finds it "extraordinary" that *Godot* and *Endgame* can move people who know nothing of the relationship beween Beckett and Joyce. A strange assumption indeed, that a matter of such local interest as the friendship of Beckett and Joyce should move people more deeply than the cosmic situations that seem, in *Godot* and in *Endgame*, to involve all mankind. One could excuse the reduction of the problem to such a trivial level if it helped to explain the devastating impact of the plays. It does not. Significantly, the most stimulating interpretations Mr Abel provides do take

---

1 *Metatheatre.*

2 *The Theatre of the Absurd*, p. 52.

the level of argument right outside the autobiographical sphere.

As already shown in Chapter 3, Beckett originally had serious thoughts about identifying Pozzo with Godot. He regarded the boy as a major obstacle to such an identification. Indeed, the boy creates a number of difficulties for the interpreter of the play on any level which equates Godot with something other than with a person. If the boy does not come at the command of a white-bearded old gentleman, who does put him up to it? The only answer can be, Pozzo. The boy must be one of Pozzo's staff, working on his estate. Pozzo must instruct him, the moment he gets out of sight of the two tramps, to tell them that the man whose name he knows from his conversation with them will not be coming. The motive? Another trick, perhaps—or pity. He knows, or feels strongly, that Godot will not come, so he puts them out of their misery until the next time. Making 'Godot's' messenger come from Pozzo does not necessarily lead to the conclusion that Pozzo is Godot, then. The equation is still

Godot = ?

In the original French production, Roger Blin as Pozzo wore a white beard, the obvious effect of which was to identify him with the description of Godot given by the boy to Vladimir. Dr Chadwick assumes from this (*art. cit.*, p. 254) that the absence of beard in the 1955 London production was "an extraordinary mistake". At the present time, however, we can view the problem with the additional insight afforded by the Royal Court Theatre production recently supervised by Samuel Beckett: he did not order any beard for Pozzo. Beckett's desire to associate Pozzo and Godot has therefore receded gradually, for reasons unknown but easily divined. Pozzo has but a fraction of the attributes which can be assigned to Godot on the basis of the textual evidence offered by this play and by Beckett's other works. To reduce Godot to Pozzo is an inexcusable diminution of the play's potential significance. To appeal to the argument (as Dr Chadwick does) that it is unlikely Pozzo would pass by three times by accident is to ignore the complex time-element in the play. Act 2 may take place aeons after Act 1; the passing of terrestrial time is but an illusion, as Pozzo implies in his attack on time in Act 2. Under these circumstances it is far from improbable that Pozzo and Lucky should come past more than once, especially as Pozzo considers it to be his land. To say that Pozzo *might* be Godot is valid, as it fits some of the pieces of the puzzle together into a satisfying pattern—but it is not the *only* pattern, as we shall now see.

CHAPTER 7

GODOT: Constant or Variable?

"Prions Dieu... Le salaud! Il n'existe pas!"—"Pas encore."
—*Fin de Partie*

Hamm's brief and appropriately violent expression about God in *Fin de Partie* illustrates the religious scepticism which is to be found throughout Beckett's works. It is of no importance; Beckett is not a writer of agnostic or atheist tracts, and he is no more interested in converting readers to his point of view than Proust was in turning his readers into pederasts. Hamm's exclamation occurs in a more open-ended way in *Godot*. Estragon appeals to God to have pity on him, and asks if God sees him (Act 2). As far as he is concerned, God and Godot are quite separate entities, but his scepticism about Godot, contrasting with Vladimir's unshakable faith in Godot, is matched by his disbelief in Vladimir's Bible stories. Beckett obviously had a good reason for giving the object of their wait the name of Godot. There is little point in stating that as Beckett wrote the play in French he would not have chosen a name similar to the English word 'God' had he intended to give it overtones of divinity. The name is a *trouvaille* of the first order, opening up several associations of ideas, through punning and analogy, in both English and French.

The suffix *-ot* is a common diminutive in French [cf. *bellot*, 'prettyish'; *brunot*, 'brownish']. It is also an indication of familiarity—*Jacquot*, *Jeannot*, *Charlot*. Of course, the suffix could have been added to a French word of divine connotation —*dieu*, *déité*, *Seigneur*... —but that would have made a religious interpretation not just possible, but inevitable. 'Godot' has the sense of 'a little god', 'a minor god', hence 'a tin god' or someone who 'thinks he's God Almighty'. This suggests reference to abuse of authority rather than to divinity. The name Godot can be associated equally with several unpleasant words in French: *godailleur*, 'loafer', *godenot*, 'a juggler's puppet', *godiche*, 'lout'. The word *godet* means a receptacle, hence perhaps something that will hold any meaning put into it.

"Surely a logical argument, without any *a priori* assumptions, must run as follows", suggests Dr Chadwick (*art. cit.*): "Godot is God, Pozzo is Godot, Pozzo is therefore God and since Pozzo is nothing but a tyrant and a slave-driver so too is God." The weakness in this logical argument is that it is assumed *a priori* that Godot is God. Dr Chadwick does put forward some evidence in support of the theory; it rests upon an exclamation-mark (shades of the hilarious court scene in *Le Mariage de Figaro*!). It will be recalled that Pozzo exclaims "De la même espèce que Pozzo! D'origine divine" (p. 17). Ronald Gray (*art. cit.*) maintains that these two sentences are separate, inferring that Pozzo is also made in the image of God. Dr Chadwick refutes this: "But surely the presence of the full-stop [*sic*] suggests that the two phrases repeat the same idea, therefore Pozzo is God." As it is in fact an exclamation-mark and not a full-stop at all (in both the English and French editions) surely it is intended as a guide to intonation? The sentences can be interpreted in either way; by themselves they offer evidence so flimsy that we must look elsewhere for anything remotely resembling 'proof' of the nature and identity of Godot.

One could push imaginative interpretation so far as to suggest some connexion between Godot and the *rue Godot de Mauroy* in Paris—a notorious place for expensive *poules*. In this street there is a shop named *Godet*. Such an interpretation would be quite in keeping with Beckett's sardonic sense of humour: the Godot so often claimed to be of divine origin may just as equally have its source in a hotbed of professional vice. Mr Beckett informs me that he was aware of the reputation of the rue Godot de Mauroy before he wrote the play.

The association seems just as likely as that between Godot and two men named *Godeau.* It has been suggested[1] that Beckett had in mind Balzac's play *Mercadet*. Mercadet has a business partner, Godeau, who never appears. All Mercadet's creditors are anxiously awaiting the return of Godeau in order to retrieve embezzled funds. At the end, it is announced that Godeau has come back, a rich man from India—but the audience never sees him. The similarities are considerable; the situation will be saved by Godeau, as it will be by Godot. But the hypothesis is not exactly helped by the fact that Mr Beckett assures me that he only came to know *Mercadet* after writing *Godot*, and that it had no influence on his own play whatever. It may seem a surprising gap in the knowledge of a Master of Arts in French, with a wide knowledge of French literature and culture. It has been maintained that education is what is left when we have forgotten all we ever learnt, and it is not impossible that although Beckett's conscious memory has released its hold on *Mercadet*, the subconscious still retained the echo of it. But the association is not an important one. For Balzac, Godot would have been just a Godeau—a missing financial figure; and although there is, as mentioned in Chapter 3, the suggestion of a business arrangement between the tramps and Godot, such an interpretation is very trivial, and is of purely genetic, not critical, interest.

The second Godeau was (or is) a veteran racing cyclist. Therefore (according to Hugh Kenner) he "typifies Cartesian Man in excelsis, the Cartesian Centaur, body and mind in close harmony . . . Cartesian Man deprived of his bicycle is a mere intelligence fastened to a dying animal".[2] As the effect of this theory is to reduce the play to the level of a recondite geometrical puzzle, it is just as well that Mr Beckett informs me he was told *after* writing Godot about the story of the little crowd of bystanders still watching and waiting at the end of a cycle race. "Qu'est-ce qu'on attend?" they were asked. "On attend

[1] By Eric Bentley, *What is Theatre*, Boston, 1956, p. 158.
[2] Hugh Kenner, *Samuel Beckett*, p. 124.

Godeau." But, it will be objected, if he could forget about *Mercadet* he could have forgotten (consciously) about being told the story before writing *Godot*.

The truth of the matter is that theorizing about the name is not a very fruitful exercise; time has been spent on it here only because some very reputable scholars and critics have spent time on it, and this the reader should know. There is, however, one possible significance of the suffix *-ot* which does take us on to interesting ground—to the very heart of the problem of Godot, in fact: it may *negate* the first syllable and imply a *need* for the first syllable. Let us note what the narrator says of his mother in *Molloy*:

> Moi je l'appelais Mag, quand je devais lui donner un nom. Et si je l'appelais Mag c'était qu'à mon idée... la lettre g abolissait la syllabe ma, et pour ainsi dire crachait dessus, mieux que toute autre lettre ne l'aurait fait (p. 23).

So much for the desire to deny and vilify the first syllable; but he goes on:

> Et en même temps je satisfaisais un besoin profond et sans doute inavoué, celui d'avoir une ma, c'est-à-dire une maman, et de l'annoncer, à haute voix.

There is little doubt that much of the anger Beckett expresses about God is caused by his belief in God's non-existence. If God does not exist, the existence of the universe and of mankind is, according to Bishop Berkeley (1685–1753), very doubtful. *Esse* is *percipi*: to be is to be an object of perception. Beckett introduces Berkeley into Lucky's speech in the Grove Press edition for reasons associated with Estragon's question, "Tu crois que Dieu me voit?" (p. 68), and Vladimir's meditation, "Moi aussi, un autre me regarde..." (p. 84). The acosmistic corollary to the theory that things exist because a mind thinks of them as existing is, that if there is no mind outside the cosmos perceiving them they cannot be said to exist in any real sense. There should be a God to give man a real existence, and Beckett is obliged to conclude that there is not. There should be some transcendent protective power, and there is not; there is only a great yawning void in the middle of which humanity hangs like an excrescence. Anger and anguish are sincere and authentic responses to this belief, whether we share it or not.

We can reasonably assume, then, that on *one level* of interpretation Beckett uses the concept of Godot in order to express his anger and disappointment at the non-existence of God. It is interesting to see, for instance, how he holds on to the syllable 'God' throughout the mispronunciations he puts into Pozzo's mouth—Godin, Godet, and not, say, Bodot or Podot—whereas Pozzo's name is mispronounced by deformation of the first syllable—Bozzo—just as Goriot's name, in Balzac's great novel, is distorted by the duchesse de Langeais by means of changing the first letter (Doriot, Foriot, Moriot, etc.).

Godot can be looked upon either as a constant or an indeterminate variable. Considered as a variable, Godot "will be an unspecified thing or state or process waiting to be defined by some constant the interpreter may elect to supply".[1] Any rôle, any function, can be assigned to Godot—a challenge to self-improvement, an anchor in a sea of doubt and uncertainty, or perhaps the hope of extrahuman help in a world likely to be totally destroyed by humans if they are left to their own devices. This is a perfectly legitimate 'lay' approach; but the scholarly approach demands greater controls and limitations strictly according to what we know to be the author's own preoccupations and concerns. These concerns are illuminated by Beckett's other works, particularly *Watt*, *L'Innommable*, and *Comment c'est*. They lead one to the conclusion that the idea behind Godot is in fact a constant. "In this fictional universe of the imprecision of the self and the uncertainty of knowledge, the only constant is the tyrant, the mysterious overlord who, from Mr Knott onwards, haunts, even governs, the destiny of the Beckettian hero. His existence, like Godot's, is never certain, because he never appears in person."[2] The

---

[1] J. Ashmore, *art. cit.*, p. 299.

[2] J. Fletcher, *The Novels of Samuel Beckett*, p. 144.

image of Godot torments the two tramps, playing on their hopes and expectations, just as Mr Knott does with his successive servants. "Little by little Watt abandoned all hope, all fear, of ever seeing Mr Knott face to face." Watt's account of his relationship with Mr Knott prefigures several elements of *Godot*. "Side by side, two men" [Vladimir and Estragon]. "All day, part of night. Dumb, numb, blind" [Pozzo and Lucky]. "Knott look at Watt? No." ["Moi aussi", says Vladimir, "un autre me regarde... " (p. 84)]: "Knott talk to Watt? No." ['divine aphasie']; "What then did us do? Niks, niks, niks." ["Rien ne se passe, personne ne vient, personne ne s'en va, c'est terrible" (p. 36)]. Both Mr Knott and Godot retain their hold over the *homunculi* by passive non-revelation of themselves. There is no evidence that Godot exists as an objective reality outside the tramps' consciousness. It is surely unjustifiable to impute an attitude to Godot in relation to the tramps, as Dr Metman does: "Godot's function seems to be to keep his dependents unconscious . . . he obviously expects unconditional patience and obedience . . ." (*art. cit.*). All we can say with certainty is that the tramps *think* Godot would punish them if they left.

In *L'Innommable* the last incarnation, Worm, is Absolute Negation, the ultimate Nothingness of the Self, "a tiny blur in the depths of the pot". Mahood struggles to coalesce with Worm, but his efforts fail because Worm merely becomes a projection of himself. Godot can similarly be regarded as a projection of Gogo and Didi; he has the elements of them within himself (G+ D+ ot)—or so one can maintain if one consents to play the name-game—so no amount of waiting or struggling can bring about the desired conjunction of the Self (divided into the *pseudocouple*) and Godot, who is the absolute non-being which surpasses all understanding.

Looking at the problem from the standpoint provided by *Comment c'est*, a similar picture emerges: "Pim's rôle . . . is very much like that of the Absent One in *Godot*: it is, presumably, in his image that the narrator dimly descries (as do Gogo and Didi in Godot) a presence and a power to be united with which is to be no longer under the dominance of meaninglessness and despair."[1] But it is only a presence and a power which they *hope* to find. Judging by what the narrator finds when he does meet Pim, their hopes would be negated if they were to see Godot. It is far better, Beckett implies, to wait even with diminishing hope, than to have the certainty of the worst. As Goethe has said, in *Faust*, "Whoever aspires unweariedly is not beyond redemption."

The narrator of *Comment c'est* assumes a sadistic attitude towards Pim (similar to that of Pozzo towards Lucky) out of sheer frustration and disappointment. It has been suggested that Pozzo is Lucky's Godot, but following *this* analogy it is Lucky who was once Pozzo's Godot (he used to think for him), and Pozzo's savagery is therefore the rage of frustrated hopes like that of the narrator of *Comment c'est*.[2]

The concept that goes under the name of Godot can be interpreted in a very different fashion opening up another set of problems: of Time, Infinity, Identity, Memory, and Reality. The issues involved have already been sketched in, and now we should look at them again with particular reference to *Godot*.

Vladimir and Estragon are waiting for the end to come; 'the end' is given a name: Godot. They are waiting, like the heroes of the *Trilogy*, to merge with the Nothing at the core of the void. As they approach the deliverance of the end, time, as they perceive it, decelerates imperceptibly (as it does for Malone). Moving along the infinitely diminishing series from one recurring decimal point to another, with each point slightly less significant than the last, they realize, like Malone, that time has no end; that time is, in Pozzo's English word, "accursed"; that the death of the Self—as distinct from the death of the physical body—will never come. For Vladimir and Estragon must not be envisaged as just physical entities

---

[1] N. A. Scott, *Samuel Beckett*, p. 77.

[2] In the first edition of *Godot*, Pozzo and Lucky are likened to the Bim (=Pim) and Bom of *Comment c'est* and other works (see p. lix, note 1).

(although they are that too, in that they are presented as sentient beings, for obvious reasons of theatrical necessity). Their thoughts of suicide, for example, become more significant to us if we consider the impossibility of suicide in terms of the impossibility of destroying the Self. *Real* death—the death of the Self, of the innermost core of personality—will only come when time has stopped, when infinity has been reached. Vladimir says hopefully, "Le temps s'est arrêté"—it is so near the end of its motion he has this impression. "Ne croyez pas ça", admonishes Pozzo: whatever you like, but not that. They are still under the spell of Pozzo's chronometric time (to which he himself is a slave, with his schedule and his total immersion in activity and motion), but Vladimir and particularly Estragon are nearer timelessness (therefore, immobility) than he is.

By its very nature infinity cannot be reached. Time slows down as it reaches its end, but it will not die. As it decelerates all impression of the passing of time is completely distorted. *L'Innommable* states it succinctly: "I say an instant, perhaps it was years." In *Endgame*, yesterday is defined as "that bloody awful day, long ago, before this bloody awful day". In the unpublished novel *Mercier et Camier* there is a long and illuminating disquisition on the tyranny and meaninglessness of time. It bears upon various points in *Godot*: Pozzo's preoccupation with keeping to his schedule, his speech about the day we are born and the day we die being the same day, the replacement of his watch (chronometric time) by his heart (existential time):

> Demandez l'heure à un passant, il vous dira n'importe quoi, au jugé, par-dessus son épaule, en s'éloignant. Mais soyez tranquille, il ne s'est pas trompé de beaucoup, lui qui consulte sa montre tous les quarts d'heure... se demande comment il va faire, pour faire tout ce qu'il a à faire, avant la fin du jour interminable. Ou il traduit, d'un geste furieux et las, l'étrange impression dont il souffre, à savoir qu'il est l'heure qu'il a toujours été et sera toujours...
>
> D'ailleurs c'est toute la journée ainsi... Oui, toute la

journée, depuis le premier tic jusqu'au dernier tac... Ou mettons du dixième jusqu'à l'x moins dixième, car il met du temps quand même, le tam-tam thoracique, à nous rappeler au rêve, et il met du temps aussi à nous en congédier. Mais les autres on les entend, chaque grain de millet on l'entend, on se retourne et on se voit, chaque fois un peu plus près, toute la vie un peu plus près. La joie par cuillerées à sel, comme l'eau aux grands déshydratés, et une gentille petite agonie à doses homéopathiques, qu'est-ce qu'il vous faut encore? Un cœur à la place du cœur? Allons, allons.

The words 'chaque grain de millet' refer to the demonstration given by the Greek philosopher Zeno that by halving a heap of millet and adding to one half exactly one half of the remaining half, then half the remainder, then half the remainder of that, and so on, one would never complete the task of transferring all the millet to one heap.[1] Similarly each 'day' of waiting is but half the quantity of yesterday added to the heap of time. Hamm uses the same image in *Fin de Partie* as he feels "Instants sur instants, plouff, plouff, comme les grains de mil de ce vieux Grec, et toute la vie on attend que ça vous fasse une vie" (p. 93).

How long will the tramps have to wait for Godot? Perhaps the answer lies in *Malone meurt*:

...qui a assez attendu attendra toujours, et passé un certain délai il ne peut plus rien arriver, ni venir personne, ni y avoir autre chose que l'attente se sachant vaine.

The waiting is not for death; that is far too simple, for death will certainly come (even Malone feels that "quand on meurt (par exemple), c'est trop tard, on a trop attendu, on ne vit plus assez pour pouvoir s'arrêter"). Then, after death, the waiting begins in earnest—for a Nothing placed at infinity, in the endless void; as Estragon says, "Ce n'est pas le vide qui manque" (p. 58).

---

[1] See R. Coe, *op. cit.*, Ch. VI, for a clear account of time elements in Beckett's work.

Infinity is reached (theoretically) when what we popularly think of as past and future meet in the present. As the past closes up and dwindles, the problem of establishing the nature of the Self becomes more and more acute. It is felt with great anguish by Vladimir and more so by Pozzo, as they try to hold on to the three elements of time (past, present, and future): Vladimir with his memories and thoughts for the morrow, Pozzo with his business projects and his distress at losing his grip on the passing of time. Time, memory, and personal identity (or self-identity) are inseparable aspects of the same problem.[1] To state it in simple terms: If I say 'I saw you yesterday', the statement assumes the identity of the 'I' making the statement with the 'I' who did the seeing, and of the 'you' being addressed with the person seen. The statement also claims to impose certain time limits within which the seeing was done. Now, although these assumptions are very commonly made in our everyday lives, they are far from being irrefutably true. A considerable amount of very complex psycho-philosophical reasoning is necessary to *prove* the truth of the statement. If we do not usually question the truth of such statements it is because we have faith in our memory,

---

[1] The enquiring reader is referred to the excellent study by Dr S. Shoemaker, *Self-Knowledge and Self-Identity*, Cornell University Press, 1963. All of it is relevant to Beckett's preoccupation with the search for Self (or the substantival ego). *E.g.*, "...a philosopher may close his eyes, furrow his brow, and 'attend' ever so closely to the contents of his mind, but he cannot be said to be looking for the 'I' (the subject of his experience) unless he knows what it would be like to find it—i.e., could identify a subject as such if he found one" (p. 8). All Beckett's solipsistic characters, or 'vice-existers' are engaged in this epistemological search, which would seem to be doomed to failure. Similarly, the tramps cannot succeed in their desire to meet Godot, because they will not know him even if he does come. Also of striking relevance, in relation to the tramps' seeing the tree, is the analysis Dr Shoemaker gives of the question 'How do I know that I see a tree?' (pp. 83–85).

on account of its previous reliability. Nevertheless, this faith is very precarious. If forgetfulness about past events becomes frequent or generalized, the effect is no longer simply irritating or inconvenient; it destroys the very essence of our pattern of existence. The 'I', the Self, of yesterday, no longer exists, except perhaps in the memories of others. This makes us utterly dependent on others for the proof of our existence for every moment up to the present which is ceaselessly melting into the past and into oblivion. In Sartrian terms, for example, Vladimir—who is very acutely aware of this problem—is fluctuating between being *pour-soi* (negative consciousness) and *en-soi* (positive unconsciousness). As *pour-soi* he sees events as his creation. As *en-soi* he envisages himself as the object of *l'Autre*—the someone who is looking at him. *L'Autre* (possibly Godot) is a fearsome concept in the Sartrian universe, a tyrannical entity who is hated and yet essential as a witness to one's existence, which thus becomes an object *pour-autrui*.

This is the situation in which many of Beckett's characters find themselves. Vladimir is the only one who recalls the boy and Pozzo from the previous occasion, and his confidence becomes rudely shaken. He is trying to hold valiantly on to the extension of himself into the past, and the anguish he suffers when he receives hesitant corroboration from others is that of any human personality being robbed of one of its dimensions without which its very reality will become highly uncertain. Estragon does not suffer so much in this way, as his consciousness is not so acute, but he realizes that he needs Vladimir to give him the impression he exists. They are each other's 'Other', hence their love-hate relationship. Pozzo suffers greatly, on the other hand, from having to answer Vladimir's probing questions about 'accursed time'.

The past being a very doubtful factor, what of the future? Does this offer any more comfort or certainty? Our conception of the future depends on our imaginative ability to project ourselves into probable situations resulting from the present as we understand it. Apart from the limitations we impose on ourselves for personal reasons, or have imposed on us by others (by society, in the case of imprisonment, for example), there are very many possible directions in which we can extend our experience of reality and existence at any given moment. But even this is denied to the two waiting tramps in *Godot*. They are restricted, in their projection into the future, to one place, for one purpose: by the tree, to wait. Like the sunrise and the sunset and the moonrise, the future for them is compounded of eternal repetition.

No account, however brief, of Beckett's attitude to the problems of time, memory, and identity, would be complete without mention of Marcel Proust, for whom involuntary memory constituted the only way through to reality and to the true Self. In writing his study of Proust Beckett was made aware of the fact that the individual has to *wait* for an intuition of reality, through the agency of involuntary memory. But the escape-route Proust opened up for himself *via* the magical transformation wrought by art is closed to Beckett.[1]

In trying to understand the implications of the concept called 'Godot' we have found that it can be likened to a catalyst, bringing about many different reactions without being changed itself. No single view of the nature of Godot invalidates the others. Invalidation comes only from irrelevance to Beckett's sphere of interest.

---

[1] Whereas Winnie in *Oh les Beaux Jours* is being 'decanted' and sucked down in the flow of time (cf. *Proust*, p. 15), in *Godot* the conception of time is more complex. It owes as much to Vico (whose cyclical theory of time, involving the eternal recurrence of situation, was revived by James Joyce) as to Zeno (see p. cxxi). Time and structure are inextricably connected in *Godot*.

CHAPTER 8

Conclusions

"Thus the play ends in a comic impasse, not in a tragic resolution."[1] How could this 'tragicomedy' (as Beckett calls the English version) end, except in the way it does? One can think of at least four possibilities:

Suicide. Vladimir and Estragon consider this, but lack the means and the courage. They will no doubt be deterred again, even if they do bring a good bit of rope, by the fact that one of them must be left alone momentarily.

Giving up. They could lose heart and go away; Estragon is clearly inclined to do this. We can be sure, though, that their *solidarité*, their dependence on each other and on Godot will prove too strong.

The arrival of Godot. This would be either an anti-climax (for example, he would really offer them a job) or a shattering disillusion (as in the case of the narrator of *Comment c'est*). If Godot came, he could be a ludicrous pantomime fairy-godmother; or a true angel or divine power—which would make the play a religious drama of a superficial and suspect kind, totally out of character for Beckett. Such an ending would create all the difficulties of portraying sublimity which even Dante failed to overcome (*Paradise* has none of the inexhaustible imaginative force of the *Inferno*).

The fourth possibility is that Vladimir and Estragon should continue to wait. In choosing this outcome, Beckett has left the field open for each one of us to complete, through our active—and preferably well-informed—participation. The existentialist philosopher Jaspers called this participation "the beating of the other wing". The writer is one wing only—the

---

[1] J. Moore, *art. cit.*, p. 59.

reader the other, and both must beat if the work is to soar upwards.

In compelling the reader to complete the creative act by his own inner action, thus completing the communication, Beckett shows he is writing literature for adults who are aware—or willing to make themselves aware—of the feeling of urgency and anguish about man's tragic estrangement in the universe once the comfort of spiritual belief has gone. This estrangement is not a mere figment of Beckett's imagination; it has received the attention of a small number of seminal writers throughout the last hundred years—for example, Nietzsche, Dostoevsky, Kafka, Jaspers, C. G. Jung, Martin Heidegger, O'Neill, and Sartre. Heidegger stated this sense of universal abandonment in these terms:

> This is the time of the gods that have fled and of the god that is coming. It is the time of need, because it lies under a double lack and a double Not: the No-more of the gods that have fled and the Not-yet of the god that is coming.[1]

Those who are able to cast aside religio-metaphysical and epistemological problems with an uncomplicated "God's in His heaven—all's right with the world!" and a self-assured "I know I am me", will have little time for the writings of Beckett or the other writers mentioned above. For those admirably simple souls such preoccupations will be mere pseudo-problems which melt away in the warmth of faith in a God who gives meaning to Self and to the universe. Yet it must be stressed that Beckett is not writing as a theologian or as a philosopher. He is an artist in words and verbal patterns using fundamental problems as a *point de départ*. Our approach to Beckett must, therefore, be different from that to Dante or Sartre, in whom we expect to find imaginative elaborations based firmly on a theological or philosophical system. Dr Colin Smith has written of "the sort of quasi-emotional response to reality from which philosophizing can legitimately arise."[2]

---

[1] *Existence and Being*, Regnery, Chicago, 1949, p. 313.
[2] *Contemporary French Philosophy*, p. 253.

The mainspring of Beckett's talent is emotional, not rational. "J'ai conçu *Molloy* et la suite le jour où j'ai pris conscience de ma bêtise. Alors je me suis mis à écrire les choses que je sens", Beckett once said to a French interviewer.[1] The violence of his emotional responses to matters that other writers are able to think about logically and coolly takes him close to Flaubert and Céline.

Although *Godot* is a unique and highly original piece of experimental theatre, it has roots in a theatrical tradition. In fact, the renewal of interest in the plays of Strindberg can partly be explained by the public-conditioning process provided by the success of *Godot*.[2] In Strindberg's expressionistic drama *The Ghost Sonata* (1907) for example, we find themes and attitudes which recur in the serious drama of the next half-century—including *Godot* and *Fin de Partie*. There is a dream-like and occasionally nightmarish atmosphere in which the areas of probability or improbability are ill-defined and overlapping, in which the existence of time and space is uncertain and meaning is embedded in a half-explained symbolism rich in imagery and poetic revelation. Facets of a single consciousness become separate characters, one of whom, the Student, addresses these final words to the dead girl:

> You poor little child—you child of a world of illusion, guilt, suffering and death—a world of eternal change, disappointment and pain—may the Lord of Heaven deal mercifully with you on your journey.

The tragedy of this 'world of illusion' is the central concern in what has become known as the 'theatre of the absurd'. The absurdity or meaninglessness of existence results from either the fickleness or the non-existence of God. The theatre of the absurd has been described by Martin Esslin as "a theatre of situation as against a theatre of events in sequence".[3] As in

---

[1] Quoted by J. Fletcher, *The Novels of Samuel Beckett*, p. 176.
[2] See J. L. Styan, *The Dark Comedy: The Development of Modern Comic Tragedy*, C.U.P., 1962.
[3] *The Theatre of the Absurd*, p. 293.

many plays of the post-Symbolist and Surrealist eras, there is usually no 'story' or 'plot', and it has thus earned the name of 'anti-theatre'. It is a theatre without theses, but certainly not without ideas. More intellectual discussion has been sparked off by the *best* of these plays than by the social realists of the last fifty years. Ionesco has summed up its potentialities as "un théâtre non pas symboliste, mais symbolique; non pas allégorique, mais mythique; ayant sa source dans nos angoisses éternelles; ...théâtre qui aveuglerait les sociologues, mais qui donnerait à penser, à vivre au savant dans ce qui n'est pas savant en lui; à l'homme commun, par-delà son ignorance". A theatre based on the fact that "La condition essentielle de l'homme n'est pas sa condition de citoyen mais sa condition de mortel."[1]

Apart from religious and metaphysical absolutists there is one other category of the reading and theatre-going public which finds Beckett anathema: the partisans of socialist realism. For being non-political is no guarantee that the politically-minded will not attack one's work. In May 1963 the International Theatre Institute (a body sponsored by UNESCO) held a World Congress in Warsaw. Michel Saint-Denis reported on it as follows:

> Before the closing of the Congress, in full session, the Russian delegation in the person of an eminent Moscow dramatic critic launched a violent attack on modern Western plays. This attack developed the usual theme: since the war, the work of our most representative playwrights had become DECADENT and PESSIMISTIC, not to mention FORMALISTIC; all they depicted of man's destiny was its misery; they were degrading humanity and cheapening the human condition at a time when the true rôle of the theatre was to give men reasons for confidence and hope so that they might improve their lot and build the new society on the basis of justice.
>
> It was necessary for one of us to point out that if the plays of our best writers were indeed 'negative' in outlook, they

[1] *Notes et contre-notes*, Gallimard, 1962, pp. 206 and 205.

> nevertheless mirrored in an authentic way modern man's consciousness, weighed down with the recent memory of so many horrors, so much suffering; we believed that authenticity was worth more than false optimism and we thought it was impossible to nourish artistically valuable work in theatre and literature by imposing upon the writers themes which they couldn't really feel strongly about.[1]

In 1965 another international conference was held, but in a different atmosphere: it was that of the Vienna Drama Conference, organized by the Austrian Society for Literature. Martin Esslin compared it with the Edinburgh Drama Conference of 1963, which he described as "dispiriting". In 1963 the Eastern bloc representatives had

> immediately entrenched themselves behind a smokescreen of sentimental clichés about "the sacredness of art" and "the artist's duty to serve humanity" . . .

But in 1965

> the Eastern representatives steadfastly declined to defend the political function of the theatre, the value of socialist realism, or to oppose the introspective pessimistic work of playwrights like Beckett and Ionesco.[2]

The great pity of such controversies is that it should be felt necessary to exclude from serious consideration any work of originality on the grounds that it either does or does not fulfil a social function. There are promising signs, however—and the performances of *Godot* that have taken place in communist countries are among them—that it may be possible to discuss such plays the whole world over before very long in their own terms, and not in terms of issues quite alien to their authors. Discussion is brought up to a relevant level when we "remember that attempts to confront their contemporaries

---

[1] 'Peaceful Co-existence in the Theatre?', *Flourish*, Spring 1965.

[2] 'The End of Socialist Realism?', *Encounter*, June 1965, pp. 51–52.

with a deeper awareness of the spiritual void of our time are a central issue . . . altogether in the air".[1]

"I have been brooding in my bath for the last hour and have come to the conclusion that the success of *Waiting for Godot* means the end of the theatre as we know it." Such was the *pronunciamento* Robert Morley issued to the Pozzo of the Arts Theatre production, Peter Bull.[2] The tone was intended to be wittily disparaging; it betrays a nostalgic regret for the possible disappearance of a theatre aimed at being an amusing, informative, and logical account of a readily understandable dilemma set in an immediately recognizable social setting. It does not, however, reflect the true situation which has been developing in a particular form of serious drama since the days of static Symbolist drama in the late nineteenth century. There is no doubt that the lack of social or psychological motivation in many of these plays—*Godot* among them—is genuinely bewildering. Symbols and patterns of images are not so easily comprehensible as representations of social reality. It is not easy to admit the validity of the harsh view expressed by Beckett of "our smug will to live, of our pernicious and incurable optimism",[3] but we may be certain that this is an authentic view which, furthermore, has been transformed by what Hugo once called "la baguette magique de l'art" into a form of literature which does not compromise.

How should we react to this? With the puzzled frown, possibly; but not the sneer.[4] The success of Beckett's plays with

---

[1] E. Metman, *art. cit.*, p. 50.

[2] Peter Bull, 'Waiting for God Knows What', *Plays and Players*, May 1956.

[3] *Proust*, p. 15.

[4] Cf. P.-Aimé Touchard (administrateur honoraire de la Comédie Française): "Certes, nous avons plus de mal encore à nous reconnaître dans l'univers de Beckett que dans celui d'Ionesco... Mais il nous faut bien prendre conscience que toute une jeunesse intellectuelle y découvre le visage même de l'homme contemporain. Le succès universel de telles œuvres près des adolescents de tous pays suffirait ainsi à mettre en garde contre un ricanement trop facile ceux qui refusent un

a younger, more open-minded and less conventionally fixated generation is gratifying. It indicates an awareness of the anguish caused by man's condition in the context of the universe as well as in that of society. None of this makes for bovine contentment, of course, but the Pascalian reaction to the horrors of "cette confusion monstrueuse" is still open to those who need it: "Le silence éternel de ces espaces infinis m'effraie... Il est bon d'être lassé et fatigué par l'inutile recherche du vrai bien, afin de tendre les bras au Libérateur." As far as Beckett is concerned such a reaction would be a sterile, facile, cowardly, and undignified failure to come to terms with the universe in which we live and to accept it fearlessly. The choice lies with each one of us. The important thing with regard to *En attendant Godot* is that at least this tragicomedy of two old men waiting endlessly beside a tree will have made us think deeply about *la beauté du chemin, et la bonté des voyageurs*. Even out of nothingness, the true artist can draw beauty.[1]

In October 1969 it was announced that Samuel Beckett had been awarded the Nobel Prize for Literature. The *Times* third leader for 24 October was optimistically headed 'GODOT HAS ARRIVED'. M. Lindon, Beckett's French publisher, was quoted as saying that Beckett was distressed by the announcement. Beckett was at the time on holiday in Tunisia, and went into hiding to avoid publicity.

---

verdict aussi catégorique sur l'aventure humaine." 'Un Théâtre Nouveau', *L'Avant-Scène*, no. 156, pp. 1–2 [*numéro spécial*, no date].

[1] This is the starting-point of the present writer's further study of Beckett's plays, *Angels of Darkness: Dramatic Effect in Beckett and Ionesco* (Allen & Unwin). He compares performances, audience reactions and more recent interpretations of *En attendant Godot*, and analyses the play in greater depth in an attempt to explain its impact. This is seen as a largely subconscious response to Beckett's own exploration of mind.

BIBLIOGRAPHY

I. PRINCIPAL WORKS OF SAMUEL BECKETT

A. WORKS ORIGINALLY WRITTEN IN FRENCH

1. *Novels and Stories.*

Molloy. Éd. de Minuit, 1951.
Malone meurt. Éd. de Minuit, 1951.
L'Innommable. Éd. de Minuit, 1953.
[These appear in *Three Novels*, published by John Calder, 1959.]
Nouvelles et Textes pour rien. Éd. de Minuit, 1955.
Comment c'est. Éd. de Minuit, 1961.
[*How it is*. Grove Press, New York, 1964; Calder, 1964.]
Mercier et Camier. Éd. de Minuit, 1970.

2. *Dramatic Works.*

Eleutheria (written *c*. 1947). *Unpublished.*
En attendant Godot. Éd. de Minuit, 1952.
[*Waiting for Godot*. Grove Press, 1954; Faber, 1956.]
Fin de Partie. Éd. de Minuit, 1957. Suivi de *Acte sans Paroles I*.
[*Endgame*, followed by *Act without Words I*. Grove Press, 1958; Faber, 1958.]
Cascando. Éd. de Minuit, 1963. [Radio play.]
Acte sans paroles II. [Mime written in French, published in English: see below.]

B. WORKS ORIGINALLY WRITTEN IN ENGLISH

1. *Novels and Stories.*

More Pricks than Kicks. [A collection of ten short stories.] Chatto and Windus, 1934.
Murphy. Routledge, 1938.
[*Murphy*, transl. Éd. de Minuit, 1953.]
Watt. Olympia Press (Paris), 1953; Calder, 1961.

2. *Dramatic Works.*

All that Fall. Faber, 1957.

[*Tous ceux qui tombent.* Éd. de Minuit, 1957.]

Krapp's Last Tape and Other Dramatic Pieces. Grove Press, 1960; Faber, 1959.

[*La Dernière Bande.* Éd. de Minuit, 1959.]

Embers. Faber, 1959. [Radio play.]

[*Cendres.* Éd. de Minuit, 1959.]

Act without Words II. Grove Press, 1960.

Happy Days. Faber, 1962.

[*Oh les Beaux Jours.* Éd. de Minuit, 1963.]

Play. Faber, 1964.

[*Comédie.* Published by Éd. de Minuit in 1966 together with *Cascando*, *Acte sans paroles II*, and Samuel Beckett's translations of *Words and Music*, *Eh Joe* (television play), and *Come and Go.*]

3. *Criticism.*

'Dante . . . Bruno. Vico . . . Joyce', in *Our Exagmination round his Factification for Incamination of Work in Progress.* 1929. Reprinted, Faber, 1961.

Proust. Chatto and Windus, 1931. Reprinted by Calder, 1965.

II. SUGGESTIONS FOR FURTHER READING

Articles listed in notes to the Introduction are not given here.

A. GENERAL

Abel, Lionel. *Metatheatre: A New View of Dramatic Form.* Hill and Wang, New York, 1963.

Bentley, Eric. *What is Theatre?* Beacon Press, Boston, 1956.

Brown, J. R., and Harris, B., eds. *Contemporary Theatre.* Stratford-upon-Avon Studies, 4.

Corvin, Michel. *Le Théâtre Nouveau.* Presses Universitaires de France (*Que sais-je?* series), 1963.

Esslin, Martin. *The Theatre of the Absurd.* Eyre and Spottiswoode, 1964.

GROSSVOGEL, David. *The Self-Conscious Stage in Modern French Theatre.* Columbia University Press, N. Y., 1958.

GUICHARNAUD, Jacques. *Modern French Theater from Giraudoux to Beckett.* Yale Romantic Studies: 2nd Series, 7. Yale University Press, New Haven, 1961.

HUNT, Hugh. *The Live Theatre.* Oxford University Press, 1962.

MAURIAC, Claude. *L'Alittérature Contemporaine.* Albin Michel, Paris, 1958.

PRONKO, L. C. *Avant-Garde: The Experimental Theatre in France.* University of California Press, 1962.

ROUSSEAUX, André. 'L'Homme désintégré de Samuel Beckett', *Littérature du XXème siècle*, Paris, 1955.

STYAN, J. L. *The Dark Comedy: The Development of Modern Comic Tragedy.* Cambridge University Press, 1962.

B. SOME STUDIES OF BECKETT'S WORK

COE, Richard N. *Samuel Beckett.* Oliver and Boyd, 1964; revised edition, Grove Press, 1970.

COHN, Ruby. *Samuel Beckett: The Comic Gamut.* Rutgers University Press, New Jersey, 1962.

COHN, Ruby (ed.). *Casebook on Waiting for Godot.* Grove Press, 1967.

DUCKWORTH, Colin. *Angels of Darkness: Dramatic Effect in Beckett and Ionesco.* Allen and Unwin, 1972.

ESSLIN, Martin. 'Samuel Beckett', in *The Novelist as Philosopher*, ed. John Cruickshank, pp. 128–146. Oxford University Press, 1962.

ESSLIN, Martin, ed. *Samuel Beckett: A Collection of Critical Essays.* Prentice-Hall, New Jersey, 1965.

FLETCHER, John. *Samuel Beckett's Art.* Chatto and Windus, 1967; *Waiting for Godot*, edition with afterword and notes, Faber and Faber, 1971; (with J. Spurling) *Beckett: A Study of his plays.* Eyre Methuen, 1972.

FRIEDMAN, M. J., ed. *Configuration Critique de Samuel Beckett.* Minard, 1964. [Contains eight essays on Beckett by different authors, and a useful *sélection bibliographique* by J. R. Bryer.]

HAYMAN, Ronald. *Samuel Beckett.* Heinemann, 1968.

HOFFMAN, F. J. *Samuel Beckett: The Language of Self.* Carbondale: Southern Illinois University Press, 1962.

JACOBSEN, J. and MUELLER, W. R. *The Testament of Samuel Beckett.* Faber, 1966.
KENNER, Hugh. *Samuel Beckett.* Calder, 1962.
MARISSEL, André. *Beckett.* Éditions Universitaires, 1963.
ONIMUS, Jean. *Beckett.* ("Les Écrivains devant Dieu"). Desclée de Brouwer, 1968.
REID, Alec. *All I Can Manage, More Than I Could: An Approach to the Plays of Samuel Beckett.* The Dolmen Press, 1968.
ROBINSON, Michael. *The long sonata of the dead. A study of Samuel Beckett.* Rupert Hart-Davis, 1969.
SCOTT, Nathan A. Jr. *Samuel Beckett.* Bowes and Bowes, 1965.
TINDALL, W. *Samuel Beckett.* Columbia University Press, 1964.

Fuller bibliographies are contained in the studies by Coe, Cohn, Fletcher, Kenner, and Scott. Readers seeking further information are referred to the critical bibliography by R. Federman and J. Fletcher, *Samuel Beckett, His Works and His Critics*, University of California Press, 1970.

III. MAJOR AUTHORIZED TRANSLATIONS OF "*EN ATTENDANT GODOT*"

Language	*Publisher*	*Date of authorization*
English	Grove Press (U.S.A.)	2.6.1953
English	Faber and Faber (U.K.)	29.9.1955
German	Suhrkamp Verlag	15.6.1953
Spanish	Poseidon (Argentina)	13.5.1954
Italian	Einaudi	21.7.1954
Japanese	Hakusui-sha	7.5.1956
Danish	Arena	23.1.1957
Catalan	Raixa	1958
Portuguese	Arcadia	19.11.1960
Finnish	Otava	7.6.1962
Norwegian	Gyldendal	20.3.1964
Serbo-Croat	Srpska Književna Zadruga (Jugoslavia)	22.6.1964
Dutch	Bezige Bij	3.9.1964
Swedish	Bonniers	?

(Details kindly supplied by Les Éditions de Minuit)

En attendant Godot

*Pièce en deux actes**

Note

An asterisk in the text indicates that the word, phrase, or passage so marked is dealt with in the Notes beginning on page 91.

ACTE PREMIER

Route à la campagne, avec arbre.

Soir.

Estragon, assis par terre, * *essaie d'enlever sa chaussure. Il s'y acharne des deux mains, en ahanant. Il s'arrête, à bout de forces, se repose en haletant, recommence. Même jeu.*

Entre Vladimir.

ESTRAGON (*renonçant à nouveau*). Rien à faire.*

VLADIMIR (*s'approchant à petits pas raides, les jambes écartées*). Je commence à le croire.* (*Il s'immobilise.*) J'ai longtemps résisté à cette pensée, en me disant, Vladimir,* sois raisonnable, tu n'as pas encore tout essayé. Et je reprenais le combat. (*Il se recueille, songeant au combat. A Estragon.*) Alors, te revoilà, toi.

ESTRAGON. Tu crois?

VLADIMIR. Je suis content de te revoir. Je te croyais parti pour toujours.

ESTRAGON. Moi aussi.

VLADIMIR. Que faire * pour fêter cette réunion? (*Il réfléchit.*) Lève-toi que je t'embrasse. (*Il tend la main à Estragon.*)

ESTRAGON (*avec irritation*). Tout à l'heure, tout à l'heure.

Silence.

VLADIMIR(*froissé, froidement*). Peut-on savoir où Monsieur * a passé la nuit?

ESTRAGON. Dans un fossé.

VLADIMIR (*épaté*). Un fossé! Où ça?

ESTRAGON (*sans geste*). Par là.

VLADIMIR. Et on ne t'a pas battu?

ESTRAGON. Si... Pas trop.*

VLADIMIR. Toujours les mêmes?

ESTRAGON. Les mêmes? Je ne sais pas.

Silence.

VLADIMIR. Quand j'y pense... depuis le temps... je me

demande... ce que tu serais devenu... sans moi... (*Avec décision.*) Tu ne serais plus qu'un petit tas d'ossements à l'heure qu'il est, pas d'erreur.*

ESTRAGON (*piqué au vif*). Et après ?

VLADIMIR (*accablé*). C'est trop pour un seul homme. (*Un temps. Avec vivacité.*) D'un autre côté, à quoi bon se décourager à présent, voilà ce que je me dis. Il fallait y penser il y a une éternité, vers 1900.*

ESTRAGON. Assez. Aide-moi à enlever cette saloperie.*

VLADIMIR. La main dans la main on se serait jeté en bas de la Tour Eiffel, parmi les premiers. On portait beau alors. Maintenant il est trop tard. On ne nous laisserait même pas monter. (*Estragon s'acharne sur sa chaussure.*) Qu'est-ce que tu fais ?

ESTRAGON. Je me déchausse. Ça ne t'est jamais arrivé, à toi ?

VLADIMIR. Depuis le temps que je te dis qu'il faut les enlever tous les jours. Tu ferais mieux de m'écouter.

ESTRAGON (*faiblement*). Aide-moi !

VLADIMIR. Tu as mal ?

ESTRAGON. Mal ! Il me demande si j'ai mal !

VLADIMIR (*avec emportement*). Il n'y a jamais que toi qui souffres ! Moi je ne compte pas. Je voudrais pourtant te voir à ma place. Tu m'en dirais des nouvelles.

ESTRAGON. Tu as eu mal ?

VLADIMIR. Mal ! Il me demande si j'ai eu mal !

ESTRAGON (*pointant l'index*). Ce n'est pas une raison pour ne pas te boutonner.

VLADIMIR (*se penchant*). C'est vrai. (*Il se boutonne.*) Pas de laisser-aller dans les petites choses.

ESTRAGON. Qu'est-ce que tu veux que je te dise, tu attends toujours le dernier moment.

VLADIMIR (*rêveusement*). Le dernier moment... (*Il médite.*) C'est long, mais ce sera bon.* Qui disait ça ?

ESTRAGON. Tu ne veux pas m'aider ?

VLADIMIR. Des fois je me dis que ça vient quand même. Alors je me sens tout drôle. (*Il ôte son chapeau, regarde dedans, y promène sa main, le secoue, le remet.*) Comment dire ? Soulagé et en même temps... (*il cherche*) ...épouvanté.

(*Avec emphase.*) É-POU-VAN-TÉ. (*Il ôte à nouveau son chapeau, regarde dedans.*) Ça alors ! (*Il tape dessus comme pour en faire tomber quelque chose, regarde à nouveau dedans, le remet.*) Enfin...

(*Estragon, au prix d'un suprême effort,** *parvient à enlever sa chaussure. Il regarde dedans, y promène sa main, la retourne, la secoue, cherche par terre s'il n'en est pas tombé quelque chose, ne trouve rien, passe sa main à nouveau dans sa chaussure, les yeux vagues*). Alors ?

ESTRAGON. Rien.

VLADIMIR. Fais voir.

ESTRAGON. Il n'y a rien à voir.

VLADIMIR. Essaie de la remettre.

ESTRAGON (*ayant examiné son pied*). Je vais le laisser respirer un peu.

VLADIMIR. Voilà l'homme tout entier, s'en prenant à sa chaussure alors que c'est son pied le coupable. (*Il enlève encore une fois son chapeau, regarde dedans, y passe la main, le secoue, tape dessus, souffle dedans, le remet.*) Ça devient inquiétant. (*Silence. Estragon agite son pied, en faisant jouer les orteils, afin que l'air y circule mieux.*) Un des larrons fut sauvé. (*Un temps.*) C'est un pourcentage honnête.* (*Un temps.*) Gogo...

ESTRAGON. Quoi ?

VLADIMIR. Si on se repentait ?

ESTRAGON. De quoi ?

VLADIMIR. Eh bien... (*Il cherche.*) On n'aurait pas besoin d'entrer dans les détails.

ESTRAGON. D'être né ?*

Vladimir part d'un bon rire qu'il réprime aussitôt, en portant sa main au pubis, le visage crispé.

VLADIMIR. On n'ose même plus rire.

ESTRAGON. Tu parles d'une privation.

VLADIMIR. Seulement sourire.* (*Son visage se fend dans un sourire maximum qui se fige, dure un bon moment, puis subitement s'éteint.*) Ce n'est pas la même chose. Enfin... (*Un temps.*) Gogo...

ESTRAGON (*agacé*). Qu'est-ce qu'il y a ?

VLADIMIR. Tu as lu la Bible ?

ESTRAGON. La Bible... (*Il réfléchit.*) J'ai dû y jeter un coup d'œil.

VLADIMIR (*étonné*). A l'école sans Dieu ?

ESTRAGON. Sais pas si elle était sans ou avec.

VLADIMIR. Tu dois confondre avec la Roquette.*

ESTRAGON. Possible. Je me rappelle les cartes de la Terre-Sainte. En couleur. Très jolies. La Mer-Morte était bleu pâle. J'avais soif rien qu'en la regardant. Je me disais, c'est là que nous irons passer notre lune de miel. Nous nagerons. Nous serons heureux.

VLADIMIR. Tu aurais dû être poète.

ESTRAGON. Je l'ai été. (*Geste vers ses haillons.*) Ça ne se voit pas ?

Silence.

VLADIMIR. Qu'est-ce que je disais... Comment va ton pied ?

ESTRAGON. Il enfle.*

VLADIMIR. Ah oui, j'y suis, cette histoire de larrons. Tu t'en souviens ?

ESTRAGON. Non.

VLADIMIR. Tu veux que je te la raconte ?

ESTRAGON. Non.

VLADIMIR. Ça passera le temps. (*Un temps.*) C'étaient deux voleurs, crucifiés en même temps que le Sauveur. On...

ESTRAGON. Le quoi ?

VLADIMIR. Le Sauveur. Deux voleurs. On dit que l'un fut sauvé et l'autre... (*il cherche le contraire de sauvé*) ...damné.

ESTRAGON. Sauvé de quoi ?

VLADIMIR. De l'enfer.

ESTRAGON. Je m'en vais. (*Il ne bouge pas.*)

VLADIMIR. Et cependant... (*Un temps.*) Comment se fait-il que... Je ne t'ennuie pas, j'espère.

ESTRAGON. Je n'écoute pas.

VLADIMIR. Comment se fait-il que des quatre évangélistes un

seul présente es faits de cette façon ? Ils étaient cependant là tous les quatre — enfin, pas loin. Et un seul parle d'un larron de sauvé.* (*Un temps.*) Voyons, Gogo, il faut me renvoyer la balle de temps en temps.

ESTRAGON. J'écoute.

VLADIMIR. Un sur quatre. Des trois autres, deux n'en parlent pas du tout et le troisième dit qu'ils l'ont engueulé tous les deux.

ESTRAGON. Qui ?

VLADIMIR. Comment ?

ESTRAGON. Je ne comprends rien... (*Un temps.*) Engueulé qui ?

VLADIMIR. Le Sauveur.

ESTRAGON. Pourquoi ?

VLADIMIR. Parce qu'il n'a pas voulu les sauver.

ESTRAGON. De l'enfer ?

VLADIMIR. Mais non, voyons ! De la mort.

ESTRAGON. Et alors ?

VLADIMIR. Alors ils ont dû être damnés tous les deux.

ESTRAGON. Et après ?

VLADIMIR. Mais l'autre dit qu'il y en a eu un de sauvé.

ESTRAGON. Eh bien ? Ils ne sont pas d'accord, un point c'est tout.

VLADIMIR. Ils étaient là tous les quatre. Et un seul parle d'un larron de sauvé. Pourquoi le croire plutôt que les autres ?

ESTRAGON. Qui le croit ?

VLADIMIR. Mais tout le monde. On ne connaît que cette version-là.

ESTRAGON. Les gens sont des cons.*

Il se lève péniblement, va en boitillant vers la coulisse gauche, s'arrête, regarde au loin, la main en écran devant les yeux, se retourne, va vers la coulisse droite, regarde au loin. Vladimir le suit des yeux, puis va ramasser la chaussure, regarde dedans, la lâche précipitamment.

VLADIMIR. Pah ! (*Il crache par terre.*)

Estragon revient au centre de la scène, regarde vers le fond.

ESTRAGON. Endroit délicieux. (*Il se retourne, avance jusqu'à la rampe, regarde vers le public.*) Aspects riants. (*Il se tourne vers Vladimir.*) Allons-nous-en.

VLADIMIR. On ne peut pas.

ESTRAGON. Pourquoi ?

VLADIMIR. On attend Godot.

ESTRAGON. C'est vrai. (*Un temps.*) Tu es sûr que c'est ici ?

VLADIMIR. Quoi ?

ESTRAGON. Qu'il faut attendre.

VLADIMIR. Il a dit devant l'arbre. (*Ils regardent l'arbre.*) Tu en vois d'autres ?

ESTRAGON. Qu'est-ce que c'est ?

VLADIMIR. On dirait un saule.

ESTRAGON. Où sont les feuilles ?

VLADIMIR. Il doit être mort.

ESTRAGON. Finis les pleurs.

VLADIMIR. A moins que ce ne soit pas la saison.

ESTRAGON. Ce ne serait pas plutôt un arbrisseau ?

VLADIMIR. Un arbuste.

ESTRAGON. Un arbrisseau.

VLADIMIR. Un — (*Il se reprend.*) Qu'est-ce que tu veux insinuer ? Qu'on s'est trompé d'endroit ?

ESTRAGON. Il devrait être là.

VLADIMIR. Il n'a pas dit ferme qu'il viendrait.

ESTRAGON. Et s'il ne vient pas ?

VLADIMIR. Nous reviendrons demain.

ESTRAGON. Et puis après-demain.

VLADIMIR. Peut-être.

ESTRAGON. Et ainsi de suite.

VLADIMIR. C'est-à-dire...

ESTRAGON. Jusqu'à ce qu'il vienne.

VLADIMIR. Tu es impitoyable.

ESTRAGON. Nous sommes déjà venus hier.

VLADIMIR. Ah non, là tu te goures.*

ESTRAGON. Qu'est-ce que nous avons fait hier ?

VLADIMIR. Ce que nous avons fait hier ?

1. "Lucky pleure." *Act 1, p. 25.*

[?—The tree has no leaves in Act 1, and Pozzo does not sit on his stool in Act 2].
Photograph taken of the Roger Blin production on tour in Germany, 1953.

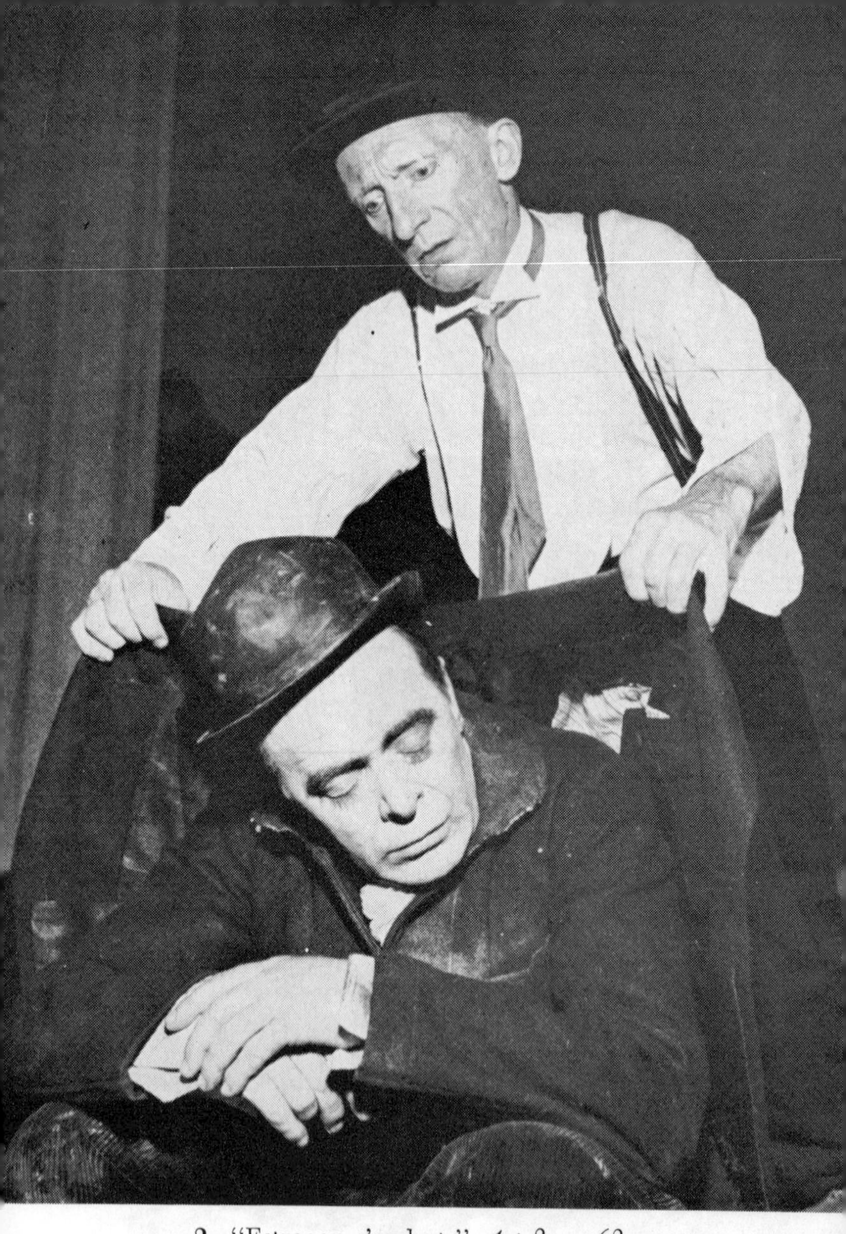

2. "Estragon s'endort." *Act 2, p. 62.*

French company on tour, 1953.

ESTRAGON. Oui.

VLADIMIR. Ma foi... (*Se fâchant.*) Pour jeter le doute, à toi le pompon.*

ESTRAGON. Pour moi,* nous étions ici.

VLADIMIR (*regard circulaire*). L'endroit te semble familier?

ESTRAGON. Je ne dis pas ça.

VLADIMIR. Alors?

ESTRAGON. Ça n'empêche pas.

VLADIMIR. Tout de même... cet arbre... (*se tournant vers le public*) ...cette tourbière.

ESTRAGON. Tu es sûr que c'était ce soir?

VLADIMIR. Quoi?

ESTRAGON. Qu'il fallait attendre?

VLADIMIR. Il a dit samedi. (*Un temps.*) Il me semble.

ESTRAGON. Après le turbin.

VLADIMIR. J'ai dû le noter. (*Il fouille dans ses poches, archi-bondées de saletés de toutes sortes.*)

ESTRAGON. Mais quel samedi? Et sommes-nous samedi? Ne serait-on pas plutôt dimanche? Ou lundi? Ou vendredi?

VLADIMIR (*regardant avec affolement autour de lui, comme si la date était inscrite dans le paysage*). Ce n'est pas possible.

ESTRAGON. Ou jeudi.

VLADIMIR. Comment faire?

ESTRAGON. S'il s'est dérangé pour rien hier soir, tu penses bien qu'il ne viendra pas aujourd'hui.

VLADIMIR. Mais tu dis que nous sommes venus hier soir.

ESTRAGON. Je peux me tromper. (*Un temps.*) Taisons-nous un peu, tu veux?

VLADIMIR (*faiblement*). Je veux bien. (*Estragon se rassied par terre. Vladimir arpente la scène avec agitation, s'arrête de temps en temps pour scruter l'horizon. Estragon s'endort. Vladimir s'arrête devant Estragon.*) Gogo... (*Silence.*) Gogo... (*Silence.*) GOGO!

Estragon se réveille en sursaut.

ESTRAGON (*rendu à toute l'horreur de sa situation.*) Je dormais. (*Avec reproche.*) Pourquoi tu ne me laisses jamais dormir ?

VLADIMIR. Je me sentais seul.

ESTRAGON. J'ai fait un rêve.

VLADIMIR. Ne le raconte pas !

ESTRAGON. Je rêvais que...

VLADIMIR. *NE LE RACONTE PAS !*

ESTRAGON (*geste vers l'univers*). Celui-ci te suffit ? (*Silence.*) Tu n'es pas gentil, Didi. A qui veux-tu que je raconte mes cauchemars privés, sinon à toi ?

VLADIMIR. Qu'ils restent privés. Tu sais bien que je ne supporte pas ça.

ESTRAGON (*froidement*). Il y a des moments où je me demande si on ne ferait pas mieux de se quitter.

VLADIMIR. Tu n'irais pas loin.

ESTRAGON. Ce serait là, en effet, un grave inconvénient. (*Un temps.*) N'est-ce pas, Didi, que ce serait là un grave inconvénient ? (*Un temps.*) Étant donné la beauté du chemin. (*Un temps.*) Et la bonté des voyageurs. (*Un temps. Câlin.*) N'est-ce pas, Didi ?

VLADIMIR. Du calme.

ESTRAGON (*avec volupté*). Calme... Calme... (*Rêveusement*). Les Anglais disent cââârn. Ce sont des gens cââârns. (*Un temps.*) Tu connais l'histoire de l'Anglais au bordel ?*

VLADIMIR. Oui.

ESTRAGON. Raconte-la moi.

VLADIMIR. Assez.

ESTRAGON. Un Anglais s'étant enivré se rend au bordel. La sous-maîtresse lui demande s'il désire une blonde, une brune ou une rousse. Continue.

VLADIMIR. *ASSEZ !*

Vladimir sort. Estragon se lève et le suit jusqu'à la limite de la scène. Mimique d'Estragon, analogue à celle qu'arrachent au spectateur les efforts du pugiliste. Vladimir revient, passe devant Estragon, traverse la scène, les yeux baissés. Estragon fait quelques pas vers lui, s'arrête.

ESTRAGON (*avec douceur*). Tu voulais me parler ? (*Vladimir ne répond pas. Estragon fait un pas en avant.*) Tu avais quelque chose à me dire ? (*Silence. Autre pas en avant.*) Dis, Didi...

VLADIMIR (*sans se retourner*). Je n'ai rien à te dire.

ESTRAGON (*pas en avant*). Tu es fâché ? (*Silence. Pas en avant.*) Pardon ! (*Silence. Pas en avant. Il lui touche l'épaule.*) Voyons, Didi. (*Silence.*) Donne ta main ! (*Vladimir se retourne.*) Embrasse-moi ! (*Vladimir se raidit.*) Laisse-toi faire ! (*Vladimir s'amollit. Ils s'embrassent. Estragon recule.*) Tu pues l'ail !

VLADIMIR. C'est pour les reins. (*Silence. Estragon regarde l'arbre avec attention.*) Qu'est-ce qu'on fait maintenant ?

ESTRAGON. On attend.

VLADIMIR. Oui, mais en attendant.

ESTRAGON. Si on se pendait ? *

VLADIMIR. Ce serait un moyen de bander. *

ESTRAGON (*aguiché*). On bande ?

VLADIMIR. Avec tout ce qui s'ensuit. Là où ça tombe il pousse des mandragores. C'est pour ça qu'elles crient quand on les arrache. Tu ne savais pas ça ?

ESTRAGON. Pendons-nous tout de suite.

VLADIMIR. A une branche ? (*Ils s'approchent de l'arbre et le regardent.*) Je n'aurais pas confiance.

ESTRAGON. On peut toujours essayer.

VLADIMIR. Essaie.

ESTRAGON. Après toi.

VLADIMIR. Mais non, toi d'abord.

ESTRAGON. Pourquoi ?

VLADIMIR. Tu pèses moins lourd que moi.

ESTRAGON. Justement.

VLADIMIR. Je ne comprends pas.

ESTRAGON. Mais réfléchis un peu, voyons.

Vladimir réfléchit.

VLADIMIR (*finalement*). Je ne comprends pas.

ESTRAGON. Je vais t'expliquer. (*Il réfléchit.*) La branche... la branche... (*Avec colère.*) Mais essaie donc de comprendre !

VLADIMIR. Je ne compte plus que sur toi.

ESTRAGON (*avec effort*). Gogo léger — branche pas casser —

Gogo mort. Didi lourd — branche casser — Didi seul. (*Un temps.*) Tandis que... (*Il cherche l'expression juste.*)

VLADIMIR. Je n'avais pas pensé à ça.

ESTRAGON (*ayant trouvé*). Qui peut le plus peut le moins.

VLADIMIR. Mais est-ce que je pèse plus lourd que toi ?

ESTRAGON. C'est toi qui le dis. Moi je n'en sais rien. Il y a une chance sur deux. Ou presque.

VLADIMIR. Alors quoi faire ?

ESTRAGON. Ne faisons rien. C'est plus prudent.

VLADIMIR. Attendons voir ce qu'il va nous dire.

ESTRAGON. Qui ?

VLADIMIR. Godot.

ESTRAGON. Voilà.

VLADIMIR. Attendons d'être fixés d'abord.

ESTRAGON. D'un autre côté, on ferait peut-être mieux de battre le fer avant qu'il soit glacé.

VLADIMIR. Je suis curieux de savoir ce qu'il va nous dire. Ça ne nous engage à rien.

ESTRAGON. Qu'est-ce qu'on lui a demandé au juste ?

VLADIMIR. Tu n'étais pas là ?

ESTRAGON. Je n'ai pas fait attention.

VLADIMIR. Eh bien... Rien de bien précis.

ESTRAGON. Une sorte de prière.

VLADIMIR. Voilà.

ESTRAGON. Une vague supplique.

VLADIMIR. Si tu veux.*

ESTRAGON. Et qu'a-t-il répondu ?

VLADIMIR. Qu'il verrait.

ESTRAGON. Qu'il ne pouvait rien promettre.

VLADIMIR. Qu'il lui fallait réfléchir.

ESTRAGON. A tête reposée.

VLADIMIR. Consulter sa famille.

ESTRAGON. Ses amis.

VLADIMIR. Ses agents.

ESTRAGON. Ses correspondants.

VLADIMIR. Ses registres.

ESTRAGON. Son compte en banque.

VLADIMIR. Avant de se prononcer.

ESTRAGON. C'est normal.

VLADIMIR. N'est-ce pas ?

ESTRAGON. Il me semble.

VLADIMIR. A moi aussi.

Repos.

ESTRAGON (*inquiet*). Et nous ?

VLADIMIR. Plaît-il ?

ESTRAGON. Je dis, Et nous ?

VLADIMIR. Je ne comprends pas.

ESTRAGON. Quel est notre rôle là-dedans ?

VLADIMIR. Notre rôle ?

ESTRAGON. Prends ton temps.

VLADIMIR. Notre rôle ? Celui du suppliant.

ESTRAGON. A ce point-là ?

VLADIMIR. Monsieur a des exigences à faire valoir ?

ESTRAGON. On n'a plus de droits ?

Rire de Vladimir, auquel il coupe court comme au précédent. Même jeu, moins le sourire.

VLADIMIR. Tu me ferais rire, si cela m'était permis.

ESTRAGON. Nous les avons perdus ?

VLADIMIR (*avec netteté*). Nous les avons bazardés.*

Silence. Ils demeurent immobiles, bras ballants, tête sur la poitrine, cassés aux genoux.

ESTRAGON (*faiblement*). On n'est pas lié ? (*Un temps.*) Hein ?

VLADIMIR (*levant la main*). Écoute !

Ils écoutent, grotesquement figés.

ESTRAGON. Je n'entends rien.

VLADIMIR. Hsst ! (*Ils écoutent. Estragon perd l'équilibre, manque de tomber. Il s'agrippe au bras de Vladimir qui chancelle. Ils écoutent, tassés l'un contre l'autre, les yeux dans les yeux.*) Moi non plus. (*Soupirs de soulagement. Détente. Ils s'éloignent l'un de l'autre.*)

ESTRAGON. Tu m'as fait peur.

VLADIMIR. J'ai cru que c'était lui.

ESTRAGON. Qui ?

VLADIMIR. Godot.

ESTRAGON. Pah ! Le vent dans les roseaux.

VLADIMIR. J'aurais juré des cris.

ESTRAGON. Et pourquoi crierait-il ?

VLADIMIR. Après son cheval.

Silence.

ESTRAGON. Allons-nous-en.

VLADIMIR. Où ? (*Un temps.*) Ce soir on couchera peut-être chez lui, au chaud, au sec, le ventre plein, sur la paille. Ça vaut la peine qu'on attende. Non ?

ESTRAGON. Pas toute la nuit.

VLADIMIR. Il fait encore jour.*

Silence.

ESTRAGON. J'ai faim.

VLADIMIR. Veux-tu une carotte ?

ESTRAGON. Il n'y a pas autre chose ?

VLADIMIR. Je dois avoir quelques navets.

ESTRAGON. Donne-moi une carotte. (*Vladimir fouille dans ses poches, en retire un navet et le donne à Estragon.*) Merci. (*Il mord dedans. Plaintivement.*) C'est un navet !

VLADIMIR. Oh pardon ! J'aurais juré une carotte. (*Il fouille à nouveau dans ses poches, n'y trouve que des navets.*) Tout ça c'est des navets. (*Il cherche toujours.*) Tu as dû manger la dernière. (*Il cherche.*) Attends, ça y est. (*Il sort enfin une carotte et la donne à Estragon.*) Voilà, mon cher. (*Estragon l'essuie sur sa manche et commence à la manger.*) Rends-moi le navet. (*Estragon lui rend le navet.*) Fais-la durer, il n'y en a plus.

ESTRAGON (*tout en mâchant*). Je t'ai posé une question.

VLADIMIR. Ah.

ESTRAGON. Est-ce que tu m'as répondu ?

VLADIMIR. Elle est bonne, ta carotte ?

ESTRAGON. Elle est sucrée.

VLADIMIR. Tant mieux, tant mieux. (*Un temps.*) Qu'est-ce que tu voulais savoir ?

ESTRAGON. Je ne me rappelle plus. (*Il mâche.*) C'est ça qui m'embête. (*Il regarde la carotte avec appréciation, la fait tourner en l'air du bout des doigts.*) Délicieuse, ta carotte. (*Il en suce méditativement le bout.*) Attends, ça me revient. (*Il arrache une bouchée.*)

VLADIMIR. Alors ?

ESTRAGON (*la bouche pleine, distraitement*). On n'est pas lié ?

VLADIMIR. Je n'entends rien.

ESTRAGON (*mâche, avale*). Je demande si on est lié.

VLADIMIR. Lié ?

ESTRAGON. Lié.

VLADIMIR. Comment lié ?

ESTRAGON. Pieds et poings.

VLADIMIR. Mais à qui ? Par qui ?

ESTRAGON. A ton bonhomme.

VLADIMIR. A Godot ? Lié à Godot ? Quelle idée ! Jamais de la vie ! (*Un temps.*) Pas encore. (*Il ne fait pas la liaison.*)

ESTRAGON. Il s'appelle Godot ?

VLADIMIR. Je crois.

ESTRAGON. Tiens ! (*Il soulève le restant de carotte par le bout de fane et le fait tourner devant ses yeux.*) C'est curieux, plus on va, moins c'est bon.

VLADIMIR. Pour moi c'est le contraire.

ESTRAGON. C'est-à-dire ?

VLADIMIR. Je me fais au goût au fur et à mesure.*

ESTRAGON (*ayant longuement réfléchi*). C'est ça, le contraire ?

VLADIMIR. Question de tempérament.

ESTRAGON. De caractère.

VLADIMIR. On n'y peut rien.

ESTRAGON. On a beau se démener.

VLADIMIR. On reste ce qu'on est.

ESTRAGON. On a beau se tortiller.

VLADIMIR. Le fond ne change pas.

ESTRAGON. Rien à faire. (*Il tend le restant de carotte à Vladimir.*) Veux-tu la finir ?

Un cri terrible retentit, tout proche. Estragon lâche la carotte. Ils se figent, puis se précipitent vers la coulisse. Estragon s'arrête à mi-chemin, retourne sur ses pas, ramasse la carotte, la fourre dans sa poche, s'élance vers Vladimir qui l'attend, s'arrête à nouveau, retourne sur ses pas, ramasse sa chaussure, puis court rejoindre Vladimir. Enlacés, la tête dans les épaules, se détournant de la menace, ils attendent.

Entrent Pozzo et Lucky. Celui-là dirige celui-ci au moyen d'une corde passée autour du cou, de sorte qu'on ne voit d'abord que Lucky suivi de la corde, assez longue pour qu'il puisse arriver au milieu du plateau avant que Pozzo débouche de la coulisse. Lucky porte une lourde valise, un siège pliant, un panier à provisions et un manteau (sur le bras); Pozzo un fouet.*

POZZO (*en coulisse*). Plus vite ! (*Bruit de fouet. Pozzo paraît. Ils traversent la scène. Lucky passe devant Vladimir et Estragon et sort. Pozzo, ayant vu Vladimir et Estragon, s'arrête. La corde se tend. Pozzo tire violemment dessus.*) Arrière ! (*Bruit de chute. C'est Lucky qui tombe avec tout son chargement. Vladimir et Estragon le regardent, partagés entre l'envie d'aller à son secours et la peur de se mêler de ce qui ne les regarde pas. Vladimir fait un pas vers Lucky, Estragon le retient par la manche.*)

VLADIMIR. Lâche-moi !

ESTRAGON. Reste tranquille.

POZZO. Attention ! Il est méchant.* (*Estragon et Vladimir le regardent.*) Avec les étrangers.

ESTRAGON (*bas*). C'est lui ?

VLADIMIR. Qui ?

ESTRAGON. Voyons...

VLADIMIR. Godot ?

ESTRAGON. Voilà.

POZZO. Je me présente : Pozzo.*

VLADIMIR. Mais non.

ESTRAGON. Il a dit Godot.

VLADIMIR. Mais non.

ESTRAGON (*à Pozzo*). Vous n'êtes pas Monsieur Godot, Monsieur ?

POZZO (*d'une voix terrible*). Je suis Pozzo ! (*Silence.*) Ce nom ne vous dit rien ? (*Silence.*) Je vous demande si ce nom ne vous dit rien ?

Vladimir et Estragon s'interrogent du regard.

ESTRAGON (*faisant semblant de chercher*). Bozzo... Bozzo...

VLADIMIR (*de même*). Pozzo...

POZZO. *PPPOZZO !*

ESTRAGON. Ah ! Pozzo... voyons... Pozzo...

VLADIMIR. C'est Pozzo ou Bozzo ?

ESTRAGON. Pozzo... non, je ne vois pas.

VLADIMIR (*conciliant*). J'ai connu une famille Gozzo. La mère brodait au tambour.*

Pozzo avance, menaçant.

ESTRAGON (*vivement*). Nous ne sommes pas d'ici,* Monsieur.

POZZO (*s'arrêtant*). Vous êtes bien des êtres humains cependant. (*Il met ses lunettes.*) A ce que je vois. (*Il enlève ses lunettes.*) De la même espèce que moi. (*Il éclate d'un rire énorme.*) De la même espèce que Pozzo ! D'origine divine !

VLADIMIR. C'est-à-dire...

POZZO (*tranchant*). Qui est Godot ?

ESTRAGON. Godot ?

POZZO. Vous m'avez pris pour Godot.

VLADIMIR. Oh non, Monsieur, pas un seul instant, Monsieur.

POZZO. Qui est-ce ?

VLADIMIR. Eh bien, c'est un... c'est une connaissance.

ESTRAGON. Mais non, voyons, on le connaît à peine.

VLADIMIR. Évidemment... on ne le connaît pas très bien... mais tout de même...

ESTRAGON. Pour ma part je ne le reconnaîtrai même pas.

POZZO. Vous m'avez pris pour lui.

ESTRAGON. C'est-à-dire... l'obscurité... la fatigue... la faiblesse... l'attente... j'avoue... j'ai cru... un instant...

VLADIMIR. Ne l'écoutez pas, Monsieur, ne l'écoutez pas !

POZZO. L'attente ? Vous l'attendiez donc ?

VLADIMIR. C'est-à-dire...

POZZO. Ici ? Sur mes terres ?

VLADIMIR. On ne pensait pas à mal.

ESTRAGON. C'était dans une bonne intention.

POZZO. La route est à tout le monde.

VLADIMIR. C'est ce qu'on se disait.

POZZO. C'est une honte, mais c'est ainsi.

ESTRAGON. On n'y peut rien.

POZZO (*d'un geste large*). Ne parlons plus de ça. (*Il tire sur la corde.*) Debout ! (*Un temps.*) Chaque fois qu'il tombe il s'endort. (*Il tire sur la corde.*) Debout, charogne ! (*Bruit de Lucky qui se relève et ramasse ses affaires. Pozzo tire sur la corde.*) Arrière ! (*Lucky entre à reculons.*) Arrêt ! (*Lucky s'arrête.*) Tourne ! (*Lucky se retourne. A Vladimir et Estragon, affablement.*) Mes amis, je suis heureux de vous avoir rencontrés. (*Devant leur expression incrédule.*) Mais oui, sincèrement heureux. (*Il tire sur la corde.*) Plus près ! (*Lucky avance.*) Arrêt ! (*Lucky s'arrête. A Vladimir et Estragon.*) Voyez-vous, la route est longue quand on chemine tout seul pendant... (*il regarde sa montre*) ...pendant... (*il calcule*) ...six heures, oui, c'est bien ça, six heures à la file, sans rencontrer âme qui vive. (*A Lucky.*) Manteau ! (*Lucky dépose la valise, avance, donne le manteau, recule, reprend la valise.*) Tiens ça. (*Pozzo lui tend le fouet, Lucky avance et, n'ayant plus de mains, se penche et prend le fouet entre ses dents, puis recule. Pozzo commence à mettre son manteau, s'arrête.*) Manteau ! (*Lucky dépose tout, avance, aide Pozzo à mettre son manteau, recule, reprend tout.*) Le fond de l'air est frais. (*Il finit de boutonner son manteau, se penche, s'inspecte, se relève.*) Fouet ! (*Lucky avance, se penche, Pozzo lui arrache le fouet de la bouche, Lucky recule.*) Voyez-vous, mes amis, je ne peux me passer longtemps de la société de mes semblables (*il regarde les deux semblables*) même quand ils ne me ressemblent qu'imparfaitement. (*A Lucky.*) Pliant ! (*Lucky dépose valise et panier, avance, ouvre le pliant, le pose par terre, recule, reprend valise et panier. Pozzo regarde le pliant.*) Plus près ! (*Lucky dépose valise et panier, avance, déplace le pliant, recule, reprend valise et panier. Pozzo s'assied, pose le bout de son fouet contre la poitrine de Lucky et pousse.*) Arrière ! (*Lucky recule.*) Encore. (*Lucky recule encore.*) Arrêt ! (*Lucky s'arrête. A Vladimir et Estragon.*) C'est pourquoi, avec votre permission, je m'en vais rester un moment auprès de vous, avant de m'aventurer plus avant. (*A Lucky.*) Panier ! (*Lucky avance, donne le panier, recule.*) Le grand air, ça creuse. (*Il ouvre le panier, en retire un morceau de poulet, un morceau de pain et une bouteille de vin. A Lucky.*) Panier ! (*Lucky avance, prend le panier, recule, s'immobilise.*) Plus loin ! (*Lucky recule.*) Là ! (*Lucky s'arrête.*) Il pue. (*Il boit une rasade à même le goulot.*) A la bonne nôtre. (*Il dépose la bouteille et se met à manger.*)

Silence. Estragon et Vladimir, s'enhardissant peu à peu, tournent autour de Lucky, l'inspectent sur toutes les coutures. Pozzo mord dans son poulet avec voracité, jette les os après les avoir sucés. Lucky ploie lentement, jusqu'à ce que la valise frôle le sol, se redresse brusquement, recommence à ployer. Rythme de celui qui dort debout.

ESTRAGON. Qu'est-ce qu'il a ?

VLADIMIR. Il a l'air fatigué.

ESTRAGON. Pourquoi ne dépose-t-il pas ses bagages ?

VLADIMIR. Est-ce que je sais ? (*Ils le serrent de plus près.*) Attention !

ESTRAGON. Si on lui parlait ?

VLADIMIR. Regarde-moi ça !

ESTRAGON. Quoi ?

VLADIMIR (*indiquant*). Le cou.

ESTRAGON (*regardant le cou*). Je ne vois rien.

VLADIMIR. Mets-toi ici.

Estragon se met à la place de Vladimir.

ESTRAGON. En effet.

VLADIMIR. A vif.

ESTRAGON. C'est la corde.

VLADIMIR. A force de frotter.

ESTRAGON. Qu'est-ce que tu veux.

VLADIMIR. C'est le nœud.

ESTRAGON. C'est fatal.

Ils reprennent leur inspection, s'arrêtent au visage.

VLADIMIR. Il n'est pas mal.

ESTRAGON (*levant les épaules, faisant la moue*). Tu trouves ?

VLADIMIR. Un peu efféminé.

ESTRAGON. Il bave.

VLADIMIR. C'est forcé.

ESTRAGON. Il écume.

VLADIMIR. C'est peut-être un idiot.

ESTRAGON. Un crétin.

VLADIMIR (*avançant la tête*). On dirait un goitre.

ESTRAGON (*même jeu*). Ce n'est pas sûr.

VLADIMIR. Il halète.

ESTRAGON. C'est normal.

VLADIMIR. Et ses yeux !

ESTRAGON. Qu'est-ce qu'ils ont ?

VLADIMIR. Ils sortent.

ESTRAGON. Pour moi il est en train de crever.

VLADIMIR. Ce n'est pas sûr. (*Un temps.*) Pose-lui une question.

ESTRAGON. Tu crois ?

VLADIMIR. Qu'est-ce qu'on risque ?

ESTRAGON (*timidement*). Monsieur...

VLADIMIR. Plus fort.

ESTRAGON (*plus fort*). Monsieur...

POZZO. Foutez-lui la paix ! (*Ils se tournent vers Pozzo qui, ayant fini de manger, s'essuie la bouche du revers de la main.*) Vous ne voyez pas qu'il veut se reposer ? (*Il sort sa pipe et commence à la bourrer. Estragon remarque les os de poulet par terre, les fixe avec avidité. Pozzo frotte une allumette et commence à allumer sa pipe.*) Panier ! (*Lucky ne bougeant pas, Pozzo jette l'allumette avec emportement et tire sur la corde.*) Panier ! (*Lucky manque de tomber, revient à lui, avance, met la bouteille dans le panier, retourne à sa place, reprend son attitude. Estragon fixe les os, Pozzo frotte une seconde allumette et allume sa pipe.*) Que voulez-vous, ce n'est pas son travail. (*Il aspire une bouffée, allonge les jambes.*) Ah ! ça va mieux.

ESTRAGON (*timidement*). Monsieur...

POZZO. Qu'est-ce que c'est, mon brave ?

ESTRAGON. Heu... vous ne mangez pas... heu... vous n'avez plus besoin... des os... Monsieur ?

VLADIMIR (*outré*). Tu ne pouvais pas attendre ?

POZZO. Mais non, mais non, c'est tout naturel. Si j'ai besoin des os ? (*Il les remue du bout de son fouet.*) Non, personnellement je n'en ai plus besoin. (*Estragon fait un pas vers les os.*) Mais... (*Estragon s'arrête*) mais en principe les os reviennent au porteur. C'est donc à lui qu'il faut demander. (*Estragon se tourne vers Lucky, hésite.*) Mais demandez-lui, demandez-lui, n'ayez pas peur, il vous le dira.

Estragon va vers Lucky, s'arrête devant lui.

ESTRAGON. Monsieur... pardon, Monsieur...

Lucky ne réagit pas. Pozzo fait claquer son fouet. Lucky relève la tête.

POZZO. On te parle, porc. Réponds. (*A Estragon.*) Allez-y.

ESTRAGON. Pardon, Monsieur, les os, vous les voulez.

Lucky regarde Estragon longuement.

POZZO (*aux anges*). Monsieur ! (*Lucky baisse la tête.*) Réponds ! Tu les veux ou tu ne les veux pas ? (*Silence de Lucky. A Estragon.*) Ils sont à vous. (*Estragon se jette sur les os, les ramasse et commence à les ronger.*) C'est pourtant bizarre. C'est bien la première fois qu'il me refuse un os. (*Il regarde Lucky avec inquiétude.*) J'espère qu'il ne va pas me faire la blague de tomber malade. (*Il tire sur sa pipe.*)

VLADIMIR (*éclatant*). C'est une honte !

Silence. Estragon, stupéfait, s'arrête de ronger, regarde Vladimir et Pozzo tour à tour. Pozzo très calme. Vladimir de plus en plus gêné.

POZZO (*à Vladimir*). Faites-vous allusion à quelque chose de particulier ?

VLADIMIR (*résolu et bafouillant*). Traiter un homme (*geste vers Lucky*) de cette façon... je trouve ça... un être humain... non... c'est une honte !

ESTRAGON (*ne voulant pas être en reste*). Un scandale ! (*Il se remet à ronger.*)

POZZO. Vous êtes sévères. (*A Vladimir.*) Quel âge avez-vous, sans indiscrétion ?* (*Silence.*) Soixante ?... Soixante-dix ?... (*A Estragon.*) Quel âge peut-il bien avoir ?

ESTRAGON. Demandez-lui.*

POZZO. Je suis indiscret. (*Il vide sa pipe en la tapant contre son fouet, se lève.*) Je vais vous quitter. Merci de m'avoir tenu compagnie. (*Il réfléchit.*) A moins que je ne fume encore une pipe avec vous. Qu'en dites-vous ? (*Ils n'en disent rien.*) Oh ! je ne suis qu'un petit fumeur, un tout petit fumeur, il n'est pas dans mes habitudes de fumer deux pipes coup sur coup, ça (*il porte sa main au cœur*) fait battre mon cœur. (*Un temps.*) C'est la nicotine, on en absorbe, malgré ses précautions. (*Il soupire.*) Que voulez-vous. (*Silence.*) Mais peut-être que vous n'êtes pas des fumeurs. Si ? Non ? Enfin, c'est un détail. (*Silence.*) Mais comment me rasseoir maintenant avec naturel, maintenant que je me suis mis debout ? Sans avoir l'air de — comment dire — de fléchir ? (*A Vladimir.*) Vous dites ? (*Silence.*) Peut-être n'avez-vous rien dit ? (*Silence.*) C'est sans importance. Voyons... (*Il réfléchit.*)

ESTRAGON. Ah ! Ça va mieux. (*Il jette les os.*)

VLADIMIR. Partons.

ESTRAGON. Déjà ?

POZZO. Un instant ! (*Il tire sur la corde.*) Pliant ! (*Il montre avec son fouet. Lucky déplace le pliant.*) Encore ! Là ! (*Il se rassied. Lucky recule, reprend valise et panier.*) Me voilà réinstallé ! (*Il commence à bourrer sa pipe.*)

VLADIMIR. Partons.

POZZO. J'espère que ce n'est pas moi qui vous chasse. Restez encore un peu, vous ne le regretterez pas.

ESTRAGON (*flairant l'aumône*). Nous avons le temps.

POZZO (*ayant allumé sa pipe*). La deuxième est toujours moins bonne (*il enlève la pipe de sa bouche, la contemple*) que la première, je veux dire. (*Il remet la pipe dans sa bouche.*) Mais elle est bonne quand même.

VLADIMIR. Je m'en vais.

POZZO. Il ne peut plus supporter ma présence. Je suis sans doute peu humain, mais est-ce une raison ? (*A Vladimir.*) Réfléchissez, avant de commettre une imprudence. Mettons que vous partiez maintenant, pendant qu'il fait encore jour car malgré tout il fait encore jour. (*Tous les trois regardent le ciel.*) Bon. Que devient en ce cas — (*il ôte sa pipe de la bouche, la regarde*) — je suis éteint — (*il rallume sa pipe*) — en ce cas... en ce cas... que devient en ce cas votre rendez-vous avec ce... Godet... Godot... Godin... (*silence*)... enfin vous voyez qui je veux dire, dont votre avenir dépend (*silence*) ...enfin votre avenir immédiat.

ESTRAGON. Il a raison.

VLADIMIR. Comment le saviez-vous ? *

POZZO. Voilà qu'il m'adresse à nouveau la parole ! Nous finirons par nous prendre en affection.

ESTRAGON. Pourquoi ne dépose-t-il pas ses bagages ?

POZZO. Moi aussi je serais heureux de le rencontrer. Plus je rencontre de gens, plus je suis heureux. Avec la moindre créature on s'instruit, on s'enrichit, on goûte mieux son bonheur. Vous-mêmes (*il les regarde attentivement l'un après l'autre, afin qu'ils se sachent visés tous les deux*) vous-mêmes, qui sait, vous m'aurez peut-être apporté quelque chose.

ESTRAGON. Pourquoi ne dépose-t-il pas ses bagages ?

POZZO. Mais ça m'étonnerait.

VLADIMIR. On vous pose une question.

POZZO (*ravi*). Une question ? Qui ? Laquelle ? (*Silence.*) Tout à l'heure vous me disiez Monsieur, en tremblant. Maintenant vous me posez des questions. Ça va mal finir.

VLADIMIR (*à Estragon*). Je crois qu'il t'écoute.

ESTRAGON (*qui s'est remis à tourner autour de Lucky*). Quoi ?

VLADIMIR. Tu peux lui demander maintenant. Il est alerté.

ESTRAGON. Lui demander quoi ?

VLADIMIR. Pourquoi il ne dépose pas ses bagages.

ESTRAGON. Je me le demande.

VLADIMIR. Mais demande-lui, voyons.

POZZO (*qui a suivi ses échanges avec une attention anxieuse, craignant que la question ne se perde*). Vous me demandez pourquoi il ne dépose pas ses bagages, comme vous dites.

VLADIMIR. Voilà.

POZZO (*à Estragon*). Vous êtes bien d'accord ?

ESTRAGON (*continuant à tourner autour de Lucky*). Il souffle comme un phoque.

POZZO. Je vais vous répondre. (*A Estragon.*) Mais restez tranquille, je vous en supplie, vous me rendez nerveux.

VLADIMIR. Viens ici.

ESTRAGON. Qu'est-ce qu'il y a ?

VLADIMIR. Il va parler.

Immobiles, l'un contre l'autre, ils attendent.

POZZO. C'est parfait. Tout le monde y est ? Tout le monde me regarde ? (*Il regarde Lucky, tire sur la corde. Lucky lève la tête.*) Regarde-moi, porc ! (*Lucky le regarde.*) Parfait. (*Il met la pipe dans sa poche, sort un petit vaporisateur et se vaporise la gorge, remet le vaporisateur dans sa poche, se râcle la gorge, crache, ressort le vaporisateur, se revaporise la gorge, remet le vaporisateur dans sa poche.*) Je suis prêt. Tout le monde m'écoute ? (*Il regarde Lucky, tire sur la corde.*) Avance ! (*Lucky avance.*) Là ! (*Lucky s'arrête.*) Tout le monde est prêt ? (*Il les regarde tous les trois, Lucky en dernier, tire sur la corde.*) Alors quoi ? (*Lucky lève la tête.*) Je n'aime pas parler dans le vide. Bon. Voyons. (*Il réfléchit.*)

ESTRAGON. Je m'en vais.

POZZO. Qu'est-ce que vous m'avez demandé au juste ?

VLADIMIR. Pourquoi il —

POZZO (*avec colère*). Ne me coupez pas la parole ! (*Un temps. Plus calme.*) Si nous parlons tous en même temps nous n'en sortirons jamais. (*Un temps.*) Qu'est-ce que je disais ? (*Un temps. Plus fort.*) Qu'est-ce que je disais ?

Vladimir mime celui qui porte une lourde charge. Pozzo le regarde sans comprendre.

ESTRAGON (*avec force*). Bagages ! (*Il pointe son doigt vers Lucky.*) Pourquoi ? Toujours tenir. (*Il fait celui qui ploie, en haletant.*) Jamais déposer. (*Il ouvre les mains, se redresse avec soulagement.*) Pourquoi ?

POZZO. J'y suis. Il fallait me le dire plus tôt. Pourquoi il ne se met pas à son aise. Essayons d'y voir clair. N'en a-t-il pas le droit ? Si. C'est donc qu'il ne veut pas ? Voilà qui est raisonné. Et pourquoi ne veut-il pas ? (*Un temps.*) Messieurs, je vais vous le dire.

VLADIMIR. Attention !

POZZO. C'est pour m'impressionner, pour que je le garde.

ESTRAGON. Comment ?

POZZO. Je me suis peut-être mal exprimé. Il cherche à m'apitoyer, pour que je renonce à me séparer de lui. Non, ce n'est pas tout à fait ça.

VLADIMIR. Vous voulez vous en débarrasser ?

POZZO. Il veut m'avoir, mais il ne m'aura pas.

VLADIMIR. Vous voulez vous en débarrasser ?

POZZO. Il s'imagine qu'en le voyant bon porteur je serai tenté de l'employer à l'avenir dans cette capacité.

ESTRAGON. Vous n'en voulez plus ?

POZZO. En réalité il porte comme un porc. Ce n'est pas son métier.

VLADIMIR. Vous voulez vous en débarrasser ?

POZZO. Il se figure qu'en le voyant infatigable je vais regretter ma décision. Tel est son misérable calcul. Comme si j'étais à court d'hommes de peine ! (*Tous les trois regardent Lucky.*) Atlas, fils de Jupiter ! (*Silence.*) Et voilà. Je pense avoir répondu à votre question. En avez-vous d'autres ? (*Jeu du vaporisateur.*)

VLADIMIR. Vous voulez vous en débarrasser ?

POZZO. Remarquez que j'aurais pu être à sa place et lui à la mienne. Si le hasard ne s'y était pas opposé. A chacun son dû.

VLADIMIR. Vous voulez vous en débarrasser ?

POZZO. Vous dites ?

VLADIMIR. Vous voulez vous en débarrasser ?

POZZO. En effet. Mais au lieu de le chasser, comme j'aurais pu, je veux dire au lieu de le mettre tout simplement à la porte, à coups de pied dans le cul, je l'emmène, telle est ma bonté, au marché de Saint-Sauveur,* où je compte bien en tirer quelque chose. A vrai dire, chasser de tels êtres, ce n'est pas possible. Pour bien faire, il faudrait les tuer.

Lucky pleure.

ESTRAGON. Il pleure.

POZZO. Les vieux chiens ont plus de dignité. (*Il tend son mouchoir à Estragon.*) Consolez-le, puisque vous le plaignez.

(*Estragon hésite.*) Prenez. (*Estragon prend le mouchoir.*) Essuyez-lui les yeux. Comme ça il se sentira moins abandonné.

Estragon hésite toujours.

VLADIMIR. Donne, je le ferai moi.

Estragon ne veut pas donner le mouchoir. Gestes d'enfant.

POZZO. Dépêchez-vous. Bientôt il ne pleurera plus. (*Estragon s'approche de Lucky et se met en posture de lui essuyer les yeux. Lucky lui décoche un violent coup de pied dans les tibias. Estragon lâche le mouchoir, se jette en arrière, fait le tour du plateau en boitant et en hurlant de douleur.*) Mouchoir! (*Lucky dépose valise et panier, ramasse le mouchoir, avance, le donne à Pozzo, recule, reprend valise et panier.*)

ESTRAGON. Le salaud ! La vache ! (*Il relève son pantalon.*) Il m'a estropié !

POZZO. Je vous avais dit qu'il n'aime pas les étrangers.

VLADIMIR (*à Estragon*). Fais voir. (*Estragon lui montre sa jambe. A Pozzo, avec colère.*) Il saigne !

POZZO. C'est bon signe.

ESTRAGON (*la jambe blessée en l'air*). Je ne pourrai plus marcher !

VLADIMIR (*tendrement*). Je te porterai. (*Un temps.*) Le cas échéant.*

POZZO. Il ne pleure plus. (*A Estragon.*) Vous l'avez remplacé en quelque sorte. (*Rêveusement.*) Les larmes du monde sont immuables.* Pour chacun qui se met à pleurer, quelque part un autre s'arrête. Il en va de même du rire. (*Il rit.*) Ne disons donc pas de mal de notre époque, elle n'est pas plus malheureuse que les précédentes. (*Silence.*) N'en disons pas de bien non plus. (*Silence.*) N'en parlons pas. (*Silence.*) Il est vrai que la population a augmenté.

VLADIMIR. Essaie de marcher.

Estragon part en boitillant, s'arrête devant Lucky et crache sur lui, puis va s'asseoir là où il était assis au lever du rideau.

POZZO. Savez-vous qui m'a appris toutes ces belles choses? (*Un temps. Dardant son doigt vers Lucky.*) Lui !

VLADIMIR (*regardant le ciel*). La nuit ne viendra-t-elle donc jamais?

POZZO. Sans lui je n'aurais jamais pensé, jamais senti, que des choses basses, ayant trait à mon métier de — peu importe. La beauté, la grâce, la vérité de première classe, je m'en savais incapable. Alors j'ai pris un knouk.

VLADIMIR (*malgré lui, cessant d'interroger le ciel*). Un knouk ?

POZZO. Il y aura bientôt soixante ans que ça dure...* (*il calcule mentalement*) ...oui, bientôt soixante. (*Se redressant fièrement.*) On ne me les donnerait pas, n'est-ce pas ? (*Vladimir regarde Lucky.*) A côté de lui j'ai l'air d'un jeune homme, non ? (*Un temps. A Lucky.*) Chapeau ! (*Lucky dépose le panier, enlève son chapeau. Une abondante chevelure blanche lui tombe autour du visage. Il met son chapeau sous le bras et reprend le panier.*) Maintenant regardez. (*Pozzo ôte son chapeau.* Il est complètement chauve. Il remet son chapeau.*) Vous avez vu ?

VLADIMIR. Qu'est-ce que c'est, un knouk ?*

POZZO. Vous n'êtes pas d'ici. Êtes-vous seulement du siècle ?* Autrefois on avait des bouffons. Maintenant on a des knouks. Ceux qui peuvent se le permettre.

VLADIMIR. Et vous le chassez à présent ? Un si vieux, un si fidèle serviteur ?

ESTRAGON. Fumier !

Pozzo de plus en plus agité.

VLADIMIR. Après en avoir sucé la substance vous le jetez comme un... (*il cherche*) ...comme une peau de banane. Avouez que...

POZZO (*gémissant, portant ses mains à sa tête*). Je n'en peux plus... plus supporter... ce qu'il fait... pouvez pas savoir... c'est affreux... faut qu'il s'en aille... (*Il brandit les bras.*) ...je deviens fou...* (*Il s'effondre, la tête dans les bras.*) Je n'en peux plus... peux plus...

Silence. Tous regardent Pozzo. Lucky tressaille.*

VLADIMIR. Il n'en peut plus.

ESTRAGON. C'est affreux.

VLADIMIR. Il devient fou.

ESTRAGON. C'est dégoûtant.

VLADIMIR (*à Lucky*). Comment osez-vous ? C'est honteux !

Un si bon maître ! Le faire souffrir ainsi ! Après tant d'années ! Vraiment !

POZZO (*sanglotant*). Autrefois... il était gentil... il m'aidait... me distrayait... il me rendait meilleur... maintenant... il m'assassine...

ESTRAGON (*à Vladimir*). Est-ce qu'il veut le remplacer ?

VLADIMIR. Comment ?

ESTRAGON. Je n'ai pas compris s'il veut le remplacer ou s'il n'en veut plus après lui.

VLADIMIR. Je ne crois pas.

ESTRAGON. Comment ?

VLADIMIR. Je ne sais pas.

ESTRAGON. Faut lui demander.

POZZO (*calmé*). Messieurs, je ne sais pas ce qui m'est arrivé. Je vous demande pardon. Oubliez tout ça. (*De plus en plus maître de lui.*) Je ne sais plus très bien ce que j'ai dit, mais vous pouvez être sûrs qu'il n'y avait pas un mot de vrai là-dedans. (*Se redresse, se frappe la poitrine.*) Est-ce que j'ai l'air d'un homme qu'on fait souffrir, moi ? Voyons ! (*Il fouille dans ses poches.*) Qu'est-ce que j'ai fait de ma pipe ?

VLADIMIR. Charmante soirée.

ESTRAGON. Inoubliable.

VLADIMIR. Et ce n'est pas fini.

ESTRAGON. On dirait que non.

VLADIMIR. Ça ne fait que commencer.

ESTRAGON. C'est terrible.

VLADIMIR. On se croirait au spectacle.*

ESTRAGON. Au cirque.

VLADIMIR. Au music-hall.

ESTRAGON. Au cirque.

POZZO. Mais qu'ai-je donc fait de ma bruyère !

ESTRAGON. Il est marrant ! Il a perdu sa bouffarde ! (*Rit bruyamment.*)

VLADIMIR. Je reviens. (*Il se dirige vers la coulisse.*)

ESTRAGON. Au fond du couloir, à gauche.

VLADIMIR. Garde ma place. (*Il sort.*)

POZZO. J'ai perdu mon Abdullah !

ESTRAGON (*se tordant*). Il est tordant !

POZZO (*levant la tête*). Vous n'auriez pas vu — (*Il s'aperçoit de l'absence de Vladimir. Désolé.*) Oh ! Il est parti !... Sans me dire au revoir ! Ce n'est pas chic ! Vous auriez dû le retenir.

ESTRAGON. Il s'est retenu tout seul.

POZZO. Oh ! (*Un temps.*) A la bonne heure.

ESTRAGON. Venez par ici.

POZZO. Pour quoi faire ?

ESTRAGON. Vous allez voir.

POZZO. Vous voulez que je me lève ?

ESTRAGON. Venez... venez... vite.

Pozzo se lève et va vers Estragon.

ESTRAGON. Regardez !

POZZO. Oh ! là là !

ESTRAGON. C'est fini.

Vladimir revient, sombre, bouscule Lucky, renverse le pliant d'un coup de pied, va et vient avec agitation.

POZZO. Il n'est pas content ?

ESTRAGON. Tu as raté des choses formidables. Dommage.

Vladimir s'arrête, redresse le pliant, reprend son va-et-vient, plus calme.

POZZO. Il s'apaise. (*Regard circulaire.*) D'ailleurs tout s'apaise, je le sens. Une grande paix descend. Écoutez. (*Il lève la main.*) Pan dort.

VLADIMIR (*s'arrêtant*). La nuit ne viendra-t-elle jamais ?

Tous les trois regardent le ciel.

POZZO. Vous ne tenez pas à partir avant ?

ESTRAGON. C'est-à-dire... vous comprenez...

POZZO. Mais c'est tout naturel, c'est tout naturel. Moi-même, à votre place, si j'avais rendez-vous avec un Godin... Godet... Godot... enfin vous voyez qui je veux dire, j'attendrais qu'il fasse nuit noire avant d'abandonner. (*Il regarde le pliant.*) J'aimerais bien me rasseoir, mais je ne sais pas trop comment m'y prendre.

ESTRAGON. Puis-je vous aider ?

POZZO. Si vous me demandiez peut-être.

ESTRAGON. Quoi ?

POZZO. Si vous me demandiez de me rasseoir.

ESTRAGON. Ça vous aiderait ?

POZZO. Il me semble.

ESTRAGON. Allons-y. Rasseyez-vous, Monsieur, je vous en prie.

POZZO. Non non, ce n'est pas la peine. (*Un temps. A voix basse.*) * Insistez un peu.

ESTRAGON. Mais voyons, ne restez pas debout comme ça, vous allez attraper froid.

POZZO. Vous croyez ?

ESTRAGON. Mais c'est absolument certain. *

POZZO. Vous avez sans doute raison. (*Il se rassied.*) Merci, mon cher. Me voilà réinstallé. (*Il regarde sa montre.*) Mais il est temps que je vous quitte, si je ne veux pas me mettre en retard.

VLADIMIR. Le temps s'est arrêté.

POZZO (*mettant sa montre contre son oreille*). Ne croyez pas ça. Monsieur, ne croyez pas ça. (*Il remet la montre dans sa poche.*) Tout ce que vous voulez, mais pas ça.

ESTRAGON (*à Pozzo*). Il voit tout en noir aujourd'hui.

POZZO. Sauf le firmament. (*Il rit, content de ce bon mot.*) Patience, ça va venir. Mais je vois ce que c'est, vous n'êtes pas d'ici, vous ne savez pas encore ce que c'est que le crépuscule chez nous. Voulez-vous que je vous le dise ? (*Silence. Estragon et Vladimir se sont remis à examiner, celui-là sa chaussure, celui-ci son chapeau. Le chapeau de Lucky tombe, sans qu'il s'en aperçoive.*) Je veux bien vous satisfaire. (*Jeu du vaporisateur.*) Un peu d'attention, s'il vous plaît. (*Estragon et Vladimir continuent leur manège, Lucky dort à moitié. Pozzo fait claquer son fouet qui ne rend qu'un bruit très faible.*) Qu'est-ce qu'il a, ce fouet. (*Il se lève et le fait claquer plus vigoureusement, finalement avec succès. Lucky sursaute. La chaussure d'Estragon, le chapeau de Vladimir, leur tombent des mains. Pozzo jette le fouet.*) Il ne vaut plus rien, ce fouet. (*Il regarde son auditoire.*) Qu'est-ce que je disais ?

VLADIMIR. Partons.

ESTRAGON. Mais ne restez pas debout comme ça, vous allez attraper la crève.

POZZO. C'est vrai. (*Il se rassied. A Estragon.*) Comment vous appelez-vous ?

ESTRAGON (*du tic au tac*). Catulle.*

POZZO (*qui n'a pas écouté*). Ah oui, la nuit. (*Lève la tête.*) Mais soyez donc un peu plus attentifs, sinon nous n'arriverons jamais à rien. (*Regarde le ciel.*) Regardez. (*Tous regardent le ciel, sauf Lucky qui s'est remis à somnoler. Pozzo, s'en apercevant, tire sur la corde.*) Veux-tu regarder le ciel, porc !* (*Lucky renverse la tête.*) Bon, ça suffit. (*Ils baissent la tête.*) Qu'est-ce qu'il a de si extraordinaire ? En tant que ciel ? Il est pâle et lumineux, comme n'importe quel ciel à cette heure de la journée. (*Un temps.*) Dans ces latitudes. (*Un temps.*) Quand il fait beau. (*Sa voix se fait chantante.*) Il y a une heure (*il regarde sa montre, ton prosaïque*) environ (*ton à nouveau lyrique*), après nous avoir versé depuis (*il hésite, le ton baisse*) mettons dix heures du matin (*le ton s'élève*) sans faiblir des torrents de lumière rouge et blanche, il s'est mis à perdre de son éclat, à pâlir (*geste des deux mains qui descendent par paliers*), à pâlir, toujours un peu plus, un peu plus, jusqu'à ce que (*pause dramatique, large geste horizontal des deux mains qui s'écartent*) vlan ! fini ! il ne bouge plus ! (*Silence.*) Mais (*il lève une main admonitrice*) — mais, derrière ce voile de douceur et de calme (*il lève les yeux au ciel, les autres l'imitent, sauf Lucky*) la nuit galope (*la voix se fait plus vibrante*) et viendra se jeter sur nous (*il fait claquer ses doigts*) pfft ! comme ça (*l'inspiration le quitte*) au moment où nous nous y attendrons le moins.* (*Silence. Voix morne.*) C'est comme ça que ça se passe sur cette putain de terre.

Long silence.

ESTRAGON. Du moment qu'on est prévenu.

VLADIMIR. On peut patienter.

ESTRAGON. On sait à quoi s'en tenir.

VLADIMIR. Plus d'inquiétude à avoir.

ESTRAGON. Il n'y a qu'à attendre.

VLADIMIR. Nous en avons l'habitude. (*Il ramasse son chapeau, regarde dedans, le secoue, le remet.*)

POZZO. Comment m'avez-vous trouvé ? (*Estragon et Vladimir le regardent sans comprendre.*) Bon ? Moyen ? Passable ? Quelconque ? Franchement mauvais ?

VLADIMIR (*comprenant le premier*). Oh très bien, tout à fait bien.

POZZO (*à Estragon*). Et vous, monsieur ?

ESTRAGON (*accent anglais*). Oh très bon, très très très bon. *

POZZO (*avec élan*). Merci, messieurs ! (*Un temps.*) J'ai tant besoin d'encouragement. (*Il réfléchit.*) J'ai un peu faibli sur la fin. Vous n'avez pas remarqué ?

VLADIMIR. Oh, peut-être un tout petit peu.

ESTRAGON. J'ai cru que c'était exprès. *

POZZO. C'est que ma mémoire est défectueuse.

Silence.

ESTRAGON. En attendant, * il ne se passe rien.

POZZO (*désolé*). Vous vous ennuyez ?

ESTRAGON. Plutôt.

POZZO (*à Vladimir*). Et vous, monsieur ?

VLADIMIR. Ce n'est pas folichon. *

Silence. Pozzo se livre une bataille intérieure.

POZZO. Messieurs, vous avez été... (*il cherche*) ...convenables avec moi.

ESTRAGON. Mais non !

VLADIMIR. Quelle idée !

POZZO. Mais si, mais si, vous avez été corrects. De sorte que je me demande... Que puis-je faire à mon tour pour ces braves gens qui sont en train de s'ennuyer ?

ESTRAGON. Même un louis * serait le bienvenu.

VLADIMIR. Nous ne sommes pas des mendiants.

POZZO. Que puis-je faire, voilà ce que je me dis, pour que le temps leur semble moins long ? Je leur ai donné des os, je leur ai parlé de choses et d'autres, je leur ai expliqué le crépuscule, c'est une affaire entendue. Et j'en passe. Mais est-ce suffisant, voilà ce qui me torture, est-ce suffisant ?

ESTRAGON. Même cent sous. *

VLADIMIR. Tais-toi !

ESTRAGON. J'en prends le chemin.*

POZZO. Est-ce suffisant? Sans doute. Mais je suis large. C'est ma nature. Aujourd'hui. Tant pis pour moi. (*Il tire sur la corde. Lucky le regarde.*) Car je vais souffrir, cela est certain. (*Sans se lever, il se penche et reprend son fouet.*) Que préférez-vous? Qu'il danse, qu'il chante, qu'il récite, qu'il pense, qu'il...

ESTRAGON. Qui?

POZZO. Qui! Vous savez penser, vous autres?*

VLADIMIR. Il pense?

POZZO. Parfaitement. A haute voix. Il pensait même très joliment autrefois, je pouvais l'écouter pendant des heures. Maintenant... (*Il frissonne.*) Enfin, tant pis. Alors, vous voulez qu'il nous pense quelque chose?

ESTRAGON. J'aimerais mieux qu'il danse, ce serait plus gai.

POZZO. Pas forcément.

ESTRAGON. N'est-ce pas, Didi, que ce serait plus gai?

VLADIMIR. J'aimerais bien l'entendre penser.

ESTRAGON. Il pourrait peut-être danser d'abord et penser ensuite? Si ce n'est pas trop lui demander.

VLADIMIR (*à Pozzo*). Est-ce possible?

POZZO. Mais certainement, rien de plus facile. C'est d'ailleurs l'ordre naturel. (*Rire bref.*)

VLADIMIR. Alors qu'il danse.

Silence.

POZZO (*à Lucky*). Tu entends?

ESTRAGON. Il ne refuse jamais?

POZZO. Je vous expliquerai ça tout à l'heure. (*A Lucky.*) Danse, pouacre!*

Lucky dépose valise et panier, avance un peu vers la rampe, se tourne vers Pozzo. Estragon se lève pour mieux voir. Lucky danse. Il s'arrête.

ESTRAGON. C'est tout?

POZZO. Encore!

Lucky répète les mêmes mouvements, s'arrête.

ESTRAGON. Eh ben, mon cochon! (*Il imite les mouvements de Lucky.*) J'en ferais autant. (*Il imite, manque de tomber.*) Avec un peu d'entraînement.

VLADIMIR. Il est fatigué.

POZZO. Autrefois, il dansait la farandole, l'almée, le branle, la gigue, le fandango et même le hornpipe. Il bondissait. Maintenant il ne fait plus que ça. Savez-vous comment il l'appelle ?

ESTRAGON. La mort du lampiste.

VLADIMIR. Le cancer des vieillards.*

POZZO. La danse du filet. Il se croit empêtré dans un filet.

VLADIMIR (*avec des tortillements d'esthète*). Il y a quelque chose...

Lucky s'apprête à retourner vers ses fardeaux.

POZZO (*comme à un cheval*). Woooa !*

Lucky s'immobilise.

ESTRAGON. Il ne refuse jamais ?

POZZO. Je vais vous expliquer ça. (*Il fouille dans ses poches.*) Attendez. (*Il fouille.*) Qu'est-ce que j'ai fait de ma poire ? (*Il fouille.*) Ça alors ! (*Il lève une tête ahurie. D'une voix mourante.*) J'ai perdu mon pulvérisateur !

ESTRAGON (*d'une voix mourante*). Mon poumon gauche est très faible. (*Il tousse faiblement. D'une voix tonitruante.*) Mais mon poumon droit est en parfait état !

POZZO (*voix normale*). Tant pis, je m'en passerai. Qu'est-ce que je disais. (*Il réfléchit.*) Attendez ! (*Réfléchit.*) Ça alors ! (*Il lève la tête.*) Aidez-moi !

ESTRAGON. Je cherche.

VLADIMIR. Moi aussi.

POZZO. Attendez !

Tous les trois se découvrent simultanément, portent la main au front, se concentrent, crispés. Long silence.

ESTRAGON (*triomphant*). Ah !

VLADIMIR. Il a trouvé.

POZZO (*impatient*). Et alors ?

ESTRAGON. Pourquoi ne dépose-t-il pas ses bagages ?

VLADIMIR. Mais non !

POZZO. Vous êtes sûr ?

VLADIMIR. Mais voyons, vous nous l'avez déjà dit.

POZZO. Je vous l'ai déjà dit ?

ESTRAGON. Il nous l'a déjà dit?

VLADIMIR. D'ailleurs il les a déposés.

ESTRAGON (*coup d'œil vers Lucky*). C'est vrai. Et après?

VLADIMIR. Puisqu'il a déposé ses bagages, il est impossible que nous ayons demandé pourquoi il ne les dépose pas.

POZZO. Fortement raisonné!

ESTRAGON. Et pourquoi les a-t-il déposés?

POZZO. Voilà.

VLADIMIR. Afin de danser.

ESTRAGON. C'est vrai.*

POZZO (*levant la main*). Attendez! (*Un temps.*) Ne dites rien! (*Un temps.*) Ça y est. (*Il remet son chapeau.*) J'y suis.

Estragon et Vladimir remettent leurs chapeaux.

VLADIMIR. Il a trouvé.

POZZO. Voici comment ça se passe.

ESTRAGON. De quoi s'agit-il?

POZZO. Vous allez voir. Mais c'est difficile à dire.

VLADIMIR. Ne le dites pas.

POZZO. Oh! n'ayez pas peur, j'y arriverai. Mais je veux être bref, car il se fait tard. Et le moyen d'être bref et en même temps clair, je vous le demande. Laissez-moi réfléchir.

ESTRAGON. Soyez long, ce sera moins long.

POZZO (*ayant réfléchi*). Ça va aller. Voyez-vous, de deux choses l'une.

ESTRAGON. C'est le délire.

POZZO. Ou je lui demande quelque chose, de danser, chanter, penser...

VLADIMIR. Ça va, ça va, nous avons compris.

POZZO. Ou je ne lui demande rien. Bon. Ne m'interrompez pas. Mettons que je lui demande de... danser, par exemple. Qu'est-ce qui se produit?

ESTRAGON. Il se met à siffler.

POZZO (*fâché*). Je ne dirai plus rien.

VLADIMIR. Je vous en prie, continuez.

POZZO. Vous m'interrompez tout le temps.

VLADIMIR. Continuez, continuez, c'est passionnant.

POZZO. Insistez un peu.

ESTRAGON (*joignant les mains*). Je vous en supplie, Monsieur, poursuivez votre relation.

POZZO. Où en étais-je ?

VLADIMIR. Vous lui demandez de danser.

ESTRAGON. De chanter.

POZZO. C'est ça, je lui demande de chanter. Qu'est-ce qui se passe ? Ou bien il chante, comme je le lui avais demandé ; ou bien, au lieu de chanter, comme je le lui avais demandé, il se met à danser, par exemple, ou à penser, ou à...

VLADIMIR. C'est clair, c'est clair, enchaînez.

ESTRAGON. Assez !

VLADIMIR. Pourtant ce soir, il fait tout ce que vous lui demandez.

POZZO. C'est pour m'attendrir, pour que je le garde.

ESTRAGON. Tout ça c'est des histoires.

VLADIMIR. Ce n'est pas sûr.

ESTRAGON. Tout à l'heure il va nous dire qu'il n'y avait pas un mot de vrai là-dedans.

VLADIMIR (*à Pozzo*). Vous ne protestez pas ?

POZZO. Je suis fatigué.

Silence.

ESTRAGON. Rien ne se passe, personne ne vient, personne ne s'en va, c'est terrible.

VLADIMIR (*à Pozzo*). Dites-lui de penser.

POZZO. Donnez-lui son chapeau.

VLADIMIR. Son chapeau ?

POZZO. Il ne peut pas penser sans chapeau.

VLADIMIR (à *Estragon*). Donne-lui son chapeau.

ESTRAGON. Moi ! Après le coup qu'il m'a fait ! Jamais !

VLADIMIR. Je vais le lui donner moi. (*Il ne bouge pas.*)

ESTRAGON. Qu'il aille le chercher.

POZZO. Il vaut mieux le lui donner.

VLADIMIR. Je vais le lui donner.

Il ramasse le chapeau et le tend à Lucky à bout de bras. Lucky ne bouge pas.

POZZO. Il faut le lui mettre.

ESTRAGON (*à Pozzo*). Dites-lui de le prendre.

POZZO. Il vaut mieux le lui mettre.

VLADIMIR. Je vais le lui mettre.

Il contourne Lucky avec précaution, s'en approche doucement par derrière, lui met le chapeau sur la tête et recule vivement. Lucky ne bouge pas. Silence.

ESTRAGON. Qu'est-ce qu'il attend ?

POZZO. Éloignez-vous. (*Estragon et Vladimir s'éloignent de Lucky. Pozzo tire sur la corde. Lucky le regarde.*) Pense, porc ! (*Un temps. Lucky se met à danser.*) Arrête ! (*Lucky s'arrête.*) Avance ! (*Lucky va vers Pozzo.*) Là ! (*Lucky s'arrête.*) Pense ! (*Un temps.*)

LUCKY. D'autre part, pour ce qui est...

POZZO. Arrête! (*Lucky se tait.*) Arrière! (*Lucky recule.*) Là! (*Lucky s'arrête.*) Hue ! (*Lucky se tourne vers le public.*) Pense !

LUCKY (*débit monotone*).* Étant donné l'existence telle qu'elle jaillit* des récents travaux publics de Poinçon et Wattmann d'un Dieu personnel quaquaquaqua à barbe blanche quaqua* hors du temps de l'étendue qui du haut de sa divine apathie sa divine athambie sa divine aphasie nous aime bien à quelques exceptions près on ne sait pourquoi mais ça viendra et souffre à l'instar de la divine Miranda* avec ceux qui sont on ne sait pourquoi mais on a le temps dans le tourment dans les feux dont les feux les flammes pour peu que ça dure encore un peu et qui peut en douter mettront à la fin le feu aux poutres assavoir porteront l'enfer aux nues si bleues par moments encore aujourd'hui et calmes si calmes d'un calme qui pour être intermittent n'en est pas moins le bienvenu mais n'anticipons pas et attendu d'autre part qu'à la suite des recherches inachevées n'anticipons pas des recherches inachevées mais néanmoins couronnées par l'Acacacacadémie d'Anthropopopométrie de Berne en Bresse de Testu et Conard il est établi sans autre possibilité d'erreur que celle afférente aux calculs humains qu'à la suite des recherches inachevées inachevées de Testu et Conard il est établi tabli tabli ce qui suit qui suit qui suit assavoir mais n'anticipons pas on ne sait pourquoi à la suite des travaux de Poinçon et Wattmann il apparaît aussi clairement si clairement qu'en vue des labeurs de Fartov et Belcher inachevés inachevés on ne sait pourquoi de Testu et Conard inachevés inachevés il apparaît que l'homme contrairement à l'opinion contraire que l'homme en Bresse de Testu et Conard que l'homme enfin bref que l'homme en bref enfin malgré les progrès de l'alimentation et de l'élimination des déchets est en train de maigrir et en même temps parallèlement on ne sait pourquoi malgré l'essor de la culture physique de la pratique des sports tels tels tels le tennis le football la course et à pied et à bicyclette la natation l'équitation l'aviation la conation le tennis le camogie* le patinage et sur glace et sur asphalte le tennis l'aviation les sports les sports d'hiver d'été d'automne d'automne le tennis sur gazon sur sapin et sur terre battue l'aviation le tennis le hockey sur terre sur mer et dans les airs la pénicilline et succédanés bref je reprends en même temps parallèlement de rapetisser on ne sait pourquoi malgré le tennis je reprends l'aviation le golf tant à neuf qu'à dix-huit trous le tennis sur glace bref on ne sait pourquoi en Seine Seine-et-Oise Seine-et-Marne Marne-et-Oise assavoir en même temps parallèlement on ne sait pourquoi de maigrir rétrécir je reprends Oise Marne bref la perte sèche par tête de pipe depuis la mort de Voltaire étant de l'ordre de deux doigts cent grammes par tête de pipe environ en moyenne à peu près chiffres ronds bon poids déshabillé en Normandie on ne sait pourquoi bref enfin peu importe les faits sont là et considérant d'autre part ce qui est encore plus grave qu'il ressort ce qui est encore plus grave qu'à la lumière la lumière des expériences en cours de Steinweg et Petermann il ressort ce qui est encore plus grave qu'il ressort ce qui est encore plus grave à la lumière la lumière des expériences abandonnées de Steinweg et Petermann qu'à la campagne à la montagne et au bord de la mer et des cours et d'eau et de feu l'air est le même et la terre assavoir l'air et la terre par les grands froids l'air et la terre faits pour les pierres

Premiers murmures d'Estragon et Vladimir. Souffrances accrues de Pozzo.

Estragon et Vladimir se calment, reprennent l'écoute. Pozzo s'agite de plus en plus, fait entendre des gémissements.

Exclamations de Vladimir et Estragon. Pozzo se lève d'un bond, tire sur la corde. Tous crient. Lucky tire sur la corde, trébuche, hurle. Tous se jettent sur Lucky qui se débat, hurle son texte.

par les grands froids hélas au septième de leur ère l'éther la terre la mer pour les pierres par les grands fonds les grands froids sur mer sur terre et dans les airs peuchère je reprends on ne sait pourquoi malgré le tennis les faits sont là on ne sait pourquoi je reprends au suivant bref enfin hélas au suivant pour les pierres qui peut en douter je reprends mais n'anticipons pas je reprends la tête en même temps parallèlement on ne sait pourquoi malgré le tennis au suivant la barbe les flammes les pleurs les pierres si bleues si calmes hélas la tête la tête la tête la tête en Normandie malgré le tennis les labeurs abandonnés inachevés plus grave les pierres bref je reprends hélas hélas abandonnés inachevés la tête la tête en Normandie malgré le tennis la tête hélas les pierres Conard Conard... (*Mêlée. Lucky pousse encore quelques vociférations.*) Tennis !... Les pierres !... Si calmes !... Conard !... Inachevés !...

POZZO. Son chapeau !

Vladimir s'empare du chapeau de Lucky qui se tait et tombe. Grand silence. Halètement des vainqueurs.

ESTRAGON. Je suis vengé.

Vladimir contemple le chapeau de Lucky, regarde dedans.

POZZO. Donnez-moi ça ! (*Il arrache le chapeau des mains de Vladimir, le jette par terre, saute dessus.*) Comme ça il ne pensera plus !

VLADIMIR. Mais va-t-il pouvoir s'orienter ?

POZZO. C'est moi qui l'orienterai. (*Il donne des coups de pied à Lucky.*) Debout ! Porc !

ESTRAGON. Il est peut-être mort.

VLADIMIR. Vous allez le tuer.

POZZO. Debout ! Charogne ! (*Il tire sur la corde, Lucky glisse un peu. A Estragon et Vladimir.*) Aidez-moi.

VLADIMIR. Mais comment faire ?

POZZO. Soulevez-le !

Estragon et Vladimir mettent Lucky debout, le soutiennent un moment, puis le lâchent. Il retombe.

ESTRAGON. Il fait exprès.

POZZO. Il faut le soutenir. (*Un temps.*) Allez, allez, soulevez-le !

ESTRAGON. Moi j'en ai marre.

VLADIMIR. Allons, essayons encore une fois.

ESTRAGON. Pour qui nous prend-il ?

VLADIMIR. Allons.

Ils mettent Lucky debout, le soutiennent.

POZZO. Ne le lâchez pas ! (*Estragon et Vladimir chancellent.*) Ne bougez pas ! (*Pozzo va prendre la valise et le panier et les apporte vers Lucky.*) Tenez-le bien ! (*Il met la valise dans la main de Lucky qui la lâche aussitôt.*) Ne le lâchez pas ! (*Il recommence. Peu à peu, au contact de la valise, Lucky reprend ses esprits et ses doigts finissent par se resserrer autour de la poignée.*) Tenez-le toujours ! (*Même jeu avec le panier.*) Voilà, vous pouvez le lâcher. (*Estragon et Vladimir s'écartent de Lucky qui trébuche, chancelle, ploie, mais reste debout, valise et panier à la main. Pozzo recule, fait claquer son fouet.*) En avant ! (*Lucky avance.*) Arrière ! (*Lucky recule.*) Tourne ! (*Lucky se retourne.*) Ça y est, il peut marcher. (*Se tournant vers Estragon et Vladimir.*) Merci, Messieurs, et laissez-moi vous — (*il fouille dans ses poches*) — vous souhaiter — (*il fouille*) — vous souhaiter — (*il fouille*) — mais où ai-je donc mis ma montre ? (*Il fouille.*) Ça alors ! (*Il lève une tête défaite.*) Une véritable savonnette, Messieurs, à secondes trotteuses.* C'est mon pépé qui me l'a donnée.* (*Il fouille.*) Elle est peut-être tombée. (*Il cherche par terre, ainsi que Vladimir et Estragon. Pozzo retourne de son pied les restes du chapeau de Lucky.*) Ça par exemple !

VLADIMIR. Elle est peut-être dans votre gousset.

POZZO. Attendez. (*Il se plie en deux, approche sa tête de son ventre, écoute.*) Je n'entends rien ! (*Il leur fait signe de s'approcher.*) Venez voir. (*Estragon et Vladimir vont vers lui, se penchent sur son ventre. Silence.*) Il me semble qu'on devrait entendre le tic-tac.

VLADIMIR. Silence !

Tous écoutent, penchés.

ESTRAGON. J'entends quelque chose.

POZZO. Où ?

VLADIMIR. C'est le cœur.

POZZO (*déçu*). Merde alors !

3. "Je me présente: Pozzo." *Act 1, p. 16.*

Criterion Theatre, 1955.

4. Pozzo ôte son chapeau.''
Act 1, p. 27.

Criterion Theatre, 1955.

5. "... l'humanité c'est nous, que ça nous plaise ou non!"
Act 2, p. 71.

Criterion Theatre, 1955.

6. "Voilà l'homme tout entier, s'en prenant à sa chaussure alors que c'est son pied le coupable." *Act 1, p. 5.*

Royal Court Theatre, 1965.

VLADIMIR. Silence !

Ils écoutent.

ESTRAGON. Peut-être qu'elle s'est arrêtée.

Ils se redressent.

POZZO. Lequel de vous sent si mauvais ?

ESTRAGON. Lui pue de la bouche, moi des pieds.

POZZO. Je vais vous quitter.

ESTRAGON. Et votre savonnette ?

POZZO. J'ai dû la laisser au château.

ESTRAGON. Alors adieu.

POZZO. Adieu.

VLADIMIR. Adieu.

ESTRAGON. Adieu.

Silence. Personne ne bouge.

VLADIMIR. Adieu.

POZZO. Adieu.

ESTRAGON. Adieu.

Silence.

POZZO. Et merci.

VLADIMIR. Merci à vous.

POZZO. De rien.

ESTRAGON. Mais si.

POZZO. Mais non.

VLADIMIR. Mais si.

ESTRAGON. Mais non.

Silence.

POZZO. Je n'arrive pas... (*il hésite*) ...à partir.

ESTRAGON. C'est la vie.

Pozzo se retourne, s'éloigne de Lucky, vers la coulisse, filant la corde au fur et à mesure.

VLADIMIR. Vous allez dans le mauvais sens.

POZZO. Il me faut de l'élan. (*Arrivé au bout de la corde, c'est-à-dire dans la coulisse, il s'arrête, se retourne, crie.*) Écartez-vous ! (*Estragon et Vladimir se rangent au fond, regardent vers Pozzo. Bruit de fouet.*) En avant ! (*Lucky ne bouge pas.*)

ESTRAGON. En avant !

VLADIMIR. En avant !

Bruit de fouet. Lucky s'ébranle.

POZZO. Plus vite ! (*Il sort de la coulisse, traverse la scène à la suite de Lucky. Estragon et Vladimir se découvrent, agitent la main. Lucky sort. Pozzo fait claquer corde et fouet.*) Plus vite ! Plus vite ! (*Au moment de disparaître à son tour, Pozzo s'arrête, se retourne. La corde se tend. Bruit de Lucky qui tombe.*) Mon pliant ! (*Vladimir va chercher le pliant et le donne à Pozzo qui le jette vers Lucky.*) Adieu !

ESTRAGON, VLADIMIR (*agitant la main*). Adieu ! Adieu !

POZZO. Debout ! Porc ! (*Bruit de Lucky qui se lève.*) En avant ! (*Pozzo sort. Bruit de fouet.*) En avant ! Adieu ! Plus vite ! Porc ! Hue ! Adieu !

Silence.

VLADIMIR. Ça a fait passer le temps.

ESTRAGON. Il serait passé sans ça.

VLADIMIR. Oui. Mais moins vite.

Un temps.

ESTRAGON. Qu'est-ce qu'on fait maintenant ?

VLADIMIR. Je ne sais pas.

ESTRAGON. Allons-nous-en.

VLADIMIR. On ne peut pas.

ESTRAGON. Pourquoi ?

VLADIMIR. On attend Godot.

ESTRAGON. C'est vrai.

Un temps.

VLADIMIR. Ils ont beaucoup changé.

ESTRAGON. Qui ?

VLADIMIR. Ces deux-là.

ESTRAGON. C'est ça, faisons un peu de conversation.

VLADIMIR. N'est-ce pas qu'ils ont beaucoup changé ?

ESTRAGON. C'est probable. Il n'y a que nous qui n'y arrivons pas.

VLADIMIR. Probable ? C'est certain. Tu les as bien vus ?

ESTRAGON. Si tu veux. Mais je ne les connais pas.

VLADIMIR. Mais si, tu les connais.

ESTRAGON. Mais non.

VLADIMIR. Nous les connaissons, je te dis. Tu oublies tout. (*Un temps.*) A moins que ce ne soient pas les mêmes.

ESTRAGON. La preuve, ils ne nous ont pas reconnus.

VLADIMIR. Ça ne veut rien dire. Moi aussi j'ai fait semblant de ne pas les reconnaître. Et puis nous, on ne nous reconnaît jamais.

ESTRAGON. Assez. Ce qu'il faut — Aïe ! (*Vladimir ne bronche pas.*) Aïe !

VLADIMIR. A moins que ce ne soient pas les mêmes.

ESTRAGON. Didi ! C'est l'autre pied ! (*Il se dirige en boitillant vers l'endroit où il était assis au lever du rideau.*)

VOIX EN COULISSE. Monsieur !

Estragon s'arrête. Tous les deux regardent en direction de la voix.

ESTRAGON. Ça recommence.

VLADIMIR. Approche, mon enfant.

Entre un jeune garçon, craintivement. * *Il s'arrête.*

GARÇON. Monsieur Albert ?

VLADIMIR. C'est moi.

ESTRAGON. Qu'est-ce que tu veux ?

VLADIMIR. Avance.

Le garçon ne bouge pas.

ESTRAGON (*avec force*). Avance, on te dit !

Le garçon avance craintivement, s'arrête.

VLADIMIR. Qu'est-ce que c'est ?

GARÇON. C'est Monsieur Godot — (*Il se tait.*)

VLADIMIR. Évidemment. (*Un temps.*) Approche.

Le garçon ne bouge pas.

ESTRAGON (*avec force*). Approche, on te dit ! (*Le garçon avance craintivement, s'arrête.*) Pourquoi tu viens si tard ?

VLADIMIR. Tu as un message de Monsieur Godot ?

GARÇON. Oui Monsieur.

VLADIMIR. Eh bien, dis-le.

ESTRAGON. Pourquoi tu viens si tard ?

Le garçon les regarde l'un après l'autre, ne sachant à qui répondre.

VLADIMIR (*à Estragon*). Laisse-le tranquille.

ESTRAGON (*à Vladimir*). Fous-moi la paix toi. (*Avançant, au garçon.*) Tu sais l'heure qu'il est ?

GARÇON (*reculant*). Ce n'est pas ma faute, Monsieur !

ESTRAGON. C'est la mienne peut-être. *

GARÇON. J'avais peur, Monsieur.

ESTRAGON. Peur de quoi ? De nous ?* (*Un temps.*) Réponds !

VLADIMIR. Je vois ce que c'est, ce sont les autres qui lui ont fait peur.

ESTRAGON. Il y a combien de temps que tu es là ?

GARÇON. Il y a un moment, Monsieur.

VLADIMIR. Tu as eu peur du fouet ?

GARÇON. Oui Monsieur.

VLADIMIR. Des cris ?

GARÇON. Oui Monsieur.

VLADIMIR. Des deux messieurs ?*

GARÇON. Oui Monsieur.

VLADIMIR. Tu les connais ?

GARÇON. Non Monsieur.

VLADIMIR. Tu es d'ici ?

GARÇON. Oui Monsieur.

ESTRAGON. Tout ça c'est des mensonges ! (*Il prend le garçon par le bras, le secoue.*) Dis-nous la vérité !

GARÇON (*tremblant*). Mais c'est la vérité, Monsieur.

VLADIMIR. Mais laisse-le donc tranquille ! Qu'est-ce que tu as ? (*Estragon lâche le garçon, recule, porte ses mains au visage. Vladimir et le garçon le regardent. Estragon découvre son visage, décomposé.*) Qu'est-ce que tu as ?

ESTRAGON. Je suis malheureux.

VLADIMIR. Sans blague ! Depuis quand ?

ESTRAGON. J'avais oublié.

VLADIMIR. La mémoire nous joue de ces tours. (*Estragon veut *parler, y renonce, va en boitillant s'asseoir et commence à se déchausser. Au garçon.*) Eh bien ?

GARÇON. Monsieur Godot...

VLADIMIR (*l'interrompant*). Je t'ai déjà vu, n'est-ce pas ?

GARÇON. Je ne sais pas, Monsieur.

VLADIMIR. Tu ne me connais pas ?

GARÇON. Non Monsieur.

VLADIMIR. Tu n'es pas venu hier ?

GARÇON. Non Monsieur.

VLADIMIR. C'est la première fois que tu viens ?

GARÇON. Oui Monsieur.

Silence.

VLADIMIR. On dit ça. (*Un temps.*) Eh bien, continue.

GARÇON (*d'un trait*). Monsieur Godot m'a dit de vous dire qu'il ne viendra pas ce soir mais sûrement demain.

VLADIMIR. C'est tout ?

GARÇON. Oui Monsieur.

VLADIMIR. Tu travailles pour Monsieur Godot ?

GARÇON. Oui Monsieur.

VLADIMIR. Qu'est-ce que tu fais ?

GARÇON. Je garde les chèvres, Monsieur.

VLADIMIR. Il est gentil avec toi ?

GARÇON. Oui Monsieur.

VLADIMIR. Il ne te bat pas ?

GARÇON. Non Monsieur, pas moi.

VLADIMIR. Qui est-ce qu'il bat ?

GARÇON. Il bat mon frère, Monsieur.

VLADIMIR. Ah ! tu as un frère ?

GARÇON. Oui Monsieur.

VLADIMIR. Qu'est-ce qu'il fait ?

GARÇON. Il garde les brebis, Monsieur.

VLADIMIR. Et pourquoi il ne te bat pas, toi ?

GARÇON. Je ne sais pas, Monsieur.

VLADIMIR. Il doit t'aimer.

GARÇON. Je ne sais pas, Monsieur.

VLADIMIR. Il te donne assez à manger? (*Le garçon hésite.*) Est-ce qu'il te donne bien à manger?

GARÇON. Assez bien, Monsieur.

VLADIMIR. Tu n'es pas malheureux? (*Le garçon hésite.*) Tu entends?

GARÇON. Oui Monsieur.

VLADIMIR. Et alors?

GARÇON. Je ne sais pas, Monsieur.

VLADIMIR. Tu ne sais pas si tu es malheureux ou non?

GARÇON. Non Monsieur.

VLADIMIR. C'est comme moi. (*Un temps.*) Où c'est que tu couches?

GARÇON. Dans le grenier, Monsieur.

VLADIMIR. Avec ton frère?

GARÇON. Oui Monsieur.

VLADIMIR. Dans le foin?

GARÇON. Oui Monsieur.

Un temps.

VLADIMIR. Bon, va-t-en.

GARÇON. Qu'est-ce que je dois dire à Monsieur Godot, Monsieur?

VLADIMIR. Dis-lui... (*Il hésite.*) Dis-lui que tu nous as vus. (*Un temps.*) Tu nous a bien vus, n'est-ce pas?

GARÇON. Oui Monsieur. (*Il recule, hésite, se retourne et sort en courant.*)

La lumière se met brusquement à baisser. En un instant il fait nuit. La lune se lève, au fond, monte dans le ciel, s'immobilise, baignant la scène d'une clarté argentée.

VLADIMIR. Enfin! (*Estragon se lève et va vers Vladimir, ses deux chaussures à la main. Il les dépose près de la rampe, se redresse et regarde la lune.*) Qu'est-ce que tu fais?

ESTRAGON. Je fais comme toi, je regarde la blafarde.*

VLADIMIR. Je veux dire avec tes chaussures.

ESTRAGON. Je les laisse là. (*Un temps.*) Un autre viendra, aussi... aussi... que moi, mais chaussant moins grand, et elles feront son bonheur.

VLADIMIR. Mais tu ne peux pas aller pieds nus.

ESTRAGON. Jésus l'a fait.

VLADIMIR. Jésus ! Qu'est-ce que tu vas chercher là ! Tu ne vas tout de même pas te comparer à lui !

ESTRAGON. Toute ma vie je me suis comparé à lui.

VLADIMIR. Mais là-bas il faisait chaud ! Il faisait bon !

ESTRAGON. Oui. Et on crucifiait vite.

Silence.

VLADIMIR. Nous n'avons plus rien à faire ici.

ESTRAGON. Ni ailleurs.

VLADIMIR. Voyons, Gogo, ne sois pas comme ça. Demain tout ira mieux.

ESTRAGON. Comment ça ?

VLADIMIR. Tu n'as pas entendu ce que le gosse a dit ?

ESTRAGON. Non.

VLADIMIR. Il a dit que Godot viendra sûrement demain. (*Un temps.*) Ça ne te dit rien ?

ESTRAGON. Alors il n'y a qu'à attendre ici.

VLADIMIR. Tu es fou ! Il faut s'abriter.* (*Il prend Estragon par le bras.*) Viens. (*Il le tire. Estragon cède d'abord, puis résiste. Ils s'arrêtent.*)

ESTRAGON (*regardant l'arbre*). Dommage qu'on n'ait pas un bout de corde.

VLADIMIR. Viens. Il commence à faire froid. (*Il le tire. Même jeu.*)

ESTRAGON. Fais-moi penser d'apporter une corde demain.

VLADIMIR. Oui. Viens. (*Il le tire. Même jeu.*)

ESTRAGON. Ça fait combien de temps que nous sommes tout le temps ensemble ?

VLADIMIR. Je ne sais pas. Cinquante ans peut-être.*

ESTRAGON. Tu te rappelles le jour où je me suis jeté dans la Durance ?

VLADIMIR. On faisait les vendanges.

ESTRAGON. Tu m'as repêché.

VLADIMIR. Tout ça est mort et enterré.

ESTRAGON. Mes vêtements ont séché au soleil.

VLADIMIR. N'y pense plus, va. Viens. (*Même jeu.*)

ESTRAGON. Attends.

VLADIMIR. J'ai froid.

ESTRAGON. Je me demande si on n'aurait pas mieux fait de rester seuls, chacun de son côté. (*Un temps.*) On n'était pas fait pour le même chemin.

VLADIMIR (*sans se fâcher*). Ce n'est pas sûr.

ESTRAGON. Non, rien n'est sûr.

VLADIMIR. On peut toujours se quitter, si tu crois que ça vaut mieux.

ESTRAGON. Maintenant ce n'est plus la peine.

Silence.

VLADIMIR. C'est vrai, maintenant ce n'est plus la peine.

Silence.

ESTRAGON. Alors on y va ?

VLADIMIR. Allons-y.

Ils ne bougent pas.

RIDEAU

ACTE DEUXIÈME

Lendemain. Même heure. Même endroit.

Chaussures d'Estragon près de la rampe, talons joints, bouts écartés. Chapeau de Lucky à la même place.

*L'arbre est couvert de feuilles.**

Entre Vladimir, vivement. Il s'arrête et regarde longuement l'arbre. Puis brusquement il se met à arpenter vivement la scène dans tous les sens. Il s'immobilise à nouveau devant les chaussures, se baisse, en ramasse une, l'examine, la renifle, la remet soigneusement à sa place. Il reprend son va-et-vient précipité. Il s'arrête près de la coulisse droite, regarde longuement au loin, la main en écran devant les yeux. Va et vient. S'arrête près de la coulisse gauche, même jeu.

Va et vient. S'arrête brusquement, joint les mains sur la poitrine, rejette la tête en arrière et se met à chanter à tue-tête.

VLADIMIR :

Un chien vint dans...

Ayant commencé trop bas, il s'arrête, tousse, reprend plus haut :*

Un chien vint dans l'office
Et prit une andouillette.
Alors à coups de louche
Le chef le mit en miettes.

Les autres chiens ce voyant
Vite vite l'ensevelirent...

Il s'arrête, se recueille, puis reprend :

Les autres chiens ce voyant
Vite vite l'ensevelirent
Au pied d'une croix en bois blanc
Où le passant pouvait lire :
Un chien vint dans l'office
Et prit une andouillette.
Alors à coups de louche
Le chef le mit en miettes.

Les autres chiens ce voyant
Vite vite l'ensevelirent...

Il s'arrête. Même jeu.

Les autres chiens ce voyant
Vite vite l'ensevelirent...

Il s'arrête. Même jeu. Plus bas.

Vite vite l'ensevelirent...

Il se tait, reste un moment immobile, puis se remet à arpenter fébrilement la scène dans tous les sens. Il s'arrête à nouveau devant l'arbre, va et vient, devant les chaussures, va et vient, court à la coulisse gauche, regarde au loin, à la coulisse droite, regarde au loin. A ce moment Estragon entre par la coulisse gauche, pieds nus, tête basse, et traverse lentement la scène. Vladimir se retourne et le voit.

VLADIMIR. Encore toi ! (*Estragon s'arrête mais ne lève pas la tête. Vladimir va vers lui.*) Viens que je t'embrasse !

ESTRAGON. Ne me touche pas !

Vladimir suspend son vol, peiné. Silence.

VLADIMIR. Veux-tu que je m'en aille ? (*Un temps.*) Gogo ! (*Un temps. Vladimir le regarde avec attention.*) On t'a battu ? (*Un temps.*) Gogo ! (*Estragon se tait toujours, la tête basse.*) Où as-tu passé la nuit ? (*Silence. Vladimir avance.*)

ESTRAGON. Ne me touche pas ! Ne me demande rien ! Ne me dis rien ! Reste avec moi !

VLADIMIR. Est-ce que je t'ai jamais quitté ?

ESTRAGON. Tu m'as laissé partir.

VLADIMIR. Regarde-moi ! (*Estragon ne bouge pas. D'une voix tonnante.*) Regarde-moi, je te dis !

Estragon lève la tête. Ils se regardent longuement, en reculant, avançant, et penchant la tête comme devant un objet d'art, tremblant de plus en plus l'un vers l'autre, puis soudain s'étreignent, en se tapant sur le dos. Fin de l'étreinte. Estragon, n'étant plus soutenu, manque de tomber.

ESTRAGON. Quelle journée !

VLADIMIR. Qui t'a esquinté ? Raconte-moi.

ESTRAGON. Voilà encore une journée de tirée.

VLADIMIR. Pas encore.

ESTRAGON. Pour moi elle est terminée, quoi qu'il arrive. (*Silence.*) Tout à l'heure, tu chantais, je t'ai entendu.

VLADIMIR. C'est vrai, je me rappelle.

ESTRAGON. Cela m'a fait de la peine. Je me disais, Il est seul, il me croit parti pour toujours et il chante.

VLADIMIR. On ne commande pas à son humeur. Toute la journée je me suis senti dans une forme extraordinaire. (*Un temps.*) Je ne me suis pas levé de la nuit, pas une seule fois.

ESTRAGON (*tristement*). Tu vois, tu pisses mieux* quand je ne suis pas là.

VLADIMIR. Tu me manquais — et en même temps j'étais content. N'est-ce pas curieux?

ESTRAGON (*outré*). Content?

VLADIMIR (*ayant réfléchi*). Ce n'est peut-être pas le mot.

ESTRAGON. Et maintenant?

VLADIMIR (*s'étant consulté*). Maintenant... (*joyeux*)* te revoilà... (*neutre*) nous revoilà... (*triste*) me revoilà.

ESTRAGON. Tu vois, tu vas moins bien quand je suis là. Moi aussi, je me sens mieux seul.

VLADIMIR (*piqué*). Alors pourquoi rappliquer?

ESTRAGON. Je ne sais pas.

VLADIMIR. Mais moi je le sais. Parce que tu ne sais pas te défendre. Moi je ne t'aurais pas laissé battre.

ESTRAGON. Tu n'aurais pas pu l'empêcher.

VLADIMIR. Pourquoi?

ESTRAGON. Ils étaient dix.*

VLADIMIR. Mais non, je veux dire que je t'aurais empêché de t'exposer à être battu.

ESTRAGON. Je ne faisais rien.

VLADIMIR. Alors pourquoi ils t'ont battu?

ESTRAGON. Je ne sais pas.

VLADIMIR. Non, vois-tu, Gogo, il y a des choses qui t'échappent qui ne m'échappent pas à moi. Tu dois le sentir.

ESTRAGON. Je te dis que je ne faisais rien.

VLADIMIR. Peut-être bien que non. Mais il y a la manière, il y a la manière, si on tient à sa peau. Enfin, ne parlons plus de ça. Te voilà revenu, et j'en suis bien content.

ESTRAGON. Ils étaient dix.

VLADIMIR. Toi aussi, tu dois être content, au fond, avoue-le.

ESTRAGON. Content de quoi ?

VLADIMIR. De m'avoir retrouvé.

ESTRAGON. Tu crois ?

VLADIMIR. Dis-le, même si ce n'est pas vrai.

ESTRAGON. Qu'est-ce que je dois dire ?

VLADIMIR. Dis, Je suis content.

ESTRAGON. Je suis content.

VLADIMIR. Moi aussi.

ESTRAGON. Moi aussi.

VLADIMIR. Nous sommes contents.

ESTRAGON. Nous sommes contents. (*Silence.*) Qu'est-ce qu'on fait, maintenant qu'on est content ?

VLADIMIR. On attend Godot.

ESTRAGON. C'est vrai.

Silence.

VLADIMIR. Il y a du nouveau ici, depuis hier.

ESTRAGON. Et s'il ne vient pas ?

VLADIMIR (*après un moment d'incompréhension*). Nous aviserons. (*Un temps.*) Je te dis qu'il y a du nouveau ici, depuis hier.

ESTRAGON. Tout suinte.

VLADIMIR. Regarde-moi l'arbre.

ESTRAGON. On ne descend pas deux fois dans le même pus.

VLADIMIR. L'arbre, je te dis, regarde-le.

Estragon regarde l'arbre.

ESTRAGON. Il n'était pas là hier ?

VLADIMIR. Mais si. Tu ne te rappelles pas. Il s'en est fallu d'un cheveu qu'on ne s'y soit pendu. (*Il réfléchit.*) Oui, c'est juste (*en détachant les mots*) qu'on - ne - s'y - soit - pendu. Mais tu n'as pas voulu. Tu ne te rappelles pas ?

ESTRAGON. Tu l'as rêvé.

VLADIMIR. Est-ce possible que tu aies oublié déjà ?

ESTRAGON. Je suis comme ça. Ou j'oublie tout de suite ou je n'oublie jamais.

VLADIMIR. Et Pozzo et Lucky, tu as oublié aussi ?

ESTRAGON. Pozzo et Lucky ?

VLADIMIR. Il a tout oublié !

ESTRAGON. Je me rappelle un énergumène qui m'a foutu des coups de pied. Ensuite il a fait le con.

VLADIMIR. C'était Lucky !

ESTRAGON. Ça je m'en souviens. Mais quand c'était ?

VLADIMIR. Et l'autre qui le menait, tu t'en souviens aussi ?

ESTRAGON. Il m'a donné des os.

VLADIMIR. C'était Pozzo !

ESTRAGON. Et tu dis que c'était hier, tout ça ?

VLADIMIR. Mais oui, voyons.

ESTRAGON. Et à cet endroit ?

VLADIMIR. Mais bien sûr ! Tu ne reconnais pas ?

ESTRAGON (*soudain furieux*). Reconnais ! Qu'est-ce qu'il y a à reconnaître ? J'ai tiré ma roulure de vie au milieu des sables ! Et tu veux que j'y voie des nuances ! (*Regard circulaire.*) Regarde-moi cette saloperie ! Je n'en ai jamais bougé !

VLADIMIR. Du calme, du calme.

ESTRAGON. Alors fous-moi la paix avec tes paysages ! Parle-moi du sous-sol ! *

VLADIMIR. Tout de même, tu ne vas pas me dire que ça (*geste*) ressemble au Vaucluse ! Il y a quand même une grosse différence.

ESTRAGON. Le Vaucluse ! Qui te parle du Vaucluse ?

VLADIMIR. Mais tu as bien été dans le Vaucluse ?

ESTRAGON. Mais non, je n'ai jamais été dans le Vaucluse ! J'ai coulé toute ma chaude-pisse d'existence ici, je te dis ! Ici ! Dans la Merdecluse !

VLADIMIR. Pourtant nous avons été ensemble dans le Vaucluse, j'en mettrais ma main au feu. Nous avons fait les vendanges, tiens, chez un nommé Bonnelly, à Roussillon.

ESTRAGON (*plus calme*). C'est possible. Je n'ai rien remarqué.

VLADIMIR. Mais là-bas tout est rouge !

ESTRAGON (*excédé*). Je n'ai rien remarqué, je te dis !

Silence. Vladimir soupire profondément.

VLADIMIR. Tu es difficile à vivre, Gogo.

ESTRAGON. On ferait mieux de se séparer.

VLADIMIR. Tu dis toujours ça. Et chaque fois tu reviens.

Silence.

ESTRAGON. Pour bien faire, il faudrait me tuer, comme l'autre.

VLADIMIR. Quel autre ? (*Un temps.*) Quel autre ?

ESTRAGON. Comme des billions d'autres.

VLADIMIR (*sentencieux*). A chacun sa petite croix. (*Il soupire.*) Pendant le petit pendant et le bref après.

ESTRAGON. En attendant, essayons de converser sans nous exalter, puisque nous sommes incapables de nous taire.

VLADIMIR. C'est vrai, nous sommes intarissables.*

ESTRAGON. C'est pour ne pas penser.

VLADIMIR. Nous avons des excuses.

ESTRAGON. C'est pour ne pas entendre.

VLADIMIR. Nous avons nos raisons.

ESTRAGON. Toutes les voix mortes.

VLADIMIR. Ça fait un bruit d'ailes.

ESTRAGON. De feuilles.

VLADIMIR. De sable.

ESTRAGON. De feuilles.

Silence.

VLADIMIR. Elles parlent toutes en même temps.

ESTRAGON. Chacune à part soi.

Silence.

VLADIMIR. Plutôt elles chuchotent.

ESTRAGON. Elles murmurent.

VLADIMIR. Elles bruissent.

ESTRAGON. Elles murmurent.

Silence.

VLADIMIR. Que disent-elles ?

ESTRAGON. Elles parlent de leur vie.

VLADIMIR. Il ne leur suffit pas d'avoir vécu.
ESTRAGON. Il faut qu'elles en parlent.
VLADIMIR. Il ne leur suffit pas d'être mortes.
ESTRAGON. Ce n'est pas assez.

Silence.

VLADIMIR. Ça fait comme un bruit de plumes.
ESTRAGON. De feuilles.
VLADIMIR. De cendres.
ESTRAGON. De feuilles.

Long silence.

VLADIMIR. Dis quelque chose !
ESTRAGON. Je cherche.

Long silence.

VLADIMIR (*angoissé*). Dis n'importe quoi !
ESTRAGON. Qu'est-ce qu'on fait maintenant ?
VLADIMIR. On attend Godot.
ESTRAGON. C'est vrai.

Silence.

VLADIMIR. Ce que c'est difficile !
ESTRAGON. Si tu chantais ?
VLADIMIR. Non non. (*Il cherche.*) On n'a qu'à recommencer.
ESTRAGON. Ça ne me semble pas bien difficile en effet.
VLADIMIR. C'est le départ qui est difficile.
ESTRAGON. On peut partir de n'importe quoi.
VLADIMIR. Oui, mais il faut se décider.
ESTRAGON. C'est vrai.

Silence.

VLADIMIR. Aide-moi !
ESTRAGON. Je cherche.

Silence.

VLADIMIR. Quand on cherche on entend.
ESTRAGON. C'est vrai.
VLADIMIR. Ça empêche de trouver.
ESTRAGON. Voilà.
VLADIMIR. Ça empêche de penser.

ESTRAGON. On pense quand même.
VLADIMIR. Mais non, c'est impossible.
ESTRAGON. C'est ça, contredisons-nous.
VLADIMIR. Impossible.
ESTRAGON. Tu crois?
VLADIMIR. Nous ne risquons plus de penser.
ESTRAGON. Alors de quoi nous plaignons-nous?
VLADIMIR. Ce n'est pas le pire, de penser.
ESTRAGON. Bien sûr, bien sûr, mais c'est déjà ça.
VLADIMIR. Comment, c'est déjà ça?
ESTRAGON. C'est ça, posons-nous des questions.
VLADIMIR. Qu'est-ce que tu veux dire, c'est déjà ça?
ESTRAGON. C'est déjà ça en moins.
VLADIMIR. Évidemment.
ESTRAGON. Alors? Si on s'estimait heureux?
VLADIMIR. Ce qui est terrible, c'est d'avoir pensé.
ESTRAGON. Mais cela nous est-il jamais arrivé?
VLADIMIR. D'où viennent tous ces cadavres?
ESTRAGON. Ces ossements.
VLADIMIR. Voilà.
ESTRAGON. Évidemment.
VLADIMIR. On a dû penser un peu.
ESTRAGON. Tout à fait au commencement.
VLADIMIR. Un charnier, un charnier.
ESTRAGON. Il n'y a qu'à ne pas regarder.
VLADIMIR. Ça tire l'œil.
ESTRAGON. C'est vrai.
VLADIMIR. Malgré qu'on en ait.
ESTRAGON. Comment?
VLADIMIR. Malgré qu'on en ait.
ESTRAGON. Il faudrait se tourner résolument vers la nature.*
VLADIMIR. Nous avons essayé.
ESTRAGON. C'est vrai.
VLADIMIR. Oh, ce n'est pas le pire, bien sûr.

ESTRAGON. Quoi donc ?

VLADIMIR. D'avoir pensé.

ESTRAGON. Évidemment.

VLADIMIR. Mais on s'en serait passé.

ESTRAGON. Qu'est-ce que tu veux ?

VLADIMIR. Je sais, je sais.

Silence.

ESTRAGON. Ce n'était pas si mal comme petit galop.

VLADIMIR. Oui, mais maintenant il va falloir trouver autre chose.

ESTRAGON. Voyons.*

VLADIMIR. Voyons.

ESTRAGON. Voyons.

Ils réfléchissent.

VLADIMIR. Qu'est-ce que je disais ? On pourrait reprendre là.

ESTRAGON. Quand ?

VLADIMIR. Tout à fait au début.

ESTRAGON. Au début de quoi ?

VLADIMIR. Ce soir. Je disais... je disais...

ESTRAGON. Ma foi, là tu m'en demandes trop.

VLADIMIR. Attends... on s'est embrassé... on était content... content... qu'est-ce qu'on fait maintenant qu'on est content... on attend... voyons... ça vient... on attend... maintenant qu'on est content... on attend... voyons... ah ! L'arbre !

ESTRAGON. L'arbre ?

VLADIMIR. Tu ne te rappelles pas ?

ESTRAGON. Je suis fatigué.

VLADIMIR. Regarde-le.

Estragon regarde l'arbre.

ESTRAGON. Je ne vois rien.

VLADIMIR. Mais hier soir il était tout noir et squelettique ! Aujourd'hui il est couvert de feuilles.

ESTRAGON. De feuilles ?

VLADIMIR. Dans une seule nuit !

ESTRAGON. On doit être au printemps.

VLADIMIR. Mais dans une seule nuit !

ESTRAGON. Je te dis que nous n'étions pas là hier soir. Tu l'as cauchemardé.

VLADIMIR. Et où étions-nous hier soir, d'après toi ?

ESTRAGON. Je ne sais pas. Ailleurs. Dans un autre compartiment. Ce n'est pas le vide qui manque. *

VLADIMIR (*sûr de son fait*). Bon. Nous n'étions pas là hier soir. Maintenant qu'est-ce que nous avons fait hier soir ?

ESTRAGON. Ce que nous avons fait ?

VLADIMIR. Essaie de te rappeler.

ESTRAGON. Eh ben... nous avons dû bavarder.

VLADIMIR (*se maîtrisant*). A propos de quoi ?

ESTRAGON. Oh... à bâtons rompus peut-être, à propos de bottes. (*Avec assurance.*) Voilà, je me rappelle, hier soir nous avons bavardé, à propos de bottes. Il y a un demi-siècle que ça dure.

VLADIMIR. Tu ne te rappelles aucun fait, aucune circonstance ?

ESTRAGON (*las*). Ne me tourmente pas, Didi.

VLADIMIR. Le soleil ? La lune ? Tu ne te rappelles pas ?

ESTRAGON. Ils devaient être là, comme d'habitude.

VLADIMIR. Tu n'as rien remarqué d'insolite ?

ESTRAGON. Hélas.

VLADIMIR. Et Pozzo ? Et Lucky ?

ESTRAGON. Pozzo ?

VLADIMIR. Les os.

ESTRAGON. On aurait dit des arêtes.

VLADIMIR. C'est Pozzo qui te les a donnés.

ESTRAGON. Je ne sais pas.

VLADIMIR. Et le coup de pied.

ESTRAGON. Le coup de pied ? C'est vrai, on m'a donné des coups de pied.

VLADIMIR. C'est Lucky qui te les a donnés.

ESTRAGON. C'était hier, tout ça ?

VLADIMIR. Fais voir ta jambe.

ESTRAGON. Laquelle ?

VLADIMIR. Les deux. Relève ton pantalon. (*Estragon, sur un pied, tend la jambe vers Vladimir, manque de tomber. Vladimir prend la jambe. Estragon chancelle.*) Relève ton pantalon.

ESTRAGON (*titubant*). Je ne peux pas.

Vladimir relève le pantalon, regarde la jambe, la lâche. Estragon manque de tomber.

VLADIMIR. L'autre. (*Estragon donne la même jambe.*) L'autre, je te dis ! (*Même jeu avec l'autre jambe.*) Voilà la plaie en train de s'infecter.

ESTRAGON. Et après ?

VLADIMIR. Où sont tes chaussures ?

ESTRAGON. J'ai dû les jeter.

VLADIMIR. Quand ?

ESTRAGON. Je ne sais pas.

VLADIMIR. Pourquoi ?

ESTRAGON. Je ne me rappelle pas.

VLADIMIR. Non, je veux dire pourquoi tu les as jetées ?

ESTRAGON. Elles me faisaient mal.

VLADIMIR (*montrant les chaussures*). Les voilà. (*Estragon regarde les chaussures.*) A l'endroit même où tu les as posées hier soir.

Estragon va vers les chaussures, se penche, les inspecte de près.

ESTRAGON. Ce ne sont pas les miennes.

VLADIMIR. Pas les tiennes !

ESTRAGON. Les miennes étaient noires. Celles-ci sont jaunes.

VLADIMIR. Tu es sûr que les tiennes étaient noires ?

ESTRAGON. C'est-à-dire qu'elles étaient grises.

VLADIMIR. Et celles-ci sont jaunes ? Fais voir.

ESTRAGON (*soulevant une chaussure*). Enfin, elles sont verdâtres.

VLADIMIR (*avançant*). Fais voir. (*Estragon lui donne la chaussure. Vladimir la regarde, la jette avec colère.*) Ça alors !

ESTRAGON. Tu vois, tout ça c'est des...

VLADIMIR. Je vois ce que c'est. Oui, je vois ce qui s'est passé.

ESTRAGON. Tout ça c'est des...

VLADIMIR. C'est simple comme bonjour. Un type est venu qui a pris les tiennes et t'a laissé les siennes.

ESTRAGON. Pourquoi ?

VLADIMIR. Les siennes ne lui allaient pas. Alors il a pris les tiennes.

ESTRAGON. Mais les miennes étaient trop petites.

VLADIMIR. Pour toi. Pas pour lui.

ESTRAGON. Je suis fatigué. (*Un temps.*) Allons-nous-en.

VLADIMIR. On ne peut pas.

ESTRAGON. Pourquoi ?

VLADIMIR. On attend Godot.

ESTRAGON. C'est vrai. (*Un temps.*) Alors comment faire ?

VLADIMIR. Il n'y a rien à faire.

ESTRAGON. Mais moi je n'en peux plus.

VLADIMIR. Veux-tu un radis ?

ESTRAGON. C'est tout ce qu'il y a ?

VLADIMIR. Il y a des radis et des navets.

ESTRAGON. Il n'y a plus de carottes ?

VLADIMIR. Non. D'ailleurs tu exagères avec les carottes.

ESTRAGON. Alors donne-moi un radis. (*Vladimir fouille dans ses poches, ne trouve que des navets, sort finalement un radis qu'il donne à Estragon qui l'examine, le renifle.*) * Il est noir !

VLADIMIR. C'est un radis.

ESTRAGON. Je n'aime que les roses, tu le sais bien !

VLADIMIR. Alors tu n'en veux pas ?

ESTRAGON. Je n'aime que les roses !

VLADIMIR. Alors rends-le-moi.

Estragon le lui rend.

ESTRAGON. Je vais chercher une carotte.

Il ne bouge pas.

VLADIMIR. Ceci devient vraiment insignifiant.

ESTRAGON. Pas encore assez.

Silence.

VLADIMIR. Si tu les essayais ?

ESTRAGON. J'ai tout essayé.

VLADIMIR. Je veux dire les chaussures.

ESTRAGON. Tu crois?

VLADIMIR. Ça fera passer le temps. (*Estragon hésite.*) Je t'assure, ce sera une diversion.

ESTRAGON. Un délassement.

VLADIMIR. Une distraction.

ESTRAGON. Un délassement.

VLADIMIR. Essaie.

ESTRAGON. Tu m'aideras?

VLADIMIR. Bien sûr.

ESTRAGON. On ne se débrouille pas trop mal, hein, Didi, tous les deux ensemble?

VLADIMIR. Mais oui, mais oui. Allez, on va essayer la gauche d'abord.

ESTRAGON. On trouve toujours quelque chose, hein, Didi, pour nous donner l'impression d'exister?

VLADIMIR (*impatiemment*). Mais oui, mais oui, on est des magiciens. Mais ne nous laissons pas détourner de ce que nous avons résolu. (*Il ramasse une chaussure.*) Viens, donne ton pied. (*Estragon s'approche de lui, lève le pied.*) L'autre, porc! (*Estragon lève l'autre pied.*) Plus haut! (*Les corps emmêlés, ils titubent à travers la scène. Vladimir réussit finalement à lui mettre la chaussure.*) Essaie de marcher. (*Estragon marche.*) Alors?

ESTRAGON. Elle me va.

VLADIMIR (*prenant de la ficelle dans sa poche.*) On va la lacer.

ESTRAGON (*véhémentement*). Non, non, pas de lacet, pas de lacet! *

VLADIMIR. Tu as tort. Essayons l'autre. (*Même jeu.*) Alors?

ESTRAGON. Elle me va aussi.

VLADIMIR. Elles ne te font pas mal?

ESTRAGON (*faisant quelques pas appuyés*). Pas encore.

VLADIMIR. Alors tu peux les garder.

ESTRAGON. Elles sont trop grandes. *

VLADIMIR. Tu auras peut-être des chaussettes un jour.

ESTRAGON. C'est vrai.

VLADIMIR. Alors tu les gardes ?

ESTRAGON. Assez parlé de ces chaussures.

VLADIMIR. Oui, mais...

ESTRAGON. Assez ! (*Silence.*) Je vais quand même m'asseoir.

Il cherche des yeux où s'asseoir, puis va s'asseoir là où il était assis au début du premier acte.

VLADIMIR. C'est là où tu étais assis hier soir.

Silence.

ESTRAGON. Si je pouvais dormir.

VLADIMIR. Hier soir tu as dormi.

ESTRAGON. Je vais essayer.

Il prend une posture utérine, la tête entre les jambes.*

VLADIMIR. Attends. (*Il s'approche d'Estragon et se met à chanter d'une voix forte.*)

Do do do do

ESTRAGON (*levant la tête*). Pas si fort.

VLADIMIR (*moins fort*).

Do do do do
Do do do do
Do do do do
Do do...

Estragon s'endort. Vladimir enlève son veston et lui en couvre les épaules, puis se met à marcher de long en large en battant des bras pour se réchauffer. Estragon se réveille en sursaut, se lève, fait quelques pas affolés. Vladimir court vers lui, l'entoure de son bras.

VLADIMIR. Là... là... je suis là... n'aie pas peur.

ESTRAGON. Ah !

VLADIMIR. Là... là... c'est fini.

ESTRAGON. Je tombais.

VLADIMIR. C'est fini. N'y pense plus.

ESTRAGON. J'étais sur un...

VLADIMIR. Non non, ne dis rien. Viens, on va marcher un peu.

Il prend Estragon par le bras et le fait marcher de long en large, jusqu'à ce qu'Estragon refuse d'aller plus loin.

ESTRAGON. Assez ! Je suis fatigué.

VLADIMIR. Tu aimes mieux être planté là à ne rien faire ?

ESTRAGON. Oui.

VLADIMIR. Comme tu veux.

Il lâche Estragon, va ramasser son veston et le met.

ESTRAGON. Allons-nous-en.

VLADIMIR. On ne peut pas.

ESTRAGON. Pourquoi ?

VLADIMIR. On attend Godot.

ESTRAGON. C'est vrai. (*Vladimir reprend son va-et-vient.*) Tu ne peux pas rester tranquille ?

VLADIMIR. J'ai froid.

ESTRAGON. On est venu trop tôt.

VLADIMIR. C'est toujours à la tombée de la nuit.

ESTRAGON. Mais la nuit ne tombe pas.

VLADIMIR. Elle tombera tout d'un coup, comme hier.

ESTRAGON. Puis ce sera la nuit.

VLADIMIR. Et nous pourrons partir.

ESTRAGON. Puis ce sera encore le jour. (*Un temps.*) Que faire, que faire ?

VLADIMIR (*s'arrêtant de marcher, avec violence*). Tu as bientôt fini de te plaindre ? Tu commences à me casser les pieds, avec tes gémissements.

ESTRAGON. Je m'en vais.

VLADIMIR (*apercevant le chapeau de Lucky*). Tiens !

ESTRAGON. Adieu.

VLADIMIR. Le chapeau de Lucky ! (*Il s'en approche.*) Voilà une heure que je suis là et je ne l'avais pas vu ! (*Très content.*) C'est parfait !

ESTRAGON. Tu ne me verras plus.

VLADIMIR. Je ne me suis donc pas trompé d'endroit. Nous voilà tranquilles. (*Il ramasse le chapeau de Lucky, le contemple, le redresse.*) Ça devait être un beau chapeau. (*Il le met à la place du sien qu'il tend à Estragon.*) Tiens.

ESTRAGON. Quoi ?

VLADIMIR. Tiens-moi ça.

Estragon prend le chapeau de Vladimir. Vladimir ajuste des deux mains le chapeau de Lucky. Estragon met le chapeau de

Vladimir à la place du sien qu'il tend à Vladimir. Vladimir prend le chapeau d'Estragon. Estragon ajuste des deux mains le chapeau de Vladimir. Vladimir met le chapeau d'Estragon à la place de celui de Lucky qu'il tend à Estragon. Estragon prend le chapeau de Lucky. Vladimir ajuste des deux mains le chapeau d'Estragon. Estragon met le chapeau de Lucky à la place de celui de Vladimir qu'il tend à Vladimir. Vladimir prend son chapeau. Estragon ajuste des deux mains le chapeau de Lucky. Vladimir met son chapeau à la place de celui d'Estragon qu'il tend à Estragon. Estragon prend son chapeau. Vladimir ajuste son chapeau des deux mains. Estragon met son chapeau à la place de celui de Lucky qu'il tend à Vladimir. Vladimir prend le chapeau de Lucky. Estragon ajuste son chapeau des deux mains. Vladimir met le chapeau de Lucky à la place du sien qu'il tend à Estragon. Estragon prend le chapeau de Vladimir. Vladimir ajuste des deux mains le chapeau de Lucky. Estragon tend le chapeau de Vladimir à Vladimir qui le prend et le tend à Estragon qui le prend et le tend à Vladimir qui le prend et le jette. Tout cela dans un mouvement vif.

VLADIMIR. Il me va ?

ESTRAGON. Je ne sais pas.

VLADIMIR. Non, mais comment me trouves-tu ?

Il tourne la tête coquettement à droite et à gauche, prend des attitudes de mannequin.

ESTRAGON. Affreux.

VLADIMIR. Mais pas plus que d'habitude ?

ESTRAGON. La même chose.

VLADIMIR. Alors je peux le garder. Le mien me faisait mal. (*Un temps.*) Comment dire ? (*Un temps.*) Il me grattait.

ESTRAGON. Je m'en vais.

VLADIMIR. Tu ne veux pas jouer ?

ESTRAGON. Jouer à quoi ?

VLADIMIR. On pourrait jouer à Pozzo et Lucky.

ESTRAGON. Connais pas.

VLADIMIR. Moi je ferai Lucky, toi tu feras Pozzo. (*Il prend l'attitude de Lucky, ployant sous le poids de ses bagages. Estragon le regarde avec stupéfaction.*) Vas-y.

ESTRAGON. Qu'est-ce que je dois faire ?

VLADIMIR. Engueule-moi !

ESTRAGON. Salaud !

VLADIMIR. Plus fort !

ESTRAGON. Fumier ! Crapule !

Vladimir avance, recule, toujours ployé.

VLADIMIR. Dis-moi de penser.

ESTRAGON. Comment ?

VLADIMIR. Dis, Pense, cochon !

ESTRAGON. Pense, cochon !

Silence.

VLADIMIR. Je ne peux pas !

ESTRAGON. Assez !

VLADIMIR. Dis-moi de danser.

ESTRAGON. Je m'en vais.

VLADIMIR. Danse, porc ! (*Il se tord sur place. Estragon sort précipitamment.*) Je ne peux pas ! (*Il lève la tête, voit qu'Estragon n'est plus là, pousse un cri déchirant.*) Gogo ! (*Silence. Il se met à arpenter la scène presque en courant. Estragon rentre précipitamment, essoufflé, court vers Vladimir. Ils s'arrêtent à quelques pas l'un de l'autre.*) Te revoilà enfin !

ESTRAGON (*haletant*). Je suis maudit !

VLADIMIR. Où as-tu été ? Je t'ai cru parti pour toujours.

ESTRAGON. Jusqu'au bord de la pente.* On vient.

VLADIMIR. Qui ?

ESTRAGON. Je ne sais pas.

VLADIMIR. Combien ?

ESTRAGON. Je ne sais pas.

VLADIMIR (*triomphant*). C'est Godot ! Enfin ! (*Il embrasse Estragon avec effusion.*) Gogo ! C'est Godot ! Nous sommes sauvés ! Allons à sa rencontre ! Viens ! (*Il tire Estragon vers la coulisse. Estragon résiste, se dégage, sort en courant de l'autre côté.*) Gogo ! Reviens ! (*Silence. Vladimir court à la coulisse par où Estragon vient de rentrer, regarde au loin. Estragon rentre précipitamment, court vers Vladimir qui se retourne.*) Te revoilà à nouveau !

ESTRAGON. Je suis damné !

VLADIMIR. Tu as été loin ?

ESTRAGON. Jusqu'au bord de la pente.

VLADIMIR. En effet, nous sommes sur un plateau. Aucun doute, nous sommes servis sur un plateau.

ESTRAGON. On vient par là aussi.

VLADIMIR. Nous sommes cernés ! (*Affolé, Estragon se précipite vers la toile de fond, s'y empêtre, tombe.*) Imbécile ! Il n'y a pas d'issue par là. (*Vladimir va le relever, l'amène vers la rampe. Geste vers l'auditoire.*) Là il n'y a personne. Sauve-toi par là. Allez. (*Il le pousse vers la fosse. Estragon recule épouvanté.*) Tu ne veux pas ? Ma foi, ça se comprend. Voyons. (*Il réfléchit.*) Il ne te reste plus qu'à disparaître.

ESTRAGON. Où ?

VLADIMIR. Derrière l'arbre. (*Estragon hésite.*) Vite ! Derrière l'arbre. (*Estragon court se mettre derrière l'arbre qui ne le cache que très imparfaitement.*) Ne bouge plus ! (*Estragon sort de derrière l'arbre.*) Décidément cet arbre ne nous aura servi à rien. (*A Estragon.*) Tu n'es pas fou ?

ESTRAGON (*plus calme*). J'ai perdu la tête. (*Il baisse honteusement la tête.*) Pardon ! (*Il redresse fièrement la tête.*) C'est fini ! Maintenant tu vas voir. Dis-moi ce qu'il faut faire.

VLADIMIR. Il n'y a rien à faire.

ESTRAGON. Toi tu vas te poster là. (*Il entraîne Vladimir vers la coulisse gauche, le met dans l'axe de la route, le dos à la scène.*) Là, ne bouge plus, et ouvre l'œil. (*Il court vers l'autre coulisse. Vladimir le regarde par-dessus l'épaule. Estragon s'arrête, regarde au loin, se retourne. Les deux se regardent par-dessus l'épaule.*) Dos à dos comme au bon vieux temps ! (*Ils continuent à se regarder un petit moment, puis chacun reprend le guet. Long silence.*) Tu ne vois rien venir ?

VLADIMIR (*se retournant*). Comment ?

ESTRAGON (*plus fort*). Tu ne vois rien venir ?

VLADIMIR. Non.

ESTRAGON. Moi non plus.

Ils reprennent le guet. Long silence.

VLADIMIR. Tu as dû te tromper.

ESTRAGON (*se retournant*). Comment ?

VLADIMIR (*plus fort*). Tu as dû te tromper.

ESTRAGON. Ne crie pas.

Ils reprennent le guet. Long silence.

VLADIMIR, ESTRAGON (*se retournant simultanément*). Est-ce...

VLADIMIR. Oh pardon !

ESTRAGON. Je t'écoute.

VLADIMIR. Mais non !

ESTRAGON. Mais si !

VLADIMIR. Je t'ai coupé.

ESTRAGON. Au contraire.

Ils se regardent avec colère.

VLADIMIR. Voyons, pas de cérémonie.

ESTRAGON. Ne sois pas têtu, voyons.

VLADIMIR (*avec force*). Achève ta phrase, je te dis.

ESTRAGON (*de même*). Achève la tienne.

Silence. Ils vont l'un vers l'autre, s'arrêtent.

VLADIMIR. Misérable !

ESTRAGON. C'est ça, engueulons-nous. (*Échange d'injures.* * *Silence.*) Maintenant raccommodons-nous.

VLADIMIR. Gogo !

ESTRAGON. Didi !

VLADIMIR. Ta main !

ESTRAGON. La voilà !

VLADIMIR. Viens dans mes bras !

ESTRAGON. Tes bras ?

VLADIMIR (*ouvrant les bras*). Là-dedans !

ESTRAGON. Allons-y.

Ils s'embrassent. Silence.

VLADIMIR. Comme le temps passe quand on s'amuse !

Silence.

ESTRAGON. Qu'est-ce qu'on fait maintenant ?

VLADIMIR. En attendant.

ESTRAGON. En attendant.

Silence.

VLADIMIR. Si on faisait nos exercices ?

ESTRAGON. Nos mouvements.

VLADIMIR. D'assouplissement.

ESTRAGON. De relaxation.

VLADIMIR. De circumduction.

ESTRAGON. De relaxation.

VLADIMIR. Pous nous réchauffer.

ESTRAGON. Pour nous calmer.

VLADIMIR. Allons-y.

Il commence à sauter. Estragon l'imite.

ESTRAGON (*s'arrêtant*). Assez. Je suis fatigué.

VLADIMIR (*s'arrêtant*). Nous ne sommes pas en train. Faisons quand même quelques respirations.

ESTRAGON. Je ne veux plus respirer.

VLADIMIR. Tu as raison. (*Pause.*) Faisons quand même l'arbre, pour l'équilibre.

ESTRAGON. L'arbre ?

Vladimir fait l'arbre en titubant.

VLADIMIR (*s'arrêtant*). A toi.

Estragon fait l'arbre en titubant.

ESTRAGON. Tu crois que Dieu me voit.

VLADIMIR. Il faut fermer les yeux.

Estragon ferme les yeux, titube plus fort.

ESTRAGON (*s'arrêtant, brandissant les poings, à tue-tête*). Dieu aie pitié de moi !

VLADIMIR (*vexé*). Et moi ?

ESTRAGON (*de même*). De moi ! De moi ! Pitié ! De moi !

Entrent Pozzo et Lucky. * *Pozzo est devenu aveugle. Lucky chargé comme au premier acte. Corde comme au premier acte, mais beaucoup plus courte, pour permettre à Pozzo de suivre plus commodément. Lucky coiffé d'un nouveau chapeau. A la vue de Vladimir et Estragon il s'arrête. Pozzo, continuant son chemin, vient se heurter contre lui. Vladimir et Estragon reculent.*

POZZO (*s'agrippant à Lucky qui, sous ce nouveau poids, chancelle*). Qu'y a-t-il ? Qui a crié ?

Lucky tombe, en lâchant tout, et entraîne Pozzo dans sa chute. Ils restent étendus sans mouvement au milieu des bagages.

ESTRAGON. C'est Godot ?

VLADIMIR. Ça tombe à pic. (*Il va vers le tas, suivi d'Estragon.*) Enfin du renfort !

POZZO (*voix blanche*). Au secours.

ESTRAGON. C'est Godot ?

VLADIMIR. Nous commencions à flancher. Voilà notre fin de soirée assurée.

POZZO. A moi !

ESTRAGON. Il appelle à l'aide.

VLADIMIR. Nous ne sommes plus seuls, à attendre la nuit, à attendre Godot, à attendre — à attendre. Toute la soirée nous avons lutté, livrés à nos propres moyens. Maintenant c'est fini. Nous sommes déjà demain.

ESTRAGON. Mais ils sont seulement de passage.

POZZO. A moi !

VLADIMIR. Déjà le temps coule tout autrement. Le soleil se couchera, la lune se lèvera et nous partirons — d'ici.

ESTRAGON. Mais ils ne font que passer.

VLADIMIR. Ce sera suffisant.

POZZO. Pitié !

VLADIMIR. Pauvre Pozzo !

ESTRAGON. Je savais que c'était lui.

VLADIMIR. Qui ?

ESTRAGON. Godot.

VLADIMIR. Mais ce n'est pas Godot.

ESTRAGON. Ce n'est pas Godot !

VLADIMIR. Ce n'est pas Godot.

ESTRAGON. Qui c'est alors ?

VLADIMIR. C'est Pozzo.

POZZO. C'est moi ! C'est moi ! Relevez-moi !

VLADIMIR. Il ne peut pas se relever.

ESTRAGON. Allons-nous-en.

VLADIMIR. On ne peut pas.

ESTRAGON. Pourquoi ?

VLADIMIR. On attend Godot.

ESTRAGON. C'est vrai.

VLADIMIR. Peut-être qu'il a encore des os pour toi.

ESTRAGON. Des os ?

VLADIMIR. De poulet. Tu ne te rappelles pas ?

ESTRAGON. C'était lui ?

VLADIMIR. Oui.

ESTRAGON. Demande-lui.

VLADIMIR. Si on l'aidait d'abord ?

ESTRAGON. A quoi faire ?

VLADIMIR. A se relever.

ESTRAGON. Il ne peut pas se relever ?

VLADIMIR. Il veut se relever.

ESTRAGON. Alors qu'il se relève.

VLADIMIR. Il ne peut pas.

ESTRAGON. Qu'est-ce qu'il a ?

VLADIMIR. Je ne sais pas.

Pozzo se tord, gémit, frappe le sol avec ses poings.

ESTRAGON. Si on lui demandait les os d'abord ? Puis s'il refuse on le laissera là.

VLADIMIR. Tu veux dire que nous l'avons à notre merci ?

ESTRAGON. Oui.

VLADIMIR. Et qu'il faut mettre des conditions à nos bons offices ?

ESTRAGON. Oui.

VLADIMIR. Ça a l'air intelligent en effet. Mais je crains une chose.

ESTRAGON. Quoi ?

VLADIMIR. Que Lucky ne se mette en branle tout d'un coup. Alors nous serions baisés.*

ESTRAGON. Lucky ?

VLADIMIR. C'est lui qui t'a attaqué hier.

ESTRAGON. Je te dis qu'ils étaient dix.

VLADIMIR. Mais non, avant, celui qui t'a donné des coups de pied.

ESTRAGON. Il est là ?

VLADIMIR. Mais regarde. (*Geste.*) Pour le moment il est inerte. Mais il peut se déchaîner d'un instant à l'autre.

ESTRAGON. Si on lui donnait une bonne correction tous les deux ?

VLADIMIR. Tu veux dire si on lui tombait dessus pendant qu'il dort ?

ESTRAGON. Oui.

VLADIMIR. C'est une bonne idée. Mais en sommes-nous capables ? Dort-il vraiment ? (*Un temps.*) Non, le mieux serait de profiter de ce que Pozzo appelle au secours pour le secourir, en tablant sur sa reconnaissance.*

ESTRAGON. Il ne demande plus rien.

VLADIMIR. C'est qu'il a perdu l'espoir.

ESTRAGON. C'est possible. Mais...

VLADIMIR. Ne perdons pas notre temps en de vains discours. (*Un temps. Avec véhémence.*) Faisons quelque chose, pendant que l'occasion se présente ! Ce n'est pas tous les jours qu'on a besoin de nous. Non pas à vrai dire qu'on ait précisément besoin de nous. D'autres feraient aussi bien l'affaire, sinon mieux. L'appel que nous venons d'entendre, c'est plutôt à l'humanité tout entière qu'il s'adresse. Mais à cet endroit, en ce moment, l'humanité c'est nous, que ça nous plaise ou non. Profitons-en, avant qu'il soit trop tard. Représentons dignement pour une fois l'engeance où le malheur nous a fourrés. Qu'en dis-tu ?

ESTRAGON. Je n'ai pas écouté.

VLADIMIR. Il est vrai qu'en pesant, les bras croisés, le pour et le contre, nous faisons également honneur à notre condition. Le tigre se précipite au secours de ses congénères sans la moindre réflexion. Ou bien il se sauve au plus profond des taillis. Mais la question n'est pas là. Que faisons-nous ici, voilà ce qu'il faut se demander. Nous avons la chance de le savoir. Oui, dans cette immense confusion, une seule chose est claire : nous attendons que Godot vienne.

ESTRAGON. C'est vrai.

VLADIMIR. Ou que la nuit tombe. (*Un temps.*) Nous sommes au rendez-vous, un point c'est tout. Nous ne sommes pas des saints, mais nous sommes au rendez-vous. Combien de gens peuvent en dire autant ?

ESTRAGON. Des masses.

VLADIMIR. Tu crois ?

ESTRAGON. Je ne sais pas.

VLADIMIR. C'est possible.

POZZO. Au secours !

VLADIMIR. Ce qui est certain, c'est que le temps est long, dans ces conditions, et nous pousse à le meubler d'agissements qui, comment dire, qui peuvent à première vue paraître raisonnables, mais dont nous avons l'habitude.* Tu me diras que c'est pour empêcher notre raison de sombrer. C'est une affaire entendue. Mais n'erre-t-elle pas déjà dans la nuit permanente des grands fonds, voilà ce que je me demande parfois. Tu suis mon raisonnement ?

ESTRAGON. Nous naissons tous fous. Quelques-uns le demeurent.

POZZO. Au secours, je vous donnerai de l'argent !

ESTRAGON. Combien ?

POZZO. Cent francs.

ESTRAGON. Ce n'est pas assez.

VLADIMIR. Je n'irais pas jusque-là.

ESTRAGON. Tu trouves que c'est assez ?

VLADIMIR. Non, je veux dire jusqu'à affirmer que je n'avais pas toute ma tête en venant au monde. Mais la question n'est pas là.

POZZO. Deux cents.

VLADIMIR. Nous attendons. Nous nous ennuyons. (*Il lève la main.*) Non, ne proteste pas, nous nous ennuyons ferme, c'est incontestable. Bon. Une diversion se présente et que faisons-nous ? Nous la laissons pourrir. Allons, au travail. (*Il avance vers Pozzo, s'arrête.*) Dans un instant, tout se dissipera, nous serons à nouveau seuls, au milieu des solitudes.* (*Il rêve.*)

POZZO. Deux cents !

VLADIMIR. On arrive.

Il essaie de soulever Pozzo, n'y arrive pas, renouvelle ses

7. "Son chapeau!" *Act 1, p. 39.*

Royal Court Theatre, 1965.

8. "On n'est pas des cariatides." *Act 2, p. 78.*

Royal Court Theatre, 1965.

efforts, trébuche dans les bagages, tombe, essaie de se relever, n'y arrive pas.

ESTRAGON. Qu'est-ce que vous avez tous ?

VLADIMIR. Au secours !

ESTRAGON. Je m'en vais.

VLADIMIR. Ne m'abandonne pas ! Ils me tueront !

POZZO. Où suis-je ?

VLADIMIR. Gogo !

POZZO. A moi.

VLADIMIR. Aide-moi !

ESTRAGON. Moi je m'en vais.

VLADIMIR. Aide-moi d'abord. Puis nous partirons ensemble.

ESTRAGON. Tu le promets ?

VLADIMIR. Je le jure !

ESTRAGON. Et nous ne reviendrons jamais.

VLADIMIR. Jamais !

ESTRAGON. Nous irons dans l'Ariège.

VLADIMIR. Où tu voudras.

POZZO. Trois cents ! Quatre cents !

ESTRAGON. J'ai toujours voulu me ballader dans l'Ariège.

VLADIMIR. Tu t'y balladeras.

ESTRAGON. Qui a pété ?

VLADIMIR. C'est Pozzo.

POZZO. C'est moi ! C'est moi ! Pitié !

ESTRAGON. C'est dégoûtant.

VLADIMIR. Vite ! Vite ! Donne ta main !

ESTRAGON. Je m'en vais. (*Un temps. Plus fort.*) Je m'en vais.

VLADIMIR. Après tout, je finirai bien par me lever tout seul. (*Il essaie de se lever, retombe.*) Tôt ou tard.*

ESTRAGON. Qu'est-ce que tu as ?

VLADIMIR. Fous le camp.

ESTRAGON. Tu restes là ?

VLADIMIR. Pour le moment.

ESTRAGON. Lève-toi, voyons, tu vas attraper froid.*

VLADIMIR. Ne t'occupe pas de moi.

ESTRAGON. Voyons, Didi, ne sois pas têtu. (*Il tend la main vers Vladimir qui s'empresse de s'en saisir.*) Allez, debout !

VLADIMIR. Tire !

Estragon tire, trébuche, tombe. Long silence.

POZZO. A moi !

VLADIMIR. Nous sommes là.

POZZO. Qui êtes-vous ?

VLADIMIR. Nous sommes des hommes.

Silence.

ESTRAGON. Ce qu'on est bien, par terre !

VLADIMIR. Peux-tu te lever ?

ESTRAGON. Je ne sais pas.

VLADIMIR. Essaie.

ESTRAGON. Tout à l'heure, tout à l'heure.

Silence.

POZZO. Qu'est-ce qui s'est passé ?

VLADIMIR (*avec force*). Veux-tu te taire, toi, à la fin ! Quel choléra quand même ! Il ne pense qu'à lui.

ESTRAGON. Si on essayait de dormir ?

VLADIMIR. Tu l'as entendu ? Il veut savoir ce qui s'est passé !

ESTRAGON. Laisse-le. Dors.

Silence.

POZZO. Pitié ! Pitié !

ESTRAGON (*sursautant*). Quoi ? Qu'est-ce qu'il y a ?

VLADIMIR. Tu dormais ?

ESTRAGON. Je crois.

VLADIMIR. C'est encore ce salaud de Pozzo !

ESTRAGON. Dis-lui de la boucler ! Casse-lui la gueule !

VLADIMIR (*donnant des coups à Pozzo*). As-tu fini ? Veux-tu te taire ? Vermine ! (*Pozzo se dégage en poussant des cris de douleur et s'éloigne en rampant. De temps en temps, il s'arrête, scie l'air avec des gestes d'aveugle, en appelant Lucky. Vladimir, s'appuyant sur le coude, le suit des yeux.*) Il s'est sauvé ! (*Pozzo s'effondre. Silence.*) Il est tombé !

ESTRAGON. Il s'était donc levé ?

VLADIMIR. Non.

ESTRAGON. Et cependant tu dis qu'il est tombé.

VLADIMIR. Il s'était mis à genoux. (*Silence.*) Nous avons été peut-être un peu fort.

ESTRAGON. Cela ne nous arrive pas souvent.

VLADIMIR. Il a imploré notre aide. Nous sommes restés sourds. Il a insisté. Nous l'avons battu.

ESTRAGON. C'est vrai.

VLADIMIR. Il ne bouge plus. Il est peut-être mort.

ESTRAGON. C'est pour avoir voulu l'aider que nous sommes dans ce pétrin.

VLADIMIR. C'est vrai.

ESTRAGON. Tu n'as pas tapé trop fort ?

VLADIMIR. Je lui ai donné quelques bons coups.

ESTRAGON. Tu n'aurais pas dû.

VLADIMIR. C'est toi qui l'as voulu.

ESTRAGON. C'est vrai.* (*Un temps.*) Qu'est-ce qu'on fait maintenant ?

VLADIMIR. Si je pouvais ramper jusqu'à lui.

ESTRAGON. Ne me quitte pas !

VLADIMIR. Si je l'appelais ?

ESTRAGON. C'est ça, appelle-le.

VLADIMIR. Pozzo ! (*Un temps.*) Pozzo ! (*Un temps.*) Il ne répond plus.

ESTRAGON. Ensemble.

VLADIMIR, ESTRAGON. Pozzo ! Pozzo !

VLADIMIR. Il a bougé.

ESTRAGON. Tu es sûr qu'il s'appelle Pozzo ?

VLADIMIR (*angoissé*). Monsieur Pozzo ! Reviens ! On ne te fera pas de mal !

Silence.

ESTRAGON. Si on essayait avec d'autres noms ?

VLADIMIR. J'ai peur qu'il ne soit sérieusement touché.

ESTRAGON. Ce serait amusant.

VLADIMIR. Qu'est-ce qui serait amusant ?

ESTRAGON. D'essayer avec d'autres noms, l'un après l'autre. Ça passerait le temps. On finirait bien par tomber sur le bon.

VLADIMIR. Je te dis qu'il s'appelle Pozzo.

ESTRAGON. C'est ce que nous allons voir. Voyons. (*Il réfléchit.*) Abel ! Abel !

POZZO. A moi !

ESTRAGON. Tu vois !

VLADIMIR. Je commence à en avoir assez de ce motif.

ESTRAGON. Peut-être que l'autre s'appelle Caïn. (*Il appelle.*) Caïn ! Caïn !

POZZO. A moi !

ESTRAGON. C'est toute l'humanité. (*Silence.*) Regarde-moi ce petit nuage.

VLADIMIR (*levant les yeux*). Où ?

ESTRAGON. Là, au zénith.

VLADIMIR. Eh bien ? (*Un temps.*) Qu'est-ce qu'il a de si extraordinaire ?

Silence.

ESTRAGON. Passons maintenant à autre chose, veux-tu ?

VLADIMIR. J'allais justement te le proposer.

ESTRAGON. Mais à quoi ?

VLADIMIR. Ah voilà !

Silence.

ESTRAGON. Si on se levait pour commencer ?

VLADIMIR. Essayons toujours.

Ils se lèvent. *

ESTRAGON. Pas plus difficile que ça.

VLADIMIR. Vouloir, tout est là.

ESTRAGON. Et maintenant ?

POZZO. Au secours !

ESTRAGON. Allons-nous-en.

VLADIMIR. On ne peut pas.

ESTRAGON. Pourquoi ?

VLADIMIR. On attend Godot.

ESTRAGON. C'est vrai. (*Un temps.*) Que faire ?

POZZO. Au secours !

VLADIMIR. Si on le secourait ?

ESTRAGON. Qu'est-ce qu'il faut faire ?

VLADIMIR. Il veut se lever.

ESTRAGON. Et après ?

VLADIMIR. Il veut qu'on l'aide à se lever.

ESTRAGON. Eh bien, aidons-le. Qu'est-ce qu'on attend ?

Ils aident Pozzo à se lever, s'écartent de lui. Il retombe.

VLADIMIR. Il faut le soutenir. (*Même jeu. Pozzo reste debout entre les deux, pendu à leur cou.*) Il faut qu'il se réhabitue à la station debout. (*A Pozzo.*) Ça va mieux ?

POZZO. Qui êtes-vous ?

VLADIMIR. Vous ne nous remettez pas ?

POZZO. Je suis aveugle.

Silence.

ESTRAGON. Peut-être qu'il voit clair dans l'avenir ?

VLADIMIR (*à Pozzo*). Depuis quand ?

POZZO. J'avais une très bonne vue — mais êtes-vous des amis ?

ESTRAGON (*riant bruyamment*). Il demande si nous sommes des amis !

VLADIMIR. Non, il veut dire des amis à lui.

ESTRAGON. Et alors ?

VLADIMIR. La preuve, c'est que nous l'avons aidé.

ESTRAGON. Voilà ! Est-ce que nous l'aurions aidé si nous n'étions pas ses amis ?

VLADIMIR. Peut-être.

ESTRAGON. Évidemment.

VLADIMIR. N'ergotons pas là-dessus.

POZZO. Vous n'êtes pas des brigands ?

ESTRAGON. Des brigands ! Est-ce qu'on a l'air de brigands ?

VLADIMIR. Voyons ! Il est aveugle.

ESTRAGON. Flûte ! C'est vrai. (*Un temps.*) Qu'il dit.

POZZO. Ne me quittez pas.

VLADIMIR. Il n'en est pas question.

ESTRAGON. Pour l'instant.

POZZO. Quelle heure est-il ?

ESTRAGON (*inspectant le ciel*). Voyons...

VLADIMIR. Sept heures ?... Huit heures ?...

ESTRAGON. Ça dépend de la saison.

POZZO. C'est le soir ?

Silence. Vladimir et Estragon regardent le couchant.

ESTRAGON. On dirait qu'il remonte. *

VLADIMIR. Ce n'est pas possible.

ESTRAGON. Si c'était l'aurore ?

VLADIMIR. Ne dis pas de bêtises. C'est l'ouest par-là.

ESTRAGON. Qu'est-ce que tu en sais ?

POZZO (*avec angoisse*). Sommes-nous au soir ?

VLADIMIR. D'ailleurs, il n'a pas bougé.

ESTRAGON. Je te dis qu'il remonte.

POZZO. Pourquoi ne répondez-vous pas ?

ESTRAGON. C'est qu'on ne voudrait pas vous dire une connerie. *

VLADIMIR (*rassurant*). C'est le soir, monsieur, nous sommes arrivés au soir. Mon ami essaie de m'en faire douter, et je dois avouer que j'ai été ébranlé pendant un instant. Mais ce n'est pas pour rien que j'ai vécu cette longue journée et je peux vous assurer qu'elle est presque au bout de son répertoire. (*Un temps.*) A part ça, comment vous sentez-vous ?

ESTRAGON. Combien de temps va-t-il falloir le charrier encore ? (*Ils le lâchent à moitié, le reprennent en voyant qu'il va retomber.*) On n'est pas des cariatides.

VLADIMIR. Vous disiez que vous aviez une bonne vue, autrefois, si j'ai bien entendu ?

POZZO. Oui, elle était bien bonne.

Silence.

ESTRAGON (*avec irritation*). Développez ! Développez !

VLADIMIR. Laisse-le tranquille. Ne vois-tu pas qu'il est en train de se rappeler son bonheur. (*Un temps.*) *Memoria praeteritorum bonorum* — ça doit être pénible.

POZZO. Oui, bien bonne.

VLADIMIR. Et cela vous a pris tout d'un coup ?

POZZO. Bien bonne.

VLADIMIR. Je vous demande si cela vous a pris tout d'un coup.

POZZO. Un beau jour je me suis réveillé, aveugle comme le destin. (*Un temps.*) Je me demande parfois si je ne dors pas encore.

VLADIMIR. Quand ça ?

POZZO. Je ne sais pas.

VLADIMIR. Mais pas plus tard qu'hier...

POZZO. Ne me questionnez pas. Les aveugles n'ont pas la notion du temps. (*Un temps.*) Les choses du temps, ils ne les voient pas non plus.

VLADIMIR. Tiens ! J'aurais juré le contraire.

ESTRAGON. Je m'en vais.

POZZO. Où sommes-nous ?

VLADIMIR. Je ne sais pas.

POZZO. Ne serait-on pas au lieudit la Planche ?

VLADIMIR. Je ne connais pas.

POZZO. A quoi est-ce que ça ressemble ?

VLADIMIR (*regard circulaire*). On ne peut pas le décrire. Ça ne ressemble à rien. Il n'y a rien. Il y a un arbre.

POZZO. Alors ce n'est pas la Planche.

ESTRAGON (*ployant*). Tu parles d'une diversion.*

POZZO. Où est mon domestique ?

VLADIMIR. Il est là.

POZZO. Pourquoi ne répond-il pas quand je l'appelle ?

VLADIMIR. Je ne sais pas. Il semble dormir. Il est peut-être mort.

POZZO. Que s'est-il passé, au juste ?

ESTRAGON. Au juste !

VLADIMIR. Vous êtes tombés tous les deux.

POZZO. Allez voir s'il est blessé.

VLADIMIR. Mais on ne peut pas vous quitter.

POZZO. Vous n'avez pas besoin d'y aller tous les deux.

VLADIMIR (*à Estragon*). Vas-y toi.

POZZO. C'est ça, que votre ami y aille. Il sent si mauvais.

VLADIMIR. Va le réveiller.

ESTRAGON. Après ce qu'il m'a fait ! Jamais de la vie.

VLADIMIR. Ah, tu te rappelles enfin qu'il t'a fait quelque chose.

ESTRAGON. Je ne me rappelle rien du tout. C'est toi qui me l'as dit.

VLADIMIR. C'est vrai. (*A Pozzo.*) Mon ami a peur.

POZZO. Il n'y a rien à craindre.

VLADIMIR (*à Estragon*). A propos, ces gens que tu as vus, où sont-ils passés ?

ESTRAGON. Je ne sais pas.

VLADIMIR. Ils sont peut-être tapis quelque part, en train de nous épier.

ESTRAGON. Voilà.

VLADIMIR. Ils se sont peut-être arrêtés tout simplement.

ESTRAGON. Voilà.

VLADIMIR. Pour se reposer.

ESTRAGON. Pour se restaurer.

VLADIMIR. Ils ont peut-être rebroussé chemin ?

ESTRAGON. Voilà.

VLADIMIR. C'était peut-être une vision.

ESTRAGON. Une illusion.

VLADIMIR. Une hallucination.

ESTRAGON. Une illusion.*

POZZO. Qu'est-ce qu'il attend ?

VLADIMIR (*à Estragon*). Qu'est-ce que tu attends ?

ESTRAGON. J'attends Godot.

VLADIMIR (*à Pozzo*). Je vous ai dit que mon ami a peur. Hier votre domestique l'a attaqué, alors qu'il voulait seulement lui essuyer les larmes.

POZZO. Ah, mais il ne faut jamais être gentil avec ces gens-là. Ils ne le supportent pas.

VLADIMIR. Qu'est-ce qu'il doit faire au juste ?

POZZO. Eh bien, qu'il tire d'abord sur la corde, en faisant attention naturellement de ne pas l'étrangler. En général, ça le fait réagir. Sinon qu'il lui donne des coups de pied, dans le bas-ventre et au visage autant que possible.

VLADIMIR (*à Estragon*). Tu vois, tu n'as rien à craindre. C'est même une occasion de te venger.

ESTRAGON. Et s'il se défend ?

POZZO. Non, non, il ne se défend jamais.

VLADIMIR. Je volerai* a ton secours.

ESTRAGON. Ne me quitte pas des yeux ! (*Il va vers Lucky.*)

VLADIMIR. Regarde s'il est vivant d'abord. Pas la peine de lui taper dessus s'il est mort.

ESTRAGON (*s'étant penché sur Lucky*). Il respire.

VLADIMIR. Alors vas-y.

Subitement déchaîné, Estragon bourre Lucky de coups de pied, en hurlant. Mais il se fait mal au pied et s'éloigne en boitant et en gémissant. Lucky reprend ses sens.

ESTRAGON (*s'arrêtant sur une jambe*). Oh la vache !

Estragon s'assied, essaie d'enlever ses chaussures. Mais bientôt il y renoncera, se disposera en chien de fusil, la tête entre les jambes, les bras devant la tête.

POZZO. Que s'est-il passé encore ?

VLADIMIR. Mon ami s'est fait mal.

POZZO. Et Lucky ?

VLADIMIR. Alors c'est bien lui ?

POZZO. Comment ?

VLADIMIR. C'est bien Lucky ?

POZZO. Je ne comprends pas.

VLADIMIR. Et vous, vous êtes Pozzo ?

POZZO. Certainement je suis Pozzo.

VLADIMIR. Les mêmes qu'hier ?

POZZO. Qu'hier ?

VLADIMIR. On s'est vu hier. (*Silence.*) Vous ne vous rappelez pas ?

POZZO. Je ne me rappelle avoir rencontré personne hier. Mais demain je ne me rappellerai avoir rencontré personne aujourd'hui. Ne comptez donc pas sur moi pour vous renseigner. Et puis assez là-dessus. Debout ! *

VLADIMIR. Vous l'emmeniez à Saint-Sauveur pour le vendre. Vous nous avez parlé. Il a dansé. Il a pensé. Vous voyiez clair.

POZZO. Si vous y tenez. Lâchez-moi, s'il vous plaît. (*Vladimir s'écarte.*) Debout !

VLADIMIR. Il se lève.

Lucky se lève, ramasse les bagages.

POZZO. Il fait bien.

VLADIMIR. Où allez-vous de ce pas ?

POZZO. Je ne m'occupe pas de ça.

VLADIMIR. Comme vous avez changé ! *

Lucky, chargé des bagages, vient se placer devant Pozzo.

POZZO. Fouet ! (*Lucky dépose les bagages, cherche le fouet, le trouve, le donne à Pozzo, reprend les bagages.*) Corde ! (*Lucky dépose les bagages, met le bout de la corde dans la main de Pozzo, reprend les bagages.*)

VLADIMIR. Qu'est-ce qu'il y a dans la valise ?

POZZO. Du sable. (*Il tire sur la corde.*) En avant ! (*Lucky s'ébranle, Pozzo le suit.*)

VLADIMIR. Un instant.

Pozzo s'arrête. La corde se tend. Lucky tombe, en lâchant tout. Pozzo trébuche, lâche la corde à temps, chancelle sur place. Vladimir le soutient.

POZZO. Qu'est-ce qui se passe ?

VLADIMIR. Il est tombé.

POZZO. Vite, faites-le lever avant qu'il s'endorme.

VLADIMIR. Vous n'allez pas tomber si je vous lâche ?

POZZO. Je ne pense pas.

Vladimir donne des coups de pied à Lucky.

VLADIMIR. Debout ! Porc ! (*Lucky se relève, ramasse les bagages.*) Il est debout.

POZZO (*tendant la main*). Corde !

Lucky dépose les bagages, met le bout de la corde dans la main de Pozzo, reprend les bagages.

VLADIMIR. Ne partez pas encore.

POZZO. Je pars.

VLADIMIR. Que faites-vous quand vous tombez loin de tout secours ?

POZZO. Nous attendons de pouvoir nous relever. Puis nous repartons.*

VLADIMIR. Avant de partir, dites-lui de chanter.

POZZO. A qui ?

VLADIMIR. A Lucky.

POZZO. De chanter ?

VLADIMIR. Oui. Ou de penser. Ou de réciter.

POZZO. Mais il est muet.

VLADIMIR. Muet !

POZZO. Parfaitement. Il ne peut même pas gémir.

VLADIMIR. Muet ! Depuis quand ?

POZZO (*soudain furieux*). Vous n'avez pas fini de m'empoisonner avec vos histoires de temps ? C'est insensé ! Quand ! Quand ! Un jour, ça ne vous suffit pas, un jour pareil aux autres il est devenu muet, un jour je suis devenu aveugle, un jour nous deviendrons sourds, un jour nous sommes nés, un jour nous mourrons, le même jour, le même instant, ça ne vous suffit pas ? (*Plus posément.*) Elles accouchent à cheval sur une tombe, le jour brille un instant, puis c'est la nuit à nouveau. (*Il tire sur la corde.*) En avant !

Ils sortent. Vladimir les suit jusqu'à la limite de la scène, les regarde s'éloigner. Un bruit de chute, appuyé par la mimique de Vladimir, annonce qu'ils sont tombés à nouveau. Silence. Vladimir va vers Estragon qui dort, le contemple un moment, puis le réveille.

ESTRAGON (*gestes affolés, paroles incohérentes. Finalement*). Pourquoi tu ne me laisses jamais dormir ?

VLADIMIR. Je me sentais seul.

ESTRAGON. Je rêvais que j'étais heureux.

VLADIMIR. Ça a fait passer le temps.

ESTRAGON. Je rêvais que...

VLADIMIR. Tais-toi ! (*Silence.*) Je me demande s'il est vraiment aveugle.

ESTRAGON. Qui ?

VLADIMIR. Un vrai aveugle dirait-il qu'il n'a pas la notion du temps ?

ESTRAGON. Qui ?

VLADIMIR. Pozzo.

ESTRAGON. Il est aveugle ?

VLADIMIR. Il nous l'a dit.

ESTRAGON. Et alors ?

VLADIMIR. Il m'a semblé qu'il nous voyait.

ESTRAGON. Tu l'as rêvé.* (*Un temps.*) Allons-nous-en. On ne peut pas. C'est vrai. (*Un temps.*) Tu es sûr que ce n'était pas lui ?

VLADIMIR. Qui ?

ESTRAGON. Godot ?

VLADIMIR. Mais qui ?

ESTRAGON. Pozzo.

VLADIMIR. Mais non ! Mais non ! (*Un temps.*) Mais non.

ESTRAGON. Je vais quand même me lever. (*Se lève péniblement.*) Aïe !

VLADIMIR. Je ne sais plus quoi penser.

ESTRAGON. Mes pieds ! (*Il se rassied, essaie de se déchausser.*) Aide-moi !

VLADIMIR. Est-ce que j'ai dormi, pendant que les autres souffraient ? Est-ce que je dors en ce moment ? Demain, quand je croirai me réveiller, que dirai-je de cette journée ? Qu'avec Estragon mon ami, à cet endroit, jusqu'à la tombée de la nuit, j'ai attendu Godot ? Que Pozzo est passé, avec son porteur, et qu'il nous a parlé ? Sans doute. Mais dans tout cela qu'y aura-t-il de vrai ? (*Estragon, s'étant acharné en vain sur ses chaussures, s'est assoupi à nouveau. Vladimir regarde.*) Lui ne saura rien. Il parlera des coups qu'il a reçus et je lui donnerai une carotte. (*Un temps.*) A cheval sur une tombe et une naissance difficile. Du fond du trou, rêveusement, le fossoyeur applique ses fers. On a le temps de vieillir. L'air est plein de nos cris. (*Il écoute.*) Mais l'habitude est une grande sourdine. (*Il regarde Estragon.*) Moi aussi, un autre me regarde, en se disant, Il dort, il ne sait pas, qu'il dorme. (*Un *temps.*) Je ne peux pas continuer.* (*Un temps.*) Qu'est-ce que j'ai dit ?

Il va et vient avec agitation, s'arrête finalement près de la coulisse gauche, regarde au loin. Entre à droite le garçon de la veille. Il s'arrête. Silence.*

GARÇON. Monsieur... (*Vladimir se retourne.*) Monsieur Albert...

VLADIMIR. Reprenons. (*Un temps. Au garçon.*) Tu ne me reconnais pas ?

GARÇON. Non Monsieur.

VLADIMIR. C'est toi qui es venu hier ?

GARÇON. Non Monsieur.

VLADIMIR. C'est la première fois que tu viens ?

GARÇON. Oui Monsieur.

Silence.

VLADIMIR. C'est de la part de Monsieur Godot.

GARÇON. Oui Monsieur.

VLADIMIR. Il ne viendra pas ce soir.

GARÇON. Non Monsieur.

VLADIMIR. Mais il viendra demain.

GARÇON. Oui Monsieur.

VLADIMIR. Sûrement.

GARÇON. Oui Monsieur.

Silence.

VLADIMIR. Est-ce que tu as rencontré quelqu'un ?

GARÇON. Non Monsieur.

VLADIMIR. Deux autres (*il hésite*) ...hommes.*

GARÇON. Je n'ai vu personne, Monsieur.

Silence.

VLADIMIR. Qu'est-ce qu'il fait, Monsieur Godot ? (*Un temps.*) Tu entends ?

GARÇON. Oui Monsieur.

VLADIMIR. Et alors ?

GARÇON. Il ne fait rien, Monsieur.*

Silence.

VLADIMIR. Comment va ton frère ?

GARÇON. Il est malade Monsieur.

VLADIMIR. C'est peut-être lui qui est venu hier.

GARÇON. Je ne sais pas Monsieur.

Silence.

VLADIMIR. Il a une barbe, Monsieur Godot ?

GARÇON. Oui Monsieur.

VLADIMIR. Blonde ou... (*il hésite*) ...ou noire ?

GARÇON (*hésitant*). Je crois qu'elle est blanche, Monsieur.

Silence.

VLADIMIR. Miséricorde.

Silence.

GARÇON. Qu'est-ce que je dois dire à Monsieur Godot, Monsieur ?

VLADIMIR. Tu lui diras — (*il s'interrompt*) — tu lui diras que tu m'as vu et que — (*il réfléchit*) — que tu m'as vu. (*Un temps. Vladimir s'avance, le garçon recule, Vladimir s'arrête, le garçon s'arrête.*) Dis, tu es bien sûr de m'avoir vu, tu ne vas pas me dire demain que tu ne m'as jamais vu ?

Silence. Vladimir fait un soudain bond en avant, le garçon se sauve comme une flèche. Silence. Le soleil se couche, la lune se lève. Vladimir reste immobile. Estragon se réveille, se déchausse, se lève, les chaussures à la main, les dépose devant la rampe, va vers Vladimir, le regarde.

ESTRAGON. Qu'est-ce que tu as ?

VLADIMIR. Je n'ai rien.

ESTRAGON. Moi je m'en vais.

VLADIMIR. Moi aussi.

Silence.

ESTRAGON. Il y avait longtemps que je dormais ?

VLADIMIR. Je ne sais pas.

Silence.

ESTRAGON. Où irons-nous ?

VLADIMIR. Pas loin.

ESTRAGON. Si si, allons-nous-en loin d'ici !

VLADIMIR. On ne peut pas.

ESTRAGON. Pourquoi ?

VLADIMIR. Il faut revenir demain.*

ESTRAGON. Pour quoi faire?

VLADIMIR. Attendre Godot.

ESTRAGON. C'est vrai. (*Un temps.*) Il n'est pas venu?

VLADIMIR. Non.

ESTRAGON. Et maintenant il est trop tard.

VLADIMIR. Oui, c'est la nuit.*

ESTRAGON. Et si on le laissait tomber? (*Un temps.*) Si on le laissait tomber?

VLADIMIR. Il nous punirait. (*Silence. Il regarde l'arbre.*) Seul l'arbre vit.*

ESTRAGON (*regardant l'arbre*). Qu'est-ce que c'est?

VLADIMIR. C'est l'arbre.

ESTRAGON. Non, mais quel genre?

VLADIMIR. Je ne sais pas. Un saule.

ESTRAGON. Viens voir. (*Il entraîne Vladimir vers l'arbre. Ils s'immobilisent devant. Silence.*) Et si on se pendait?

VLADIMIR. Avec quoi?

ESTRAGON. Tu n'as pas un bout de corde?

VLADIMIR. Non.

ESTRAGON. Alors on ne peut pas.

VLADIMIR. Allons-nous-en.

ESTRAGON. Attends, il y a ma ceinture.

VLADIMIR. C'est trop court.

ESTRAGON. Tu tireras sur mes jambes.

VLADIMIR. Et qui tirera sur les miennes?

ESTRAGON. C'est vrai.

VLADIMIR. Fais voir quand même. (*Estragon dénoue la corde qui maintient son pantalon. Celui-ci, beaucoup trop large, lui tombe autour des chevilles. Ils regardent la corde.*) A la rigueur ça pourrait aller. Mais est-elle solide?

ESTRAGON. On va voir. Tiens.

Ils prennent chacun un bout de la corde et tirent. La corde se casse. Ils manquent de tomber.

VLADIMIR. Elle ne vaut rien.

Silence.

ESTRAGON. Tu dis qu'il faut revenir demain?

VLADIMIR. Oui.

ESTRAGON. Alors on apportera une bonne corde.

VLADIMIR. C'est ça.

Silence.

ESTRAGON. Didi.

VLADIMIR. Oui.

ESTRAGON. Je ne peux plus continuer comme ça.

VLADIMIR. On dit ça.

ESTRAGON. Si on se quittait? Ça irait peut-être mieux.

VLADIMIR. On se pendra demain. (*Un temps.*) A moins que Godot ne vienne.

ESTRAGON. Et s'il vient.

VLADIMIR. Nous serons sauvés.

*Vladimir enlève son chapeau — celui de Lucky — regarde dedans, y passe la main, le secoue, le remet.**

ESTRAGON. Alors on y va?

VLADIMIR. Relève ton pantalon.

ESTRAGON. Comment?

VLADIMIR. Relève ton pantalon.

ESTRAGON. Que j'enlève mon pantalon?

VLADIMIR. *RE*-lève ton pantalon.*

ESTRAGON. C'est vrai.

Il relève son pantalon. Silence.

VLADIMIR. Alors on y va?

ESTRAGON. Allons-y.

Ils ne bougent pas.

RIDEAU

NOTES

NOTES

The figures refer to pages. Words and phrases dealt with in Harrap's Shorter French and English Dictionary *are not normally included here. Interesting variants to be found in French and English versions of the play are referred to as follows:*

M: Manuscript of *En attendant Godot.*
1st ed.: Éditions de Minuit, *dépôt légal* octobre 1952.
G: Waiting for Godot, Grove Press, New York, 1954.
F: Waiting for Godot, Faber and Faber, London, 1956. This edition consists of the text used in the Criterion Theatre 1955 production, incorporating "a small number of textual deletions . . . made to satisfy the requirements of the Lord Chamberlain". Including these deletions, there are two hundred and sixty-seven examples of variation in meaning or tone in *F* compared with the second French edition (also 1952) which is the *édition de base*: one hundred and seventy-six in Act 1, ninety-one in Act 2. Many of these are too minor to be listed here.
RC: The Royal Court Theatre production of 1964/5. The version used included a few variations from *F* and *G* which, as the production was supervised by Mr Beckett, are occasionally worthy of mention here.

Title page: In *F* and *G* the play is called "a tragicomedy in two acts".

3. ***assis par terre:*** *F* and *G:* "sitting on a low mound". The scene was much clearer in Beckett's mind by the time he came to do the English translation.
Rien à faire: "Nothing to be done". Mr Beckett told me of one producer of *Waiting for Godot* (in Ireland) who insisted that the correct English must be "Nothing doing"!
Je commence à le croire: *F* and *G:* "I'm beginning to come round to that opinion". The English version introduces an immediate contrast, lacking in the French, between the highly literate speech of the two tramps and their physical condition. There is no direct indication that the two tramps are tramps,

in fact; this is now assumed because of Roger Blin's original production (which had the blessing of Mr Beckett) in which they took on many of the physical characteristics of the destitutes in Beckett's previous works. Vladimir objects strongly to Estragon's begging from Pozzo later.

Vladimir: In the manuscript this is the first mention of Vladimir's name. See Introduction, page lxii.

Que faire . . .: In *F* and *G* this question is preceded by further evidence of Vladimir's warmth of character: "Together again at last!" This also stresses the strangeness of the time factor in the play. How long is it *in fact* since they last saw each other? See Introduction, Chapters 2 and 7.

Monsieur: Heavier sarcasm in the English versions: "his Highness".

Si... pas trop: In *F* and *G* Estragon is more self-pitying: "Beat me? Certainly they beat me."

4. **Tu ne serais . . . erreur**: Cf. p. 47, where Estragon speaks of the time he was saved by Vladimir from drowning.

il y a une éternité, vers 1900: *M:* "il y a un demi-siècle, vers 1900". *F:* "when the world was young, in the nineties". *G:* "a million years ago, in the nineties".

cette saloperie: *M:* "mes godasses". *F* and *G:* "Stop blathering and help me off with this bloody thing".

C'est long, mais ce sera bon: The reader is no doubt expected to reach for the *Dictionnaire des citations* in response to Vladimir's question "Qui disait ça?". In fact, Mr Beckett heard it in the street, and the correct answer is "Un passant"! *F* and *G* read: "Hope deferred maketh the something sick". See Introduction, p. liv, concerning this variant.

5. ***un suprême effort:*** *M:* "*un effort surhumain*". What a gift this would have been to the imaginative interpreter had it remained in the final text!

un pourcentage honnête: i.e., "a reasonable percentage" (*F*, *G*). *M:* "un bon pourcentage".

D'être né?: Cf. ". . . the original and eternal sin . . . the sin of having been born." Samuel Beckett, *Proust.*

Seulement sourire: Cf. *Mercier et Camier:* "dans chaque situation la nature nous convie . . . au sourire, sinon au rire".

6. **A l'école sans Dieu . . . la Roquette**: The religious association and play on words do not appear in the manuscript:

— A l'école libre?
— Sais pas si elle était libre.
— Tu dois confondre avec la maison de correction.

F and *G* omit all reference to school. La Roquette was until 1900 a prison in Paris. The reference is probably to La *Petite* Roquette, which is a kind of Borstal for *jeunes détenus*.
Il enfle: Funnier in *F* and *G:* "Swelling visibly".

7. **un seul parle d'un larron de sauvé**: It is only St Luke who mentions (xxiii, 43) that Jesus rewarded the faith of one of the two thieves by promising "Today shalt thou be with me in paradise". The salvation of one of the two thieves is a recurrent theme in Beckett's works; he has even 'explained' Estragon's difficulty with his boots in terms of it: "one foot blessed and the other damned, like the two thieves on the cross".
Les gens sont des cons: This obscene pratfall effectively puts an end to a conversation that was boring Estragon increasingly. *F* and *G:* "People are bloody ignorant apes".
8. **Ah non, là tu te goures**: i.e., "Ah no, there you're mistaken" (*F*, *G*).
9. **Pour jeter le doute, à toi le pompon**: *F*, *G:* "Nothing is certain when you're about". *M:* "Pour semer le doute, il n'y a pas deux comme toi".
Pour moi: 'In my opinion'.
10. **Les Anglais . . . bordel**: *M:* "Les Anglais disent carrrm (*accent d'Oxford exagéré*)." *F:* "All the best people say cawm". *G:* "The English say cawm". *1st ed.:* "Ce sont des gens câââms" does not appear.
11. **Qu'est-ce qu'on fait . . . on se pendait**: In *M* the rôles are reversed for these lines:

    LÉVY. Qu'est-ce qu'on fait maintenant?
    VLADIMIR. Si on se pendait?

    Estragon gradually develops as the more despairing of the two.
    Ce serait un moyen de bander: *G:* "It'd give us an erection". Omitted from *F*, replaced in *RC*. It is not just a dirty joke, as the following comments show. "Sexual imagery, which is counterpointed with religious imagery throughout the play, supports one of the principal themes: without God there is no creation. The impotence that Gogo and Didi are constantly striving to overcome is complete, or as nearly complete as it can be while human contact is still possible. . . . they light on a

desperate expedient which brings out the full pathos and absurdity of the situation" (J. R. Moore, 'A Farewell to Something', *Tulane Drama Review*, I, 1960, p. 51). "The fact that they exist in the despairing sickness of hope makes them too weak to destroy their own existence. In fact, even their desire for suicide is a commitment to existence, to becoming, for by suicide they wish to satisfy their sexual impotency, their impotency for becoming" (Bro. John Rechtien, 'Time and Eternity meet in the Present', *Texas Studies in Literature and Language*, VI, 1964, pp. 5–21).

12. **Si tu veux**: In *F* and *G* this becomes more definite: "Exactly".
13. **bazardés**: *F:* "We waived them". *G:* "got rid of them". *RC:* "dumped them". *M* continues:

    LÉVY. Je ne veux pas discuter avec toi.
    VLADIMIR. Ni moi avec toi.
    LÉVY. Mais tu as tort.
    VLADIMIR. C'est probable. (*Silence.*) [etc.]

14. **Allons-nous-en . . . encore jour**: These lines are omitted from *F* and *G*.
15. **Je me fais au goût au fur et à mesure**: Picturesquely rendered in *F* and *G* by "I get used to the muck as I go along".
16. ***plateau:*** *M* has *scène*; *F* and *G* revert to this: *stage*.
    méchant: *M* (crossed out): "Il est sauvage".
    Je me présente: Pozzo: *M:* "Je m'appelle Pozzo". Supporters of the theory that Pozzo is really Godot may see in this change a significant refusal on Beckett's part to make Pozzo tell an outright lie about his name. He is *introducing* himself as Pozzo and not, as in *M*, saying that his *name* is Pozzo. But shortly after, he states "Je suis Pozzo" without tergiversation.
17. **brodait au tambour**: *M:* "faisait de la couture". The English versions are far removed from either embroidery or sewing. *F:* "The mother had warts". *G* and *RC:* "had the clap".
    pas d'ici: *M:* "pas du pays".
22. **sans indiscrétion**: Not in *M*.
    Demandez-lui: In *F* and *G* Estragon replies "Eleven"—an even more effective way of telling Pozzo to mind his own business.
23. **Il a raison . . . saviez-vous?**: There is no 'He's right' in *F* or *G*. *G* goes on, "Who told you?"
25. **au marché de Saint-Sauveur**: In *F* and *G* this becomes

simply "to the fair". 'Le Sauveur' invites religious interpretation, as discussed in the Introduction, Chapter 3 (p. lix).

26. **Le cas échéant:** Vladimir's amusingly human regret at being so over-helpful is not in *M*.
Les larmes du monde sont immuables: This is more graphic in the English versions: "The tears of the world are a constant quantity".

27. **soixante ans que ça dure:** *M:* "cinquante ans que ça dure. (*Il se redresse*, etc.)".
chapeau: An author's footnote in the French edition reads: "Tous ces personnages portent le chapeau melon."
Qu'est-ce que c'est, un knouk?: Vladimir's question and Pozzo's reply do not appear in *F* and *G*. *F* misprints *knook* [*G* and *RC*] as *knock*. The word *knouk* was invented by Samuel Beckett by analogy with *knout* (Russian for 'whip').
Êtes-vous seulement du siècle?: 'Can you really be so out of touch (with worldly things)?' People used to have all-licensed fools, buffoons; now they only have what we see in Lucky.
fou: *M:* "fou à lier".
Silence: *M:* "*Silence religieux*". [!].

28. **On se croirait au spectacle:** *F:* "It's worse than being at the theatre". *G* and *RC:* "pantomime". For *M* and *1st ed.* versions of these exchanges, see Introduction, Chapter 3 (p. lix).

30. **Non non . . . *basse:*** Not in *M*.
Vous croyez . . . certain: Intercalated on left-hand page in *M*.

31. **Catulle:** For explanation and variants, see Introduction, Chapter 3, p. lxiii.
porc: *M:* "cochon".
Regardez . . . nous y attendrons le moins: Cf. *Mercier et Camier:* "On parle beaucoup du ciel, les yeux s'y portent souvent, ils se détachent, histoire de se reposer, des masses permises et voulues, pour s'offrir à ce monceau de déserts transparents, c'est un fait." And *Watt:* "These northwestern skies are really extraordinary, said Goff, are they not.—So voluptuous, said Tetty. You think it is all over and then pop! up they flare, with augmented radiance" (Olympia Press, p. 16).

32. **très bon:** *M:* LÉVY (*comprenant le premier*) . . . [etc.].
VLADIMIR [no *accent anglais*]. Oh très très bien, très très très bien.
J'ai cru que c'était exprès: *M* simply has "A peine".

En attendant: 'In the meantime'.
Ce n'est pas folichon: 'It's not exactly gay'. *F*, *G:* "I've been better entertained"; it is Estragon who says this in English.
un louis: *F:* "a shilling". *G:* "ten francs".
cent sous: *F:* "sixpence". *G:* "five". *RC:* "a tanner".

33. **J'en prends le chemin**: Estragon has not registered Pozzo's last speech, and carries on from Vladimir's previous remark ("Nous ne sommes pas des mendiants"). Hence the meaning is, 'I'm on the way to becoming one'. *F* and *G* change the line completely: "I couldn't accept less".
Qui! Vous savez penser, vous autres?: Pozzo's condescending remark does not appear in *M*.
pouacre: *F*, *G:* "misery".

34. **La mort . . . vieillards**: In *M*, simply "La mort du canard". The English versions are quite different: "The Scapegoat's Agony" and "The Hard Stool". It has been suggested that the latter has an association with the penitential stool, but Mr Beckett tells me the only association is with constipation.
Woooa!: *M:* "Reste là où tu es!" For Lucky's equine origins, see Introduction, Chapter 3, p. lxiv.

35. **C'est vrai**: From here to "Je suis fatigué" (p. 36) omitted in *F* and *G*.

37. ***débit monotone:*** *M:* "*débit précipité*". For comments on Lucky's speech, see Introduction, Chapter 6, p. cvii.
jaillit: *M:* "ressort".
quaqua: *M:* "quoique".
la divine Miranda: Prospero's daughter in *The Tempest*, whom Ferdinand praises thus:

> Admir'd Miranda!
> Indeed, the top of admiration: worth
> What's dearest to the world!

38. **le camogie**: Irish hurling.

40. **Une véritable savonnette . . . à secondes trotteuses**: "A genuine half-hunter, gentlemen, with deadbeat escapement" (*F* and *G*). The French cannot render the associations of 'deadbeat escapement': loss of the watch brings loss of ability to escape becoming 'dead beat'; and the beat of Pozzo's heart—which is ailing—is nearer to being dead.
C'est mon pépé qui me l'a donnée: *1st ed.:* "Elle appartenait

à mon grand-père". The later version brings out the little-boy pathos. *F* and *G* have Pozzo "sobbing" here.

43. ***craintivement:*** *M:* "*peureusement*". The English merely has "*timidly*".

44. **C'est la mienne peut-être:** *M:* "Comment ce n'est pas ta faute?"

De nous?: *M* is less angry:

> ESTRAGON. De nous?
> GARÇON. Non, Monsieur.
> VLADIMIR. Je vois [*etc.*].

Des deux messieurs: *F* and *G* have "The two big men".

46. **Je fais comme toi . . . la blafarde:** Estragon has two poetic lines here in English, an echo of Shelley ("To the Moon", 1820):

> ESTRAGON. Pale for weariness.
> VLADIMIR. Eh?
> ESTRAGON. Of climbing heaven and gazing on the likes of us.

47. **Il faut s'abriter:** The horrors of night, vaguely suggested here, are mentioned in *Mercier et Camier:*

> Je me coucherai par terre, dit Mercier, et j'attendrai l'aube. Devant mes yeux ouverts défileront des scènes et des visages. La pluie sur la verrière fera son bruit de griffes et la nuit me contera ses douleurs. L'envie me viendra de me jeter par la fenêtre, mais je la dominerai. Il répéta, dans un rugissement, Je la dominerai!

Cinquante ans peut-être: *RC:* "Donkey's years".

ACT TWO

49. ***couvert de feuilles:*** The English versions read "four or five leaves". See Introduction, Chapter 3, p. liii, for a discussion of this.

trop bas: *F* and *G* have "too high".

51. **tu pisses mieux:** *M:* "Tu vois, tu vas mieux". Vladimir has a condition caused by enlargement of the prostate gland.

Maintenant... (*joyeux*): Between these two words the following appears in the 1st edition:

> Oui... quand je ferme les yeux (*il les ferme et les couvre de*

ses mains, pour plus de sûreté) je sens... oui... que la lumière m'abandonne. (*Il rouvre les yeux.*) Te revoilà et maintenant (*il ferme les yeux, se concentre*), maintenant je me sens devenir tout noir, à l'intérieur. N'est-ce pas curieux?

The passage is fairly obviously inspired by the philosophy of Bishop Berkeley (see Introduction, Chapter 7, p. cxvi).

dix: *M:* "quatre".

53. **sous-sol:** i.e., the grave. *F*, *G:* "the worms".
54. **nous sommes intarissables:** Cf. *Mercier et Camier:*

> Si nous n'avons rien à nous dire, dit Camier, ne nous disons rien.
> Nous avons des choses à nous dire, dit Mercier.
> Alors pourquoi ne nous les disons-nous pas? dit Camier.
> C'est que nous ne savons pas, dit Mercier.
> Alors taisons-nous, dit Camier.
> Mais nous essayons, dit Mercier.

56. **vers la nature:** In the Royal Court production, Estragon turned to look at the pathetic little tree as he said this. Cf. *Fin de Partie:*

> HAMM. La nature nous a oubliés.
> CLOV. Il n'y a plus de nature.
> HAMM. Plus de nature! Tu vas fort.
> CLOV. Dans les environs.
> HAMM. Mais nous respirons, nous changeons! Nous perdons nos cheveux, nos dents! Notre fraîcheur! Nos idéaux!
> CLOV. Alors elle ne nous a pas oubliés. (p. 25)

57. **Voyons:** In the English versions they do the same hat-doffing routine as they do with Pozzo in Act 1.
58. **Ce n'est pas le vide qui manque:** *1st ed.:* "l'espace". *F* and *G:* "There's no lack of void".
60. ***Vladimir . . . le renifle:*** Cf. this remark on progressive destitution in *Mercier et Camier:* "Sentir ses poches qui chaque jour se vident des suprêmes ressources, voilà de quoi briser les résolutions les mieux trempées".
61. **pas de lacet:** The reason for Estragon's fear of laces is obscure; possibly it is nothing more mysterious than the dislike born of wearing boots too small far too long.

Elles sont trop grandes: Mr Beckett wrote me the following comment on this: "The second day boots are no doubt same as first and Estragon's feet wasted, pined, shrunk and dwindled in interval. There's exegesis for you." *En effet!*

62. ***une posture utérine:*** i.e., "His head between his knees" (*F* and *G*).

65. **Jusqu'au bord de la pente:** For comment on omission of all mention of *la pente* (and *le plateau*) see Introduction, Chapter 3, p. lvii.

67. ***Échange d'injures:*** The insults are specified in the English versions—the last and most devastating being: "Crrritic!"

When *En attendant Godot* was produced by Roger Blin in Toulouse, the final insult was "Architecte!" Dr John Fletcher tells me that M. Blin had heard an exchange of insults between taxi-drivers in Brussels, the most virulent apparently being 'Architecte'. M. Blin's driver told him the reason was that part of Brussels was being demolished and redeveloped in a way which caused such strong public disapproval that 'architecte' had become a term of vilest abuse. The first edition of *Godot* does not contain the word.

68. ***Entrent Pozzo et Lucky:*** Their entrance is intercalated on the left-hand page of *M*.

70. **baisés:** Vulgar for 'done for'. *F* has "banjaxed".

71. **en tablant sur sa reconnaissance:** "In anticipation of some tangible return" (*F* and *G*).

72. **et nous pousse . . . l'habitude:** The English is clearer (*F* and *G*): "the hours... constrain us to beguile them with proceedings which, how shall I say, which may at first sight seem reasonable until they become a habit".

solitudes: *F* and *G* have "nothingness" (*le néant*), a more definitely philosophical concept.

73. **Après tout . . . Tôt ou tard:** The English version is more picturesque: "Well, I suppose in the end I'll get up under my own steam . . . In the fullness of time".

tu vas attraper froid: Estragon makes the same remark to Pozzo in Act 1.

75. **Il s'était donc levé . . . toi qui l'as voulu. —C'est vrai:** These lines are all omitted from the English versions.

76. ***Ils se lèvent:*** Cf. *All that Fall:* the preacher says the text for the next Sunday will be "The Lord upholdeth all that fall and raiseth up all those that be bowed down". Their not being

able to get up for some time may have no connexion with this text, however. It may be a warning that they are fast approaching the state of timelessness, which is *ipso facto* motionless. Pozzo is certainly nearer timelessness in Act 2 than in Act 1.

78. **On dirait qu'il remonte:** Cf. *Mercier et Camier:* "Seul Mercier regarda le ciel s'éteindre, l'ombre se parfaire. L'horizon englouti, il ne le quitta pas des yeux, car il connaissait ses sursauts, par expérience".
dire une connerie: Vulgar for *dire une bêtise.*
79. **Tu parles d'une diversion:** 'Marvellous time we're having'.
80. **Ah, tu te rappelles . . . Une hallucination. —Une illusion:** Omitted from English versions. Also from "Je vous ai dit que mon ami a peur" to "Ils ne le supportent pas" omitted in *F* and *G*.
81. **volerai:** *1st ed.:* "viendrai".
Debout: Not in *1st ed.*
82. **Comme vous avez changé!:** Cf. p. 42, Vladimir's question, "N'est-ce pas qu'ils ont beaucoup changé?" He is very sensitive to their evolution, whereas Estragon, being nearer the state of timelessness, is oblivious to it.
83. ***Lucky s'ébranle* . . . Puis nous repartons:** Omitted from English versions.
84. **rêvé:** *1st ed.:* "imaginé".
85. **L'air est plein de nos cris . . . peux pas continuer:** Cf. the last few pages of *L'Innommable:*

> ce sera le silence, faute de mots, plein de murmures, de cris lointains, celui prévu, celui de l'écoute, celui de l'attente, l'attente de la voix, les cris s'apaisent, comme tous les cris . . . dans le silence on ne sait pas, il faut continuer, je vais continuer (pp. 259–262).

le garçon de la veille: *F* and *G* read simply "*Enter Boy right*", thus leaving open the question of whether it is the same boy as in Act 1.
Deux . . . hommes: There is no hesitation in *M:* "Deux hommes". The hesitation could be doubt about their humanity: Pozzo is in Vladimir's eyes a monster, Lucky is more like a beast of burden.
Qu'est-ce qu'il fait . . . rien, Monsieur: These lines do not appear in *M* and *1st ed.*

87. **demain:** Not in *M*.
Il n'est pas venu? . . . c'est la nuit: Not in *M*. The main

difference between the boy scene in Act 2 and that in Act 1 is, of course, that Estragon is sleeping.

Seul l'arbre vit: Not in *M*.

88. ***Vladimir . . . le remet:*** Not in *M*.

Que j'enlève . . . ton pantalon: Not in *M*.